Anonymous

City of Kingston

street, alphabetical, general, miscellaneous and classified business directory for the

year 1889-90, including residents of Barriefield, Garden Island and Portsmouth

Anonymous

City of Kingston
street, alphabetical, general, miscellaneous and classified business directory for the year 1889-90, including residents of Barriefield, Garden Island and Portsmouth

ISBN/EAN: 9783337891497

Printed in Europe, USA, Canada, Australia, Japan

Cover: Foto ©Andreas Hilbeck / pixelio.de

More available books at **www.hansebooks.com**

CITY OF KINGSTON.

Street, Alphabetical, General, Miscellaneous

AND CLASSIFIED BUSINESS

DIRECTORY

FOR THE YEAR 1889-90.

INCLUDING THE RESIDENTS OF

Barriefield, Garden Island, and Portsmouth.

4th Biennial Edition

PRICE - $2.00.

W. H. IRWIN & CO., PUBLISHERS,
HAMILTON, ONTARIO.

KINGSTON :
PRINTED AT THE BRITISH WHIG OFFICE.
1889.

PREFACE.

The publishers, in presenting their fourth edition of the City of Kingston Directory, beg to assure their patrons that every exertion in their power has been used to render the work as complete and reliable as a compilation of this kind can be. Especial care was necessary in the arrangement of the Street Directory, owing to the great irregularity in the numbering of the houses, and we would respectfully suggest that this matter be remedied as soon as possible, and also that a change be made where two or more streets bear the same name. For any errors that may be discovered we request a lenient criticism. We return our thanks to our patrons and gratefully acknowledge the universal courtesy and generous aid our agents received during their canvas.

W. H. IRWIN & CO.,

Kingston, July, 1889.   Proprietors.

GENERAL INDEX.

The City of Kingston.

The fifth City in Ontario in population, is situated at the head of the St. Lawrence River and at the end of Lake Ontario. It is the principal port for lake navigation in Ontario, possessing the largest and finest harbor in the country. It is a station of the Grand Trunk Railway, and the headquarters of the Kingston and Pembroke Railway. The Public Buildings are very beautiful, the City Hall (the finest one in the Province,) the Court House, Post Office, Custom House, Queen's University and College, the Churches and a number of business blocks and private residences. At the Western boundary is located the Kingston Penitentiary, and about a mile West of it the Kingston Asylum for the Insane. Opposite the city is the Royal Canadian Military College, and Garden and Wolfe Islands. Kingston is a military as well as a naval city. Here is stationed "A" Battery, a local troop of cavalry, a field battery, and the 14th Princess of Wales' Own Rifles. The principal business streets are Princess, and parts of King, Wellington, Bagot, Clarence, Ontario, Brock, Market Square, Montreal, etc., all connected by the Kingston Street Railway. There are two daily papers published, *The British Whig* and the *Daily News*, both papers having weekly editions, and the *Canadian Freeman*, the leading Catholic organ of Eastern Ontario. The city returns one member for the Dominion Parliament, Sir John A. Macdonald, and one for the Local House, Mr. James H. Metcalfe. Kingston enjoys the proud position of being the soundest city financially, its merchants being considered the most prudent and safest men to deal with. The Limestone City, as it is sometimes called, is also the cleanest and healthiest city in Ontario, being built on the solid rock. The population is increasing and real estate is rapidly rising in value, and Kingston bids at no distant date to be one of the most foremost cities of the Province. Kingston is distant from Toronto 161 miles, Montreal 172, Quebec 344, Ottawa 95, Hamilton 200, London, (Ont.) 276, Detroit 386, St. John (N.B.,) 752, Halifax 828, and Liverpool 2,414 miles. Population about 20,000 ; with suburbs of Portsmouth, Barriefield, and Garden Island, 22,000.

KINGSTON STREET DIRECTORY.
1889-90.

The Odd Numbers commence on the North or East Sides, the Even on the South or West.

Adelaide st west from Division

2 Isaac Sammon, laborer
6 Fred Byrant, mason

Albert st (east side) from Union

33 Mrs. Bryan
81 Charles Wrenshall, artist

Earl st intersects.

101 Mrs Scanlan
115 Robert Pogue, shoemaker
277 H Chapman
119-121 Vacant
Solomon Boyd

Johnston st intersects

Dixon Knapp, carder.

Brock st intersects

Victoria Park

Mack st intersects

John Marshall, mariner
John Cochrane, mason
Charles Haskins, laborer
J. Redden, carpenter
Robert Downey, carpenter
Edwin Brouse, clerk
——Bendigo, laborer
W. H. Rogers, contractor

Princess st intersects

John Birmingham, laborer
John Campbell, carpenter
John McGill, laborer

Albert st (west side)

22 James Weir, steward K P
32 Vacant
42 W M Chadwick, mar. cutter
54 Vacant

Earl st intersects

94 Thomas Brooks, carpenter

2

270-272 Vacant
    James Shannon, carter
120 John Fisher, carpenter

Johnston and Brock sts intersect

    John Lockhart, colporteur
    Thos Hutchinson, carpenter
    Mrs Haffner
    Wm Allinson, boiler maker
    W H Cruse, shoemaker
    James Douglas, mason
    Mrs Briggs
    John Gray, contractor

Princess st intersects

Albert st (east side) from York to Adelaide

1 George Hemley, laborer

Pine and Upper Victoria sts intersect

Albert st (west side)

48 James Devine, carter
56 Robert Smith, teamster

Alfred st (east side) n from Union

113 Neil McLeod
117 Mrs Ann Hughson
127 Francis Armstrong, laborer
131 Joel Eby, foreman
133 John Hewton, machinist
135 Mrs Isaac Asselstine
137 James Black, carpenter
153 Samuel H Harper
157 A H Miller, superintendent letter carriers
159 Geo Smallbridge, carpenter

Earl st intersects

163 John Litton, grocer
165 Wm Reid, carter
179 Vacant
181 John Murphy, carpenter
193 Philip Small, policeman
203 Miss Catharine Cartmell
205 Henry Miller, blacksmith
207 John Stacey, gardener
209 John Tarrant, carpenter
    Vacant

Johnston and Brock sts intersect

273 Thos Howland, cab driver
275 J E Hutcheson, traveller
277 H G Goodfellow, mail clerk
279 Vacant
285 John Gallivan, engineer
295 John Nichol, bookkeeper
301 James Shaw
303 Mrs Hugh McDonald

Princess st intersects

347 Bryce Davidson, clerk
349 Henry Bonnie, moulder
351 Geo Bonnie, foreman
359 John Hamer, weighman
361 Wyman Rowe, laborer
365 Vacant

Elm st intersects

427 Vacant
429 Samuel Hyland, carpenter

Sixth st intersects

436 Chas Asselstine, carpenter
439 Fred Atwood, laborer

York, Pine and Upper Victoria sts intersect

487 Francis Bushy, carpenter

Adelaide st intersects

Alfred st (west side)

Earl st intersects

176 R E Aiken, policeman
178 Samuel Ely
198 Wm Redmond, carpenter
200 Andrew Rea, mariner
204 John Darragh, guard K P
206 Edward Spooner, carpenter
210 Mrs Wm H Cassidy
212 Mrs Richard Genge
214 Chas Hallet, laborer
216 ——Wotten, carter
218 Jas Lawler, keeper, Asylum
320 W H Asselstine, carpenter

Johnston st intersects

234 David Hall, plumber
236 Robert Sherbino, carpenter
248 Wm Pannell, carpenter
250 Peter McKim, hide inspector
252 D J Dick, merchant
254 J Asselstine, piano maker
258 John McEwen, carter
260 Robert Nesbitt, policeman

Brock st intersects

Victoria Park

Mack st intersects

322 Vacant
324 J W Madden, varnish manufacturer .
326 Mrs Mary Bowen
328 Vacant

Princess st intersects

John Powers, laborer
Fair grounds

Alice st west from Gordon

W A Rockwell, traveller
James Downing
F C Ireland, city treasurer

Alma st, from junction of York and Ordnance

12 Robert Moon, carpenter
16 Edward Chrisley, hostler
20 James Downs, laborer
22 Mrs Anthony Busso
28 Thomas Cushion, laborer
34 Patrick Fanning, carter

Alwington ave (east side) from King w to Union

J G Dennison, carpenter
Jas Adams, chief trades' instructor K P

Alwington ave (west side)

Michael Lahey, trade instructor, K P
Mrs Michael Koen
Wm Hurst, guard K P
John Bannister, guard K P
Jno F Baker, com traveller
Robt Hewton, chief keeper K P

Anne st, from end of Division

Charles Smith, painter

Ann st (north side) from n Bagot to Vine

7 Thos Robinson, clerk

12   CITY OF KINGSTON.

Ann st (south side)

8   James A Tarrant, carpenter
10 Frank Spooner, carpenter
14 Thos Pyman, warehouse-
    man
16 Charles Cook, laborer

Arch st (east side) n from Stuart to Union

11 Miss Annie Sullivan
21 Thos Turnbull, laborer
23 Miss Sarah Craig
25 George Long, machinist
29 William Hyett
29 Wm Shea, keeper, Asylum

Deacon st intersects

45 Edward Hamilton, tailor
47 Thomas Tweed, grocer
51 John McCormack, janitor
53 Henry Angrove, machinist
55 Wm Patterson, student
57 James Walsh, porter
59 Mrs David Mundell
61 Vacant
65 Wm Kennedy, engineer
69 ——McDonald, carpenter
77 Thos F Taylor, inspector
79 Mrs John Mair

Arch st (west side)

    Queen's College
60 Miss Elizabeth Moffatt
62 Mrs John Walker
64 H J Spriggs, librarian
66 Mrs Mary Craik
68 James Mitchell
72 John Perryman, mechanic
74 A Arntfield, carder
76 Thos Hodgson, stone cutter

80 John Cooper
84 Joseph Branch, engineer
86 C J Warwick, carpenter
88 Mrs Annie McCrath
92 Henry Collins, laborer
94 Thos Brightman, gardener

Artillery Park Barracks, head Barrack st

    James Wotten, agent
    Mrs Patrick O'Connor
    Frank A Birch, clerk
    Dep Adj Gen Office
    R J McGee, moulder

Bagot st (east side) from the Park north

West and Union sts intersect

    Felix Shaw, merchant

Gore st intersects

125 John Smith, jeweler
127 Mrs Francis Lawson
129 Henry Mason, carpenter
133 Charles Porter, storeman
137 Martin Clayton, carpenter

Earl st intersects

151 John Green, butcher
153 Thos Barlow, contractor
155 Vacant
157 John Goodearle, watchman
161 Charles Beattie
r161 Mrs Wm Patterson
163 Robt Charlton, boilermaker
165 Charles Maund, clerk
167 I Mitchell, jeweler
169 Miss Catharine Nelson,
     dressmaker

William st intersects

Convent School ,

Johnston st intersects

211 Edward Moore, sec Gas Co
213 John Orr, merchant
217 Mrs Mary Murray
219 Miss Mary McTaggart
223 Gilbert Johnston, engineer
231 Miss Harriet Everett

Brock st intersects

T McMahon & Co, painters
Gillen & Gillen, architects
233 Dr Livingstone
237 James Massie, V S
239 Rigney & Hickey, liquors
243 Henry Wilton, saddler
245 Macnee & Minnes, wh dry
goods
Minnes & Burns, dry goods

Princess st intersects

Noxon & Rockwell, boots
A Stackhouse, dentist
Dalton & Strange's ware-
house
273 Wm Robinson, Div Court
office
275-7 Robinson Bros, painters
279 Wm Robinson, Div Court
Clerk
281 James Elder, livery

Queen st intersects

Salvation Army barracks
305 Robert Wright, mason
307 Capt Chas McWilliams

Barrack st intersects

Cavalry stables
Vinegar Works

Ordnance st intersects

James Daley, printer
Vacant
R & J H Newman, contrac-
tors
Arch Hatton, shoveller
Mrs Hickey, grocer

Bay st intersects

Chadwit's Yard {
Mrs Samuel McLeod
James Loughren, laborer
John Peters, shoemaker
Mrs John Hickey

Jacob Simmons, carpenter
Mrs John Taylor
Owen Ward, laborer
F A Forsyth, mariner
James Murphy, laborer
James Connolly, laborer

North st intersects

67 James Eggleton, laborer
69 Mrs Margaret Brick
79 Martin Meagher, laborer
Benj Lyland, shoemaker
John H King, carpenter
John Brady, laborer

Picard st intersects

John Waters, baker
Jas Hamilton, machinist
Alex Mitchell, laborer
107 Henry Roney
115 Samuel Robinson, baker
117 A W Whitfield, baker
119 Isaac Plunkett, laborer

Corrigan st intersects

121 Almond Roushorn
123 Edward Harrison, laborer
125 R J Shales, blacksmith
    Robert Burns, carpenter
    Richard Pike, blacksmith
    Wm McKee, moulder

Dufferin and Charles sts intersect

Congregational Church

James st intersects

Bagot st (west side)

94 Schuyler Shibley
98 A Strachan, merchant
100 Benj Robinson, druggist
102 John Petrie, teller, Bank B N A
104 L B Spencer
106 Allan Chadwick
108 Mrs Robert Deacon
110 Chas Chown, iron founder
122 James Minnes, merchant
126 Wm Allen, shoemaker
128 Robert Shaw, barrister
130 H J Wilkinson, merchant
134 John McKelvey, plumber
136 Samuel Birch, plumber
138 Mrs James Mills
140 Wm Moore, real estate

Earl st intersects

Geo A Wilder, grocer
156 Rev James Godfrey
158 Edward Fahey, inland rev
160 Vacant
162 Robt McCammon, jr, baker
164 R K Rowe, teacher
r164 Michael Donoghue
166 Mrs Geo Givens
168 Henry Dunbar

170 Vacant
r170 John Vail, laborer
r170 Alex O'Hagan
172 John Bunt, boiler maker
174 Robert King, machinist
176 Robert Marshall, engineer
178 Michael Anderson

William st intersects

180 D Cunningham, cabman
182 Patrick Bradley, watchman
184 Thomas McMahon
r184 Michael Hogan, laborer
r184 Miss Eliza White
    T Downey, shoemaker
    Mrs Margaret Shea
    Miss Jane Wilson
    Wm Christo, bookbinder
200 J X Lachance, grocer
    Patrick Kilcauley, engineer
202 Edward Mostyn, hotel clerk
202 Mrs J McBride
204 Mrs Samuel Phippen

Johnston st intersects

206 Thos Caulfield, grocer
208 Vacant
210 Mrs Joseph Yeomans
214 Miss Ellen Casey
214 Chas Rowe, carpenter
216 John Liston, laborer
230 C H Clark, hotel

Brock st intersects

McCammon Bros, livery
244 T Ronan, undertaker
246 Daniel Phelan, M D
248-50 E Chown & Son, stoves
252 A Chown & Son, hardware
    T Mills & Co, hatters

Princess st intersects

G S Hobart, druggist
280 David Harold, carpenter
282 Mrs Maria Quinn

Queen st intersects

Greenwood & McGuire, marble works

Artillery Park Barracks intersects

Ordnance st intersects

Chas H Hatch, ticket agent
Walter Gunn, laborer
Patrick O'Neill, laborer
Hebron Harris, lumber
James Eves, cab driver

Bay st intersects

Isaac Doherty, dyer
48 James Gormley, laborer
50 Jeremiah Sullivan, laborer
52 Patrick Connolly, laborer
54 James Bryant, laborer
58 Daniel Corrigan

North st intersects

66 Richard Brunt, blacksmith
70 Geo Henderson, engineer
72 Henry Jarrall, laborer
76 Mrs Edward Surley

Miller's Lane intersects

82 Edward Wilmot, boarding
86 Patrick Driscoll, painter
88 Wm Scanlan, printer
90 Jos Wheeler, piano maker
94 John Millane, salesman
96 Vacant

Picard st intersects

T H Phillips, bookkeeper
Henry Wilmot, contractor
102 Vacant
104 Charles Murray
106 James Rushford, laborer
Vacant
Wm Peters, engineer
3 vacant houses
116 John Davy, carpenter
118 Vacant
120 John Wemp, laborer
122 Vacant
124 Mrs John King
126 Dennis Sullivan
128 Samuel Smith, teamster
130 Mrs James McCluskey
132 John Kallagher, laborer

John st intersects

John Doolan, laborer
Robt O'Connor, shoemaker
Thos Phelan, currier
Mrs Morris Kellaher
Peter Mallen, laborer
Martin Redmond
Alex Crumley, baker
Wm Shaver, fireman
Anthony Strong, machinist

Charles st intersects

Edward Bennett, shoveller
J Whitebread, bookkeeper
George Ferrier, machinist
Vacant

Bagot St North, sometimes called Upper Bagot, (east side) from Colborne

9 George Sarsfield, merchant
21 Arch McGill, clerk
23 E McCardley, laborer

25 Mrs Catharine Maiden
29 H G Turpin, carter
33 Wm McCullough, carpenter
35 Robt Barr, teleg'h repairer
37 Alex Nicholson, moulder
39 Wm E Ricard, printer
41 Thos Nicholson, laborer
43 James Gowan, sailmaker

Ann st intersects

45 Jonathan Offord, accountant
47 Vacant
49 Wm Ada, mariner
51 John Nolan, scroll sawyer

Bagot st n (west side)

12 Robert Baird
14 Miss Redmond
16 Peter Hunter, printer

Ellice st intersects

32 John McCammon, butcher
34 Wm McMaster, laborer
36 Thos Clanahan, baker
38 Wm Graham, laborer
42 Vacant

Ann st intersects

50 Wm Smith, laborer

Balaclava st (north side) from Bay to Alma

15 Vacant
17 Wm Robbs, carter
19 Mrs Wm Elliott
21 Charles Martin, mariner
23 Mrs Rose Coyle

Redan st intersects

37 Robert Spencer, merchant
41 James Allen, engineer
51 John Bourne, pedler

Balaclava st (south side)

Burial ground

Barrack st (north side) from the harbor to Artillery Park.

Ontario st intersects

Patrick Walsh, coal dealer
Wm Stewart, station agent K & P R
D C Collins, engineer K P R
A Hoppins, manager, Rathbun Co
J E McMullen, carpenter
Wm Hall, teamster
Geo Parks, laborer
Patrick Devlin, cabman
Mrs Geo Cochrane
Chas Olive, diver

King st intersects

Thos M Fenwick, M D
51 Thos Malone, upholsterer
r51 Samuel Hall, carter
r51 Thos Gorman, laborer
Riding School

Wellington st intersects

85 S Anglin, manufacturer
87 Patrick McKegney, laborer
89 Miss M J Benson

Rideau st intersects

109 Vacant
111 Jas Donoghue, bartender
117 Francis Twiss, carter

117 James Currie, machinist
119 E T Roberts, clerk

Bagot st intersects

Artillery Park

Barrack st (south side)

Mallen's wood yard

Ontario st intersects

Hogan House
Jas Robert, laborer
Gas Works

King st intersects

Victoria Foundry
Thos Wilson, laborer
Mrs Benj Trenheill
Thos Stigney, laborer
Martin Staley, hotel

Wellington st intersects

92 Henry Thurston, engineer
96 James McBride
100 Mrs John White
102 D Hoppins
r102 Patrick Collins, carter
r102 Timothy Kennedy, carter
104 T Gallagher, cartage agent
106 John Davis, carpenter
110 Geo Wright, carter
116 James Dickson, blacksmith
116 Wm Burns, laborer
Artillery Park

Barrie st (east side) from junction of King e and King w

Park

Union st intersects

Cricket grounds
Court House
Collegiate Institute

Clergy st intersects

New Presbyterian Church

Earl st intersects

231 Wm Makins, grain buyer

William, Johnston and Brock sts intersect

295 John Sutherland, clerk
297 R F Rowan, C E
301 Miss Cardwell
303 M J Shaw, druggist
305 Miss Chapman — MAPLE ROW.
307 Mrs Fowler
309 John Stewart, M D
A Swanston, baker

Princess st intersects

327 H H Curtis, druggist
329 T J Leahy, traveller
341 Albert Chown, druggist
343 Francis Newlands, contractor

Queen and Colborne sts intersect

385 Vacant
387 Henry Locker, baker

Ordnance st intersects

397 James Boyd, livery
399 Mrs Stephen Goodell

York st intersects

407 John Sullivan, laborer
411 Wm Bennett, tinsmith
429 Mrs Wm Forbes
435 Richard Moules, laborer
437 Samuel Dutton, laborer
439 J Smith, laborer
441 John Stansbury, driver

Picard st intersects

Thos Phillips, shoemaker
— Jenkins, laborer

Barrie st (west side)

O'Kill st intersects

26 Wm Dunnet, foreman
28 P Mitchell, ship builder
34 John Strange, barrister
64 Miss B Doran
66 Miss O'Reilly
72 R T Walkem, barrister
78 W L Hamilton, Inspector
     In Rev

Stuart st intersects

80 R Waldron, merchant
82 Michael Flanagan, city
     clerk
84 Robert Ford, merchant
86 John Bower
88 Wm Bailey
90 Henry Mooers, merchant
92 Robert Kennedy, carpenter

Deacon st intersects

98 T Y Greet, banker
100 Rev George Bell, LL D
102 John Hanson, blacksmith
104 E C Hiscock, engineer
106 Henry Merritt, moulder
110 Patrick O'Neil, mechanic

112 Daniel Gourley, boilermaker
114 Mrs Mulholland
130 D C Hickey, M D
124 W D McRae
128 H S Dupuy, accountant
140 Miss Roach
144 Rev J H Nimmo
146 Capt E A Booth, merchant
148 R V Rogers, barrister
     Rev J K McMorine

Union st intersects

162 J B McIver, accountant
164 Geo Cliff, real estate
170 R M Rose, registrar
172 Geo O'Reilly, mechanic
174 Thos Coffee, laborer
180 E Morham, piano tuner
182 Shore Loynes, merchant
184 Jas Mulholland, mechanic
186 Mrs Murray
188 Arch Smith, laborer
190 Miss Brooks
192 Mrs Hastings
194 John Gilbert, grocer
198 John Veal, baker

Young st intersects

201 Andrew McKee, mason
206 Edward Hopkinson, trader
208 Jos Little, hotel keeper
212 James Wiley, engineer
216 Mrs M Dean
218 Wm Newman, carpenter
220 Mrs Rynard
222 Mrs Jane Anderson
224 Wm Atkinson, laborer
226 John McConville, butcher

Earl st intersects

228 John Turbett, grocer
230 A C McMahon, insurance

232 John Munro, mechanic
234 R G Givens, carpenter
236 Hugh Alderdice, painter
238 J H Taylor, dealer
240 Langley Bird, laborer
242 John Swift, machinist
244 Samuel McKee, riveter
246 Mary Kavanagh, grocer

William st intersects

248 Mrs Alex Adair, grocer
250 Miss Rees
250 Vacant
254 John McFaul, machinist

Johnston st intersects

286 R Beaupre
238 S W Scobell, accountant KP
292 Peter Shangrow, carpenter
294 Miss Armstrong

Brock st intersects

296 Hugh Doyle, grocer
298 James Madden, engineer
300 Mrs Hamilton
302 Geo Booth, machinist
304 Edgar Storey, carpenter
306 Thos Hodgson, stone yard
    G W Brown & Co, carriage
    manufacturers
314 Mrs Hawley
316 James Steacy, traveller
318 Thos Rice, laborer
320 Andrew Keys, shoemaker

Princess st intersects

332 Jas Agnew city solicitor

Queen st intersects

358 Chas Cunningham, confec-
    tioner
362-364 Vacant

366 Geo Kessler, cigarmaker
368 Vacant

Colborne st intersects

378 R K Funnell, mechanic
380 James Tierney, grocer
390 S McCullough, policeman
392 Patrick Mullen, carpenter
396 James Dooley, shoemaker
398 Samuel Ball, jeweller
400 George Pound, baker

York st intersects

404 Vacant
406 Thos Moore, tailor
408 H J Peters, carpenter
436 Mrs Jane Pigeon
438 John Miller, engineer
440 Wm Kennedy, carpenter

Bartlett st south, runs west from Smith st off Princess

George Osborne, sec K & P
Mining Co

Bay st (north side) from water's edge west

W B & S Anglin, lumber

Anglin's Cottages.
{ 2 James Hansen, carter
  4 John Quinliven, laborer
  6 Thos Bennett, laborer
  8 Thos Cambridge, laborer
 10 Mrs Samuel Nichols
Coal sheds
Wm Lennox, carter
Mrs Mary Cardwell

Rideau st intersects

James Reid, grocer
47 Chris Elliott, groom

HORSESHOE ISLAND.

To be maintained as a Private Family Resort. Beautiful Lots, Cheap.

20   CITY OF KINGSTON.

49 James Smith, carpenter
51 D Cunningham, carpenter
53 Chas O'Neill, laborer
57 Jos Morrison, carpenter
59 Mrs Mary Stanford
61 Wm Loke, laborer
63 Francis Clark, laborer
65 Traver Blakley, carter
67 Mrs Thos Beamish
r67 Mrs Benj Barter
69 John Crowley, sailor

Bagot st intersects

73-5 John Guild, grocer
91 John Nichol, carpenter
93 Patrick Madden, engineer

Montreal st intersects

111 David Anderson
113 Geo Hunter, carpenter
115 Wm A Kelly, engineer

Sydenham and Balaclava sts intersect

137 H McBratley, stone cutter

Bay st (south side)

John L Joyce, coal dealer

Rideau st intersects

50 Jas W Clarke, currier
52 Vacant
54 J J Bliss, blacksmith
1 Wm Gallagher, cab driver
2 A S Boutillier, A Battery
3 Ed Marchand, engineer
4 John L Joyce, merchant
5 Geo Robson, car inspector
6 Jas C McAdam, laborer
Mrs Edward Hickey, grocer

Bagot st intersects

92 Mrs Mark Nicholson
94 John Reid, machinist

Montreal st intersects

120 James Foden, fitter

Sydenham st intersects

138 A Ferguson, laborer
142 Joseph Kimpsom
144 Martin McDonald, laborer
146 Joseph Smith, laborer

Beverley st (east side) n from King, w to Union

NEWMAN'S COTTAGES.

Mrs Regan, grocer
Edward Roche, laborer
Wm Hurst, mason
John Woods, laborer
Robt Carswell, boiler maker
Jas Campbell, mariner
John O Saunders, laborer
David Fraser, fitter
John Francis, pressman
Wm Mulligan, laborer
Chas Givens, laborer
John Blakley, carter
Jas Hurst, carpenter
Isaac Tuttle, lumberman
John Breden

Beverley st (west side)

Grove Inn
Wm Phillips, laborer

Beverley Lane runs alongside of Bajus' Brewery, south side

2 Mrs Boakes
4 Mrs Wolliver

J. B. PAGE & Co. Fashionable Hatters & Furriers
138 Princess Street.

STREET DIRECTORY. 21

6 R Graham, tailor
8 Joseph Lario, cooper

Brock st (north side) from harbor to limits

Folger's Dock
J G Campbell & Son, millers
Kingston Electric Light Co
Folger Bros, bankers
Calvin Co, wharfingers

Ontario st intersects

21 Wm Doyle, hotel
25 Tierney Bros, grocers
27-29 American Hotel
31 T D Dunnill, shooting gallery
33 Luke Doney, hotel
35 John Reeve, hotel
41 Thos Farrell, liquors
43 H F Stowell, artist
43 H S Smith, bookbinder
43 A F Brabant, needles
43 E C Hill, insurance agent
43 D A Givens, barrister
43 Webster & Co, phosphate dealers
44 G A McGowan, cigar manufacturer
45 Thos Farrell, grocer
47 Express office

King st intersects

49-51 Henry Wade, druggist
53 John Halligan, grocer
55 Z Prevost, tailor
57 J A LeHeup, watchmaker
59 J S Henderson, liquors
61 J S Henderson, grocer
65 W J McNeill, flour and feed

67 Wm Adams, boots
69-71 McKelvey & Birch, plumbers
73 Mrs Gorham, ladies' wear
75-77 Livingston & Bro, tailors
79 R Spencer, tailor
81 Jas B Reid, architect
81 Wm Baillie, printer
81 Mowat & Skinner, barristers
81 Fred Ostler, ins agent
83 Mrs J Kirk, fancy goods
85 F Nisbet, bookseller

Wellington st intersects

R Waldron, dry goods
103 W J Keeley, engraver
105 Mrs E Murray, dressmaker
107 Miss M Woods, fancy goods
109 John Gleeson, purveyor
113 S Neelon, flour and feed
115 S J Lake, boarding
117 Geo Offord, sr, boots
119 Canadian Freeman office
127 Queen's Hotel
129 Bibby Bros, livery
131 T McMahon & Co, painters

Bagot st intersects

McCammon Bros, livery
147 W A Deeks, carriage maker
149 George Elliott, traveller
151 E Horsey, chief of police
153 Vacant
155 M W Sine, V S
159 E Chance, barber
163 Dr Dupuis

Montreal st intersects

Third Methodist Church
183 H M Ruttan, bookkeeper
187 Edwin Chown, merchant
189 Mrs C Livingston
191 W L Goodwin, professor

193 L W Breck, merchant
    Cooks' Church
199 W A Deeks, carriage maker
201 Mrs M J Taudy
203 Mrs S Bibby
209 Hotel Dieu
241 T Overend, contractor
243 S J Kilpatrick, stone manu-
    facturer
247 C S Marshall, traveller
249 F Fowler, M D
255 G W Clerihew, merchant
257 G Chown, merchant

Clergy st intersects

273 A R Martin, insurance ag't
275 Mrs S G Hersey
277 A W Hall, agent
279 R J Carson, merchant
    Fourth Methodist Church
291 C McMillan, auctioneer

Barrie st intersects

305 A Vanasky, laborer
307 Mrs M Comber
309 W Dunn, merchant
311 Vacant
313 H Henderson, photographer
315 Miss W H Norris
319 Thos Hilton, saddler
321 Mrs J Coughlin
323 Henry Colville, printer
325 M W Coward, clerk
329 J Nolan, sexton
331 A B Sharpe, machinist
337 G Marriott, farmer

Division st intersects

347 J Tucker, mason
349 J W Martin, carpenter
357 J Boyd, mariner
359 A W Stevenson, steward

361 J Pigion, piano maker
363 J Patton, clerk
365 E Milo, carpenter
367 W Dennison, shoemaker
369 J Francis, shoemaker
371 J Baird, stove fitter
373 A Baird, bookkeeper
375 S Chapman, contractor
379 C Rutherford, stove moun-
    ter
391 J Nugent, tinsmith
393 C DeCarteret, merchant
395 J Halligan, merchant
397 A McArthur, accountant
399 T W Moore, merchant

Gordon st intersects

421 J Collins, hatter
425 D Nicholson, plasterer
429 C Robinson, merchant
431 Vacant
433 Vacant
489 G McCullough, cabman

Alfred st intersects

Victoria Park

Albert and Victoria sts intersect

Brock st (south side)

Ontario st intersects

City Hall
Market

King st intersects

56 John L Grass, confectioner
58 Jos Salter, auctioneer
60-62 W C Horton, fishmonger
66 Neil McNeill, plumber
68 Vacant

70 Vacant
72 Octave Madran, butcher
74 John McCammon, butcher
76 John Mayell, tailor
78 Jno Schroder, pork butcher
84 Wm Allen, shoemaker
86 C H Martin, ins agent
88 Miss Egan
90 W Moore, real estate agent
92 W J B White, ins agent
92 J T White, insurance agent
94 T M Parkin, confectioner

Wellington st intersects

McRae & Co, grocers

Bagot st intersects

Asylum
Base Ball grounds
Christian Brothers' School

Clergy st intersects

St Mary's Cathedral

Barrie st intersects

304 Mrs J Armstrong
306 Mrs J Alexander
310 Henry Hughes, carpenter
312 Mrs C Cumming
314 C Linton, blacksmith
318 W Scott, carpenter
320 W Denn, laborer
322 R Wartman, mason
328 Mrs I Mitchell
330 M Smith, deputy sheriff
332 Vacant
334 A D Sawyer, clerk
336 A McMillan, storekeeper KP
338 C B Bailey, biscuit baker

Division st intersects

346 J J Burton, merchant
348 M Nolan, sailor
350 W Minshull, mechanic
351 J Connor, cabinet maker
356 W Downing, clerk
358 C Sangster, clerk

Alfred st intersects

360 W J Dick, merchant
362 J Sharpe, rag dealer
364 D Cooper, merchant
370 J Snyder, whitewasher
384 M C Cummins, laborer
386 T. Mills, merchant
388 Vacant
390 Mrs A Simmons
394 Vacant
396 R Clugston, contractor
398 I Boyd, engineer
400 S Lowe, clerk
404 Mrs McCutcheon
406 J C Metcalf, butcher

Gordon st intersects

426 E B Conley, farmer
428 G Hazlett, engineer
430 W Abernethy, contractor
432 W L Richardson, merchant
434 J Belch, agent
460 E R Martin, auctioneer
462 C Allen, guard K P
464 Geo Offord, jr, traveller
466 S Marshall, accountant
468 Vacant
470 Mrs M Weir
472 Vacant
474 J S R McCann, accountant
476 W Hazlett, boiler maker

Frontenac st intersects

480 A Malone, mariner

Albert and Victoria sts intersect

Cataraqui st (north side) from the water's edge

David Edgar, fireman
Ford's Tannery

Orchard st intersects

John Odette, teamster
A J Lalonde, machinist
Fred Munroe, laborer
Thos Murphy, painter
Thos Stanley, laborer
Railway track

Rideau st intersects

J W Dow
Wm Wilson, jr
Wm Nevens, yard boss

Cataraqui st (south side)

Kingston Cotton M'fg Co
Jas Mallen, wood merchant

Centre st (east side) from King w

Jas Wilson

Centre st (west side)

Prof D H Marshall
Thos McCormack, clerk
J G Layton, printer
Frank Fox, carpenter
V Moyle
Thomas Lonergan
A McCormick, merchant
Mrs Yates

Charles st (north side) from Rideau w

17 Jas Mallen, wood merchant
19 Wm Cannon, jr, accountant
21 Thomas Smeaton, tanner
27 Matthew Claxton, tinsmith
29 Mrs Ann Wood
35 Vacant
37 Thos Grahen, hide dealer
   Congregational Church

Bagot st intersects

Wm J Clark, carter
Wm Kearns, coal heaver

Montreal st intersects

Charles st (south side)

12 Jas Roney, carpenter

Bagot and Montreal sts intersect

Charles st, Upper (north side), from Montreal to Patrick

13 Michael Campbell, spinner
15 G F Wilson, stone cutter
17 John Murray
21 Lewis Green
25 Wm Purtell, blacksmith
31 James Quigley, engineer
33 Miss Catharine Mullett
37 Joseph Tait, mason
49 John Baker, laborer
51 E Crollian, boilermaker
53 Mrs James Martin
59 Chas Asselstine, laborer
61 John McKim, laborer
63 Ira Fisk, laborer

65 Chas Doyo, conductor
67 Vacant

Charles st, Upper (south side)

18 Edward Shook
20 John Grogan, laborer
22 Wm Davies, carpenter
24 Wm Randall, mason
26 Vacant
28 Webb Robinson, builder
34 J Gallagher, sailor
38 Daniel Smith, ragman
42 Frank McDonald, laborer
46-8 Wm Green, laborer
52-56 Vacant
58 James Purtell, carter
62 Wm McEwen, teamster
64 S Hagarman, teamster

Chatham st (east side) north from Princess to York

23 John McCulla, laborer

First st intersects

45 Joseph Jackson, grocer

Colborne st intersects

51 Wm Wood, laborer
59 Thos R Graves, blacksmith
67 Mrs John Carruthers
69 Thos Enwright, carpenter

Elm and Fifth sts intersect

79 Edward Smith, machinist
101 Wm Saunders, tinsmith

Sixth st intersects

Chatham st (west side)

20 Wm Bruce, carpenter
22 Edward Fillion, bailiff
24 George Wilson, machinist
26 John Hynds, teamster
28 Geo Davy, carpenter

First and Colborne sts intersect

66 J H Caldback, carpenter

Elm and Fifth sts intersect

100 John Bowen, carter

Sixth st intersects

134 Mrs Wm Wood
140 Mrs Alex Mahews

Cherry st (east side) from York

3 Wm Cook, blacksmith
5 Thos Slater, laborer
9 James Bennett, laborer

James st intersects

35 Samuel Cannem, sailor

Pine st intersects

63 Vacant
67 Wm Cowdy, contractor
69 Joseph Rolow, carpenter
61 Damon Snider, laborer

Cherry st (west side)

16 Fred Curtis, plasterer

James and Quebec sts intersect

28 Wm Isaac, carpenter
34 Thos O'Brien, laborer

Pine st intersects

60 Wm Holland, laborer
68 Daniel O'Barny, laborer
70 Daniel Barrett, mason

Clarence st (north side) from Kingston harbour to Bagot

K & P R offices

Ontario st intersects

Canal office
Gas Inspector's office
Weights & Measures office
45 Robt Thompson, liquors
J F Swift, coal, etc
Dominion Express Co

King st intersects

61-3 Vacant
67 Ontario Building and Savings Society
69 Britton & Whiting, barristers
71 Vacant
73 John Cridiford, barber
77 Mrs Mary Kincaid
79 Wm Clanahan, laborer
81 Mrs Susan Clanahan
83 Wah Long, laundry
85 Hide Inspector's office
87 Frontenac Loan & Investment Society
89 J A Henderssn, master in chancery
91 Mills & Kent, bankers
93 Walkem & Walkem, barristers
93 Isaac Simpson, banker
95 Strange & Strange, insurance agents

95 John Strange, barrister
95 Geo Cliff, real estate agent
Bon Ton Saloon

Wellington st intersects

Ontario Bank
J X Rogers, messenger

Bagot st intersects

Clarence st (south side)

Ontario st intersects

28 Breck & Booth, vessel agts
30 Canadian Pacific Telegraph Comp'y
34 Great North-Western Telegraph Comp'y
36 W H Sullivan, barrister
38 Steamboat Inspector's office
38 J B McIver, accountant
38 J M Machar, barrister
38 Macdonnell & Mudie, bar-
40 C F Gildersleeve, steamboat owner
42 J P Gildersleeve, ticket agt
44 H T Shibley, barrister
48 Vacant
50 James Jones, barber
British American Hotel

King st intersects

Custom House
Post Office

Wellington st intersects

112 Robt Eilbeck, grain dealer
114 Vere Hooper, bookkeeper
120 T C Wilson, livery
122 Wm Murphy, wheelwright

124 Barber & Johnson, carpenters
128 Young Women's Christian Association
132 Chas F Barber, carpenter
132 Jos Sharpe, rag dealer
134 Mrs Mary Smith

Bagot st intersects

Clergy st (east side) from Barrie to Colborne

Earl and William sts intersect

45 Mrs John Henderson
47 R E Burns, accountant
49 James McNaughton, merchant
51 N K Scott, traveller
53 James Kearns, manager G N W T Co
55 Mrs Sophia Middleton

Johnston st intersects

89 Christian Brothers' School

Brock st intersects

107 Timothy Donoghue, traveller
109 James Kavanagh, salesman
    E R Welch & Son, marble

Princess st intersects

133 Mrs Agnes Allen
135 Mrs Donald McMillan
137 Mrs Richard Jolly

Queen st intersects

    Queen st Methodist Church
151 Edward Hawkins, shoemaker

153 George Amber, carpenter
163 James Harkness, butcher

Colborne st intersects

165 Charles Purvis, traveller
167 J Boyd, baker
169 Vacant
171 Mrs Edward Lark
175 J B Forsyth
177 Henry Hunter, carpenter
181 Wm Walham, jobber
187 A Sine, merchant
189 John Russell, grocer
191 S J Horsey, manfr

Ordnance st intersects

Clergy st (west side)

Earl st intersects

38 George Sears, merchant
40 Jos E Clark, accountant
44 George J Kemp, clerk
46 Geo Offord, sr, merchant
48 A E Brockett, traveller
50 Wm Sands
52 Rev R Whiting
   Owen Tierney, merchant

Johnston st intersects

St Mary's Cathedral

Brock st intersects

Barnstaple Terrace. {
1 Rev Wm Timberlake
2 Robt Crawford, merchant
3 John Walsh
4 G H Bissonette, merchant
5 John Corbett, merchant
6 Capt James Murray
7 W G Ford, merchant

Princess st intersects

St Andrew's Church
Rev J Mackie

Queen st intersects

158 James Fitzgibbon, laborer
164 Wm Kines, carpenter

Colborne st intersects

176 George Forsyth, carriage trimmer
178 Mrs Martin D Strachan
180 Wm Copley, trader
182 J Bastow
190 James Pense, clerk P O
192 James H Jones, barber

Ordnance st intersects

Colborne st (north side) from Sydenham

7 Richard Boyd, cabman
9 G A Aylsworth, merchant
11 Sam'l Sutherland, traveller
13 John Sands, merchant
15 J A Madill, traveller
17 D F Armstrong, merchant
21 J C Hardy, merchant
25 C W Wright, merchant
27 J G Elliott, journalist
29 G F Wilson, stone cutter
31 Charles Anderson, clerk
33 Jas F Sherman, clerk

Clergy st intersects

41 G Auchinvale, grocer
45 J Gillespie, keeper, Asylum
47 I Baubih, sailor
49 A T Smith, Bell Tele Co
53 Thos Callaghan, engineer
55 M Devan, carpenter
57 Vacant

59 John Craig, conductor
67 James Kane, laborer
69 J A McDonald, inspector of weights
71 Jas Yule, traveller
73 Matthew Neilson, C E
75 A Robinson, traveller
79 Mrs S E Whitehead
81 J R Massie, pattern maker

Barrie st intersects

83 Mrs Fanny Dennis
85 Wm McCandless, machinist
87 Joseph Landeryou
105 Geo Counter, truck builder
119 S J Kilpatrick, contractor

Upper Bagot st intersects

123 W Robinson, jr, customs
127 Walter Jones
129 Mrs Jas Burgess
131 J Powers
133 Miss M Clare, dressmaker
135 Edward Orser, musician
127 S J McWaters, engineer
139 Horace Orser, laborer
147 Mrs Thomas Farley
149 Mrs John Smith
151 Alex D Pettigrew
153 E H Hubbard, barber

Division st intersects

181 N Wilmot, blacksmith
183 Vacant
185 John Oram, bookkeeper
193 Thos Lannon, blacksmith
195 Frank Somerville, engineer
197 Robert Davidson, carpenter
199 J Vanwinckle, carpenter
201 Edmund Clarke, boilerm'r
203 W P Bell, photographer
205 D J Walker, county clerk

207 Robt Eward, bookkeeper
209 J P Donnelly, traveller
211 Vacant
215 Reuben Bryant, moulder
235 Mrs Mary Crozier
243 James Gormley, mariner
245 J B Holder, carpenter

Chatham st intersects

Lewis Hubbard, carpenter
Mrs James Calback

Colborne st (south side)

2 John McIver
4 J B McKay, teacher
8 Mrs Patrick O'Neil
14 Wm Haley, shoemaker
22 J Duncan Thompson
30-34 Vacant
36 John Massey, machinist
40 James Harkness, butcher

Clergy st intersects

44 Charles Sharp, grocer
46 James McCullough, clerk
48 A W Dunlop, bookkeeper
50 James S Hogan, traveller
58 John Newton, carpenter
60 John McCullough, laborer
62 Mrs John Smith
68 William Marshall
70 Mrs Wm Hannay
74 A G Flett, merchant
78 J Bridge
80 Vacant
82 J W Bryant, butcher

Barrie st intersects

H J Myers, grocer
114 Vacant
116 Thos Lambert, merchant

118 Edwin Walsh, salesman
120 Wm Bailey, broom manufacturer
122 Geo Briden, bookkeeper
124 W J Chapman, contractor
136 Mrs Geo Booth
138 Jos Little, laborer
140 Henry Tyson, laborer
142 Wm Eves, painter
144 R J McDonald, pilot
146 Geo Forder, sailor
148 R Fraser, laborer
150 John Hamilton, laborer

Division st intersects

192 Mrs Thos Rutherford
196 John Siler, machinist
198 Geo Young, shoemaker
204 Geo Annett, carpenter
206 Patrick Lindsay
208 Alex Barnes, blacksmith
210 Jas McWater, carter
214 Wm Burke, carpenter
216 W McIlroy, traveller
240 Hugh Derry, mason
244 Jas Hynds, laborer

Chatham st intersects

College st north from Union

1 Fred Ostler, ins agent
3 Oliver Gravelle, salesman
  Mrs McFarlane

Collingwood st (east side) from King w

Thos Fraser, laborer
John Sinclair, laborer
Thos Atkinson, mason

Union st intersects

Collingwood st (west side)

Ernest Villard, laborer
Henry Schonfieldt, spinner
Mrs J Williamson
Mrs Johnston
Mrs A R McDonald
F G Norton, bookkeeper

Union st intersects

Corrigan st (north side) from Rideau to Bagot

M R Davis, ship builder

Corrigan st (south side)

Mrs James Stallard
Jas Grimshaw, grain shoveller
Arthur Kingston Knight, currier
Solomon Schultz, carpenter
Jas Bennett, laborer
D Moore, grain shoveller
John Moore, engineer

Cowdy st, from Pine

12 Hugh Peters, carpenter
16 John Thomas, mason
22 Geo Waller, laborer
24 Thos Barrett, mason
26 Mrs James Jackson

Deacon st (north side) from Barrie west to Arch

9 Robert Bryant, carriage-maker
11 Wm McNaughton
15 John Beauchamp, machinist
17 John Kennedy, machinist

Deacon st (south side)

12 George Wilson, laborer
14 Mrs Barnes
16 Herbert Peder, clerk
18 Samuel Cunningham, carpenter
22 Thomas Healey, clerk

Division st (east side) from Union to limits

1 Daniel Sharp, laborer
3 John McKenzie, coachman
5 Charles Lemon, carpenter
9 John McArthur, sailor
13 Jos Kennedy, boilermaker
17 Mrs Alice McGrogan
19 Robt Mooney, machinist
21 Francis Tracey, instructor K P
23 Lawrence Walsh, guard K P
25 Edward O'Brien, laborer
27 Thos Scott, baker
29 H J Randalls, sailor
31 John Howes, carpenter
33-35-37 Vacant

Young st intersects

41 Edwin Charles, carpenter
45 David Brown, moulder
47 David Rea, laborer
51 James Denison, stonecutter
53 David Donnelly, carpenter
55 Wm Cockade, blacksmith

Earl st intersects

71 James Maxwell, foreman
73 Charles Booth, C E
75 Vacant
79 Mrs G H Squire
83 Alpheus Turcott, carpenter

85 George Hewitt, machinist
87 Mrs Z Guy

William st intersects

93 James McArthur, banker
95 Mrs Thos McCutcheon

Johnston st intersects

Public School
125 Mrs Wm Clarke
127 Wm Neill, letter carrier

Brock st intersects

149 Mrs Mary Clark
153 Geo Bonny, jr, blacksmith
155 Mrs Margaret Allen
168 Capt Webster Augustus

Princess st intersects

179 E R Welch, marble manu-
    facturer
181 Prof Forshaw Day
188 Mrs Henry Plees
185 Charles Welch

Queen st intersects

E F Chapman, grocer

Colborne st intersects

221 John Waddell, contractor
225 R Edwards, grocer

Ellice st intersects

231 Neil McIntyre
237 Amos McDonald, teacher
239 W Dorland, tailor
249 J Waddell, harness maker
251 H A Dunlop, clerk
253 Fred Greenwood, clerk
255 Frank Booth, gardener

259 P O'Reilly, shoemaker
271 John Pound, baker
277 Vacant
285 W H Madill, keeper, Asy-
    lum
287 Alex Bennett, baker
297 Mrs Wm Allen
303 Robt Patterson, grocer

Main st intersects

327 Jas Crawford, merchant
329 Geo Crawford, mariner

York st intersects

335 Jas Stacey, manager *News*
337 Mrs Ann Virtue
353 Vacant
355 Richard Corrigan, waggon
    maker
357 Mrs Peter McMaster
359 A Moreland, grocer

Pine st intersects

363 Thomas Risbger
375 Wm Walter, laborer
379 J Stafford, carriage maker
381 Edward Dawson, machinist
387 Wesley Bryant, butcher
391 Jas Campbell, mason
393 Vacant
395 Wm J Robertson, boiler
    maker
425 John Taylor, laborer
449 R Dickinson, carpenter
451 Vacant

Ann st intersects

Wm Grundell, carpenter
Chas Bidell, driver
City Limits

Division st (west side)

18 Robt Barry, coppersmith
21 Thomas Parker, clerk
28 Albert Elmer, barber
32 John H Dickson, engineer
34 Elijah Purdy, agent

Young st intersects

F Carleton, grocer
40 John Percy, mechanic
42 Geo H Parkin, farmer
44 R Decker, blacksmith
46 John Wuintrup, machinist
48 Mrs John Hamilton
50 Henry Smith, laborer
52 Mrs Joseph Killmurray
54 Thos Coffee, laborer
56 Francis Morrison, machinist

Earl st intersects

78 Richard Edwards, grocer
80 George Comer, purser
82 Mrs John Taylor
86 Miss Ann Smith
88 J Robinson, painter
90 John Geal
92 Mrs Andrew Wallace
94 Robt Free. mason
100 Peter Asselstine, carpenter

Johnston st intersects

124 Anthony Crawford
130 Peter Donoghue, clerk
134 Donald McDonald, boiler-
    maker
136 Jos Hipson, boilermaker
    John Burton, grocer

Brock st intersects

146 Vacant
148 Richard Newlands, tobac-
    conist

152 John Jenkin, carpenter
168 Benj Asselstine, carpenter

Garratt st intersects

Princess st intersects

208 W Richardson, weaver
210 Wm Mathews
212 Leslie Minaker
214 H W Casey
216 Miss Lizzie Richardson,
    dressmaker
218 D A Harold, carpenter
220 David J Pugh, harness-
    maker

Colborne st intersects

220 Henry Peters, mariner
222 George Waldron, broom-
    maker
224 Henry Mowat, mason
226 George Mowat
230-2-4 Vacant
240 Mrs Thomas Eward
248 Mrs John Strachan

Elm st intersects

254 John Hogan, carpenter
256 Mrs George Hartrick
258 F W Eward, blacksmith
260 Mrs Robert Joyce
270 Robert Rutherford, black-
    smith
278 John Gordon, mason .
284 Silas Grimshaw, carpenter
286 John Rutherford, grinder
286a Mrs Ellen Walker
288 John Lyons, laborer
294 J Gallivan
296 Thos Puddon, laborer
318 Mrs Ann Parker
320 All Saints' Church

York st intersects

836 Jas Murray, engineer
848 A Robinson, watchman
854 Robt McIntyre, laborer
866 Robt Elliott, carpenter

Pine st intersects

368 Mrs Wm Conley
378 Thomas Abbott
384 Mrs Wm Lemon

Victoria st intersects

386 Thos Friendship, gardener
388 Samuel Bates, carpenter
390 Mrs John Jolliff
392 Jas Babcock, carter
396 Mrs James Cannon
400 Robt Thompson, knitter

Adelaide st intersects

426 Robert McVety, carpenter
438 Thos Collins, mariner
448 Chas Scott, plasterer
    City limits

Dufferin st (north side) from Rideau west to Bagot

Isaac Oliver, carpenter
John Hawkes, laborer
Chas Vanluven, miller
Thos Bell, watchman
Charles Jackson, stove polisher
B Hurst, warehouseman
M O'Connor, carpenter
Frank Somerville, carpenter
Mrs Bernard McKenna
Harvey Hoppius, weighman
John Whinton, plumber
Edmund Germain, currier
Thos Healey, brakeman

Dufferin st (south side)

John Guirey, engineer

Durham st, w from Victoria

28 Vacant
129 Walter Lamb, lumberman
131 Edward Roddy, carter
137 James Bewis, mason
139 John Brady
141 Robert Martin, laborer

Macdonnell st intersects

76 R Harris, broom maker
   Daniel Carter, quarryman

Earl st (north side) west from water's edge

Ontario st intersects

23 Edward Williams, lumber
25 Mrs Ann Fraser

King st intersects

43 James Wilson, laborer
47 Wm Irwin, machinist
49 J B Johnson, barber
53 J S Johnston, blacksmith
55 Mrs Jane Somerville
63 John Welch, accountant ·
65 Thos A Hanley telegrapher
   Thos Hanley, ticket agent
   G T R

Wellington st intersects

81 Andrew McMahon, painter
83 David Thompson, grocer
87 Isaac Kelly, carpenter
89 Timothy Lane, grocer
89a Edward LeHeup, cutler

5

91 Jeremiah Millan
r91 John O'Connor, laborer
97 Michael Foley, carter
   John Green, butcher

Bagot st intersects

113 Z Prevost, merchant
117 Wm Wormworrth, piano maker
121 Rev Malcolm Macgillivray
   Chalmers Church

Sydenham st intersects

   First Methodist Church
149 Vacant
151 R Gardiner, merchant
155 John Kerr, Manager Gas Works
161 B W Robertson, merchant
163 H Cunningham, iron founder
179 W J Crothers, manufact'r

Clergy st intersects

183 Mrs James Johnston
189 Martin James
195 Prof G D Ferguson
199 Mrs C Morrison
201 Miss M L Young

Barrie st intersects

213 Mrs Little
215 Mrs Fairbanks
217 Harry Cable, painter
219 Joseph Norris, carpenter
221 Robt Milne, mariner
223 Jas McGillivray, engineer
225 Alex McEwen, carpenter
227 Capt James Dix
229 Thomas Elmer, moulder
233 James Hickey, engineer
235 James Gillie, engineer

237 C S Crosby, shoemaker
239 Robt Agnew, moulder
243 Thomas Milne, engineer
245 Edward King, laborer
247 Wm Percy, tailor
255 Charles Green, moulder
257 Mrs James McDowall

Division st intersects

   Biscuit factory
267 Hugh Braniff, storeman
269 Wm Pollitt, baker
277 Robt Howlett, carter
289 S Self, laborer
291 Samuel Shaw, carter
293 Thos Bain, laborer
303 Robert Keys
305 Vacant
307 Wm Newell, mariner
309 Joseph Lawler, baker
311 David Gilchrist, tinsmith

Gordon st intersects

317 Mrs Walter Ross

Alfred st intersects

327 Mrs A Harvey

Frontenac st intersects

377 Wm Robertson, blacksmith
379 Geo Hanett, boiler maker
381 John Ansley, carpenter
383 Vacant

Albert and Victoria sts intersect

Earl st (south side)

Ontario st intersects

12 Mrs Harriet Parsons
12 Peter Whims, laborer

16 Mrs Ann Lovett
18 John Hunt, laborer
20 John Dunstar, mariner
22 Chas Marchand, laborer
24 Owen Rourke, laborer

King st intersects

46 John Saunders, laborer
48 Mrs G H Williams
50 Robt Meek, Sec'y Odd-Fellows' R A
52 Wm G Anglin, M D
56 W Anglin, bursar, Asylum
58 Mrs Daniel Whalen
62 Mrs J Richardson, boarding
66 Wm S R Murch, traveller
68 Michael Grady

Wellington st intersects

72 Wm Sawyer, artist
74 John Mitchell, printer
76 Jere'h, O'Sullivan, laborer
80 John Macdonnell
r80 Edward Duffy, laborer
82 Miss Bridget Moran
90 Mrs Wm Hayward
92 Joseph Roadley, steward
94 Chas Franklin, merchant
96 Thomas Hewitt, foreman
98 Rev Samuel Houston
100 Thomas O'Donnell
102 Robert McRae, grocer

Bagot st intersects

108 Mrs C Stoba
110 Mrs M Moore
114 E W Lowe, traveller
116 Geo Lee, piano maker
118 W M Drennan, merchant
120 R J Bowes, merchant
122 Capt J B Cochrane
130 Wm Nickle

132 R E Kent, banker
134 Prof J W Williamson

Sydenham st intersects

148 Thos Moore, merchant
    A McPherson, bookkeeper
    Fleming Rowland, collector
    inland revenue
    Vacant

West st intersects

164 Wm McRae, merchant

Clergy st intersects

Chalmers Church
212 Joseph Murphy, laborer
214 James Fleming, mariner
220 John Trencer, carter
222 Michael Lawless, carter
224 Benj Barney, broker
226 John Johnston, clerk
228-30-32 Vacant
234 Neil McCaig, laborer
236 Edward Martin, laborer
238 James Denny, laborer
240 Walter Keeling, laborer
242 Peter Monks, laborer
244 Patrick Hamilton
246 D J Ainslie, carpenter
248 James Hamilton, laborer
252 Mrs B Culpack

Division st intersects

254 B O'Donnell, gardener
256 Thomas Murphy, laborer
258 Wm Jamieson, boilermaker
260 Wm Bunt, blacksmith
262 Michael Purcell
264 Albert Follest, carpenter
266 Edward Verbeck, dyer
276 Mrs James Renton
278 Richard Ludlow, laborer

282 Mrs Robert Harkness
284 I Asselstine, blacksmith
288 Samuel Shaw, baker
302-4-6 Vacant
810 James Rigley, laborer

Gordon st intersects

318 David Cunningham, trade instructor
320 Wm Smallbridge, mason

Alfred and Frontenac sts intersect

380 R D Baker, tobacconist
382 Wm Baker

Albert and Victoria sts intersect

Ellerbeck Ave, runs n from King w

Samuel Kelly, machinist

Ellice st (north side) from Bagot to Division north

9 Vacant
11 James McNamee, laborer
15 J Mendell
17 Jas Martin, mariner
19 Lewis Lalonde, carpenter

Vine st intersects

21 Joseph Tait, plasterer
23 Thos Pope, shoemaker
27 Geo T Swan, grocer

Ellice st (south side)

8 Jonathan Taylor, sr, carter
18 Jonathan Taylor, jr, engineer

20 Thomas Mathews
22 John Mitchell, stonecutter
24 Jos Gascoigne, engineer
26 Patrick Conroy
28 Jas G Meagher, trader
30 Geo Kean, carpenter
32 Vacant
34 Robert Graham, shoemaker
36 Vacant
38 Charles Edwards, mason

Elm st (north side) from Division to Alfred

23 Leon Young, laborer
25 Rennie Young, laborer
35 James Bennett, shoemaker
43 Peter Rourke, laborer
47 S D Swann, machinist
59 James Volume, shoemaker
61 ——Fraser, carpenter
79 Philip Boswell, laborer

Chatham st intersects

87 Alex Finlay, bricklayer
89 Mrs Lucy Glaceon
91 Horace Attwood, laborer
99 John Doherty, laborer

Elm st (south side)

18 John Stagg, laborer
22 Edward Suddard, laborer
24 Wm Keene, fireman
26 John Lake, mechanic
28 Wm Westcott, laborer
36 Ernest Rowe, clerk
40 J McCallum, stone cutter
42 Geo Henderson, blacksmith
48 William Meek
50 B Saunders, laborer
54 James O'Neill, laborer
56 R M Hamilton, mason

Hosiery and Gloves Cheapest at Shaw's.

60 John Marsh, laborer
64 J W Marsh, storeman

Chatham st intersects

Richard Pigion, gardener

Emily st from the water to King e

M H Folger
James B Strathy
Hon G A Kirkpatrick, Q C M P

Fifth st, west from Division

Chas Fivcash, laborer

First st (north side) from Division west

3 R McMillan, piano maker

Chatham st intersects

25 Wm Grant, driver
27 John LeHeup
29 Mrs Mary McCann
33 Wesley Perry, laborer

First st (south side)

2 Mrs Mary A Thornton

Frontenac st (east side) from Union to limits

Earl st intersects

81 Joseph Bawden, barrister
83 Mrs Mary Baker
85 Thos Thompson guard K P

Johnston st intersects

148 W W Gautt, grocer

Brock st intersects

Victoria Park

Mack st intersects

Vacant

Princess st intersects

James Baker
2 vacant houses
Wm Woods, driver

Frontenac st (west side)

Arthur Frost, painter
28 R F Sargent, clerk
30 Wm Scale
32 J J Otto, bookbinder
34 John Geal, solicitor

Earl st intersects

86 Robt Sinclair, teamster
John Comper, carpenter

Johnston st intersects

152 W S Gordon, assessor
158 W H Sleeman, plasterer
164 Mrs C Cochrane

Brock st intersects

Victoria Park

Mack st intersects

Orlando Burnett, policeman
J E Harpell, laborer
C M Hamilton, inland rev
Mrs Addie Gorham

Horseshoe Island. Boats twice a day each way. Liquor prohibited from being sold.

Moses Fisher, tailor
Mrs G B Corby
John Buckley

Princess st intersects

A McIlquham, traveller
Wm Woollard, clerk
Samuel Lee, moulder

Garratt st, west from Division to Gordon

6 J J Crawford, cutter
8 Mrs G W Andrews
10 Jos Reid, cabinet maker
12 R J Reid, undertaker

George st (east side) n from King, w to Stuart

O'Kill st intersects

31 B McConville, mail carrier
33 Robt Kearns, letter carrier
35 Mrs Rollands
39 Jas F Lesslie, merchant
43 R W Vandewater, merchant
47 James Shannon, postmaster
51 Wm Harty
53 Wm Lesslie, raftsman
59 John Noon
61 David Lee, steam fitter
63 Joseph Taylor, steamboat inspector

George st (west side)

6 Mrs David Albertson
8 Wm Dousley, shoemaker
10 Mrs John Dodds
14 Henry Johnston, laborer
16 John Geary, laborer

20 Mrs Scales
22 Vacant

O'Kill st intersects

Kingston Hospital

Gordon st (east side) from King w to Princess

15 Henry Young, laborer
17 Geo Galloway, machinist
19 Mrs Ann Orrel
11 John Dolphin
25 Robt Robinson, carpenter
27 Wm Bowen, teamster
29 John Twigg, laborer

Stuart, Union and Young sts intersect

191 Robert Gaw, contractor
193 Miss A N Sutherland
195 Capt Thos Donnelly

Earl st intersects

203 Vacant
205 Robt Gilmour, letter carrier
207 Mrs Twohey
209 Mrs Catharine McDonald
     Joseph Skeggs, laborer
211 James Lawless, carter
213 Mrs Henry Patterson
215 Edward Perry, moulder
217 John Moore, laborer
223 Mrs Sarah Donnelly
227 Wm Coward, baker, K P
229 M S Burnett, canvasser
231 John McCartney, mason
241 Mrs Peter Nugent
     Wm Elliott

Johnston st intersects

J. B. PAGE & Co. FINE FURS A SPECIALTY
138 Princess St.

STREET DIRECTORY. 39

259 Albert Gissing, grocer
261-263 Vacant
265 Mrs Wm Swales
267 Mrs Robert Gill
269 R Young, guard K P

Brock st intersects

291 Wm Newlands, architect
293 D A Givens, barrister
295 D Hutcheson, manager
297 Geo W Browne, inland rev
299 Mrs John Agnew
307 John Gardiner, bailiff
309 John Hendry, salesman

Garratt st intersects

317 N C Polson, druggist
319 John L Renton, mail clerk
321 C H Martin, insurance agt

Gordon st (west side)

Stuart st intersects

G M Macdonnell, Q C
Public School

Alice st intersects

98 Geo Richardson, merchant
120 Thos Mills, merchant
122 Thos Mills, banker
124 Geo Mills, merchant
126 A F Chown, merchant
132 R E Sparks, dentist
138 P Browne, merchant
2 new houses

Union st intersects

152 John Lovick, blacksmith
154 Miss Meadows
168 Francis Wiseman, mason
176 Robert Bell

184 Wm Harold, pattern maker
186 J W Fralick
190 A Shaw, surveyor customs
192 Wm Mudie
194 J T White, insurance agent

Earl st intersects

206 Wm McCartney, contractor
208 — Rowatt, foreman
210 James Bryson, guard
216 Geo Young, agent Shedden Co
218 James Devlin, engineer
220 Robt Carson, sergt police
222 Rev Alex Drennan
224 James Reid, hatter
226 Geo C Watson, tailor
228 Alex Elsmere, instructor, K P
230 Chas McNeill, guard, K P
234 Wm Snowden, mason
236 Wm McCormack, guard, K P
238 Justus Daley
240 Capt C H Nicholson, mariner
242 John Patton, insurance agt
244 Thos Gaskin, customs
246 James Purdy, piano agent
248 Alex McCartney, mason
250 Benj Watson
252 Wm Tyner
254 David McRae, grocer
256 Wm J McKee, mariner

Johnston st intersects

Wm Spence, grocer
264 Daniel Doran, painter
268 Wm Derry, engineer
270 Alex Horn, sailmaker
272 Mrs E McLaren
274 Wm Burrows, gas inspector
282 Geo McEwen, shoemaker

Engravings at P. Ohlke's, 184 Wellington Street.

Brock st intersects

294 James Cochrane, sailor
296 Albert C Johnston, jeweller
298 C B Daley, C E
300 Rev George Porteous
302 Wm Neish, customs
304 E C Hill, real estate
306 John E McMullen
308 Robt Thomson, cashier
310 James McLeod, machinist
312 Hugh Jack, missionary
314 C I Dickson, inspector
318 Wm Adams, shoemaker
326 Samuel Bailey, manuf'r
328 Thomas Cruse
330 T H Johns, grocer
332 Alex Gallinger, contractor
334 William Meek, sup't *Whig*
346 Thos Nicholson, carpenter
348 J G Saunders, butcher
     G M Weber factory, pianos

Gore st (north side) from water's edge to Bagot

Locomotive Works

Ontario st intersects

39 Wm H Peart, ticket agent, K & P R
45 J P Gildersleeve, insurance
59 Miss E de St Remy, teacher

King st intersects

65 H S Smith, bookbinder

73 Capt Thos Merritt, inspector
75 A Hanley, inland revenue
77 Wm Potts, bartender
79 Patrick Moran, moulder
81 Mrs Wm Leslie
85 Thos Jamieson, plumber

r85 Jas Craig, coppersmith
89 Mrs Mary Wade
91 Vacant

Wellington st intersects

105 Patrick Curtis, shoemaker
     Vacant
111 Mrs Henry Kenney
115 A Williamson, contractor

Gore st (south side)

Government Dry Dock

Ontario st intersects

Wm Corrigan, pilot
P Ainslie, boiler maker
John G Smith, teamster
44 Vacant

King st intersects

64 Wm Power, shipbuilder
76 John J Walsh
78 C S Gould, engineer
82 R H Toye, confectioner
84 Adam Gilchrist, loco works
88 Jas Loftus, mariner
90 Mrs Chas Dine
92 Jas Douglas, blacksmith
94 Mrs Jane Sullivan, grocer

Wellington st intersects

104 Mrs John Melville
106 John Percy, cab driver
112-14 Joseph George, piano manufacturer
     2 vacant houses

Gray's Lane, north from Upper William

1 Miss Elizabeth Wilson

2 Mrs Margaret Pierce
3 John Gibbs, laborer

Grove st (east side), also called Rideau, from River st to Montreal

Carrington's tannery
W Hanscombe, switchman
John Bleany, coal heaver
Samuel Cearns, carpenter
Wm Lambert, trackman

Montreal st intersects

Grove st (west side)

6 J A Coggan, patternmaker
8 Alexander Boles
10 Vacant
12 Mrs J McCallum, grocer
14 Vacant
    R Halligan, grain shoveller
36 F W Clark, machinist
40 Geo Holland, engineer
42 J Linton, grain shoveller
44 Chester Wood, carpenter
46 Thos McCormack, laborer
48 Wm Cunningham, currier
50 Wm Hubbard, carpenter
    Jos Beuse, tanner
    Venandus Soles, currier

Montreal st intersects

Herchmer st, now called Stuart

James st (north side) from Montreal to Patrick

31 Wm Cullen, engineer
41 W Gillmore, carriage maker

43 John Gibson, laborer
45 F McGinnis, laborer
47 Wm Dodd, blacksmith
49 Enoch Burtch, carpenter

James st (south side)

6 Edward Hargraves, moulder
8 ——Clark, carter
10 Richard Cournen, mechanic
12 C Campbell, laborer
14 S G Herbert, laborer
16 Patrick Culle, laborer
22 A Sharow, blacksmith
26 John Lee, laborer
30 Wm Sissons, laborer
32 Alex Sly, blacksmith
34 Alex Bailey, carter
38 Mrs M McGinnis
50 John Vanhooser, moulder

James st Upper (north side)

9 John Wilson, gardener

Plum and Cherry sts intersect

41 Wm Ward, engineer
43 James T Godwin

Quebec st intersects

James st Upper (south side)

40 Henry Bates, carpenter
46 W Truesdell, carpenter

John st (north side) from Montreal to Patrick

7 Vacant
11 Francis Genau, laborer
17 Patrick, Whalen, tanner

21 Robert Cowie, carpenter
23 Thos Cowie, mason
29 Robert Dunlop, tailor
35 John O'Hearn, engineer
47 James Black, laborer
51 Mrs Andrew Cassidy
55 James Belanger, grainer
57 F McCambridge, laborer
59-61-63 Vacant

John st (south side)

8 Daniel O'Gorman, carter
10 Vacant
12 Mrs John Gunn
14 Thomas Clark, laborer
   Separate School
42 John Burns, carpenter
50 John Perryman, plasterer
54 Wm Gordon, teamster
60 E McFadden, cab driver

John st North (north side) from Montreal to Division

Vacant
Wm McQuaid, carpenter
Patrick McKenty, laborer
John McQuaid, carpenter
John Gray, mariner
Chas Dinsmore, laborer
B Keagen, laborer
James Delaney
Martin Delaney, carpenter

John st North (south side)

J W Willey, laborer
Vacant
Wm H Booth, carpenter
John Scanlan, printer
Patrick Delaney, fireman
John O'Brien, carter

Vacant
Wm Gallagher, carpenter
Patrick Killeen, cab driver

Johnston st (north side) from Kingston Harbor

James Swift & Co., wharfingers
C H Hatch, ticket agent
P Clint, hotel

Ontario st intersects

Anglo-American hotel
19 Mrs Thos Nugent
21 Mrs Alex McKillop
25 Mrs Ellen Lynch
31 Jeremiah Hurley, laborer
r31 Mrs Mary Gleason
r31 Richard Bolton, laborer
r31 Mrs John Fanning
r31 Mrs John Joyce
33 John Sughrue, laborer
37 John O'Shea, trader

King st intersects

St George's Cathedral

Wellington st intersects

Congregational Church
87 Michael Aratta, cutler
r87 Stephen Quelish, plaster worker
r87 Mrs Wm Aubin
r87 Mrs John Bondall
r87 Mrs Michael Massy
r87 Thomas Pickering
r87 Timothy Rooney
r87 Mrs Philip Phillips
93 Rev J A K Walker
99 Mrs James Gleeson
101 Mrs Ellen Larue

Bagot st intersects

Asylum
Baseball grounds
191 J B Page, merchant
193 Rev S N Jackson
195 R S Dobbs, C E
197 E Steacy, merchant

Clergy st intersects

St Mary's Cathedral
225 Bishop's Palace

Barrie st intersects

247 F Brownfield, banker
249 H Goodearle, cabinet mak'r
255 Mrs E Scott
257 Mrs C Ryan
259 Mrs M Glenn
261 J Primo, laborer
263 Vacant
267 J Scouse, painter
Louise Public School

Division st intersects

291 Mrs C Cunningham
293 J McArnen, farmer
295 Mrs A Burns
297 Vacant
301 W Hayward, blacksmith
305 J Farley, carter
307 D Manhan, laborer
309 G Boyd, engineer
311 W Hanscombe, laborer
313 T O'Reilly, engineer
315 D Scott, clerk
317 R H Light, artist
319 P Lawless, carter
321 Mrs J Fowler
323 J Sloan, painter
325 A J Spenceley
327 R Greer, laborer

335 J A LeHemp, watchmaker
337 John Smith, printer
339 W Knox, butcher

Gordon st intersects

351 E Hull, painter
353 Richard Lum, mechanic
355 Mrs L Hammond
361 H H Taylor, tinsmith

Alfred st intersects

373 J Crowley, carter
377 R Burns, laborer
385 J McGall, clerk
387 G Filtz, cabinet maker
389 J McKim, hide inspector
391 T Rutherford, moulder
393 Mrs E Lyons
395 J Williams, laborer

Frontenac st intersects

405 R Filtz, mason

*Albert, Nelson and Victoria sts
intersect*

601 Vacant

Johnston st (south side)

G T R Station

Ontario st intersects

18 Mrs Mary Kelly
20 James Quigley
24 Patrick Hurley, carter
r24 Wm O'Donnell, laborer
26 Geo Laturney, carter
28 E J Manning, saddler
32 Mrs John Sinnott
34 Thomas Sinnott, cab driver
42 Joseph Jamieson, plumber

r42 John Harris, laborer
r42 Mrs John Parson
 44 John Birkett, laborer
 46 Thomas Healey, laborer

King st intersects

 52 Dr Garrett
 54 Jas H Taylor, K & P R
 68 J A Henderson, Q C

Wellington st intersects

 76 John McNeil, moulder
 78 Roller Rink
 80 John McLeod, carter
 82 Miss Kate Mathews
 84 Geo F Palmer, carpenter
 84 S Arniel, mariner
     Notre Dame Convent

Bagot st intersects

112 Mrs C Garrett
114 Mrs James Scott
116 Mrs Wm McNamee
120 Mrs Mary Woods
122 Robert Hendry, traveller
126 Wm Rigney, merchant
128 Alex Smyth, harbor master
136 Wm S Smyth, clerk P O
138 Wm Dalton, merchant
140 Capt A G G Wurtele
142 T O Bolger, city engineer
146 T G Rudd, merchant
148 Neil McNeil, plumber
154 R Macpherson, immigration
       agent
162 John Ward, merchant

Sydenham st intersects

172 Mrs J R Dickson
176 G S Fenwick, merchant
188 Prof G B Mowat

190 Mrs J Birmingham
196 Alex Gunn, merchant

Clergy st intersects

216 John Laidlaw, merchant
218 D H Dowsley, M D
220 Mrs Richard Tossell
220 Robt J Chown, agent
222 J M Machar, barrister
224 C F Rees, traveller
226 H C Voight, accountant
228 Mrs Jane Macalister
232 R T Burns, deputy P M
238 Alex Ross, merchant
240 John Kelly, clerk P O

Barrie st intersects

242 Rev G S Eldridge
     Second Congregational Church
258 Miss Nellie Carnegie, grocer
260 Mrs Doherty
262 Frank Hollowell, laborer
264 John Fisher, contractor
266 Evan McColl, Customs
268 A G Allen, M D
270 Wm Wright, butcher
276 John Paul, sup't harbor
278 Mrs John Wright

Division st intersects

282 John Carey, moulder
284 Geo Thompson, collector
286 Mrs John Munro
288 M Brennan, keeper K P
280 Richard Bilton, sailor
292 Wm McCutcheon, baker
294 Mrs Harriet Swanston
296 Mrs Caleb Boyce
298 Wm Campion, blacksmith
302 I Asselstine, carpenter
304 James Sleeth, mason
306 Mrs E A Harper

308 Rev W Short
310 J Holden, laborer
312 Miss M Dempsey
314 Mrs M Swain
316 C Seale, laborer
320 J Chrisley, laborer
322 Wm Gates, carpenter
328 ——Guess
330 J Johnston, merchant
338 Wm McCartney, mason
340 F M Morrison, machinist

Gordon st intersects

356 Vacant
358 N B Johnston, gardener
360 G M Weber, piano maker
362 J McKenty

Alfred st intersects

382 J Rutherford, carpenter
386 James Lee, carpenter

Frontenac st intersects

410 H Wilkins, painter
412 J Kirkwood, mariner
414 P Filtz, carpenter
416 C Schermerhorn, mason
418 A Potter, sailor
420 J Megarry, policeman
422 J Ballentyne, policeman
424 J Callaghan, cabinet maker
426 T Barber, carpenter
428 G Randall, laborer
430 Mrs M Reid

*Albert, Nelson and Victoria sts
intersect*

**King st East (east side) from
Barrie to the river**

Murney Tower

Emily st intersects

31 J S Muckleston, merchant
45 C F Gildersleeve
49 E J B Pense, publisher
Andrew Maclean, grocer

Maitland st intersects

Joseph Upper
Rybert Kent

Simcoe st intersects

107 Alex Robinson, boilermaker
James A Hendry

West st intersects

John Mudie, barrister
F A Bickley, traveller
131 Vacant
133 Mrs Catherine Fraser
141 K N Fenwick, M D
Major-Gen Cameron

Union st intersects

161 Noel Kent
165 Gilbert Griffin, P O inspector
167 Thomas Briggs, manager F
L & I society
169 Donald Fraser, banker
W Ferguson, sheriff

Gore st intersects

199 Dr Herald
203 Vacant

Earl st intersects

B W Folger
223 Philip Stearne, fur dealer
Bank of Montreal

William st intersects

Merchants Bank
Mrs John Arnold
Henry O'Hara
Robert Sloan, engineer
259 Jos A B Smith, tailor

Johnston st intersects

John Hallett, laborer
Mrs Mary Lowry
277 John Bush, laborer
279 Dr Connell
British American Hotel

Clarence st intersects

J F Swift, insurance agent
297 R W Shannon, barrister
299 J B Carruthers, broker
J G King & Co, druggists

Market Square intersects

Market

Brock st intersects

327 Canadian Express Office
331 Vacant
335 Vacant
337 Bibby & Virtue, tinsmiths
339 Vacant
341 Jas McParland, wh liquors
343 Thos Peters, hairdresser
345 Smith Bros, watchmakers
347 F W Spangenburg, jeweller
349 J G Bastow, plumber
351-53 A S Oliver, M D
355 McBroom Bros, grocers

Princess st intersects

Murphy's grocery
R H Patterson, blacksmith
371 Thos Hand, second hand
       dealer
373 John Joyce, butcher

375 Peter Lamoureaux, dealer
377 Wm Cochrane, grocer
381 Wm Hayward, blacksmith
St Lawrence Hotel

Queen st intersects

395 Mrs Jane Young, dressm'r
397 M Norris, coal heaver
401 J M Jackson, ale bottler
403 G C Wylie, carpenter
405 James Young, laborer
407 John O'Donnell, inland rev
409 Capt J Monette, mariner
411 Capt J G Hurley, mariner
413 Geo Elder
415 John Dodd, engineer

Barrack st intersects

425 Bowen House
427 David Hay, laborer
429 Samuel Cairns, laborer
431 Albert Davy, grain shovel'r
433 Benj Davy, carpenter
435 Railroad House

Place d' Armes intersects

King st East (west side)

City Park

West st intersects

130 Miss Mary Fowler
132 Isaac Simpson, banker
140 Jas Swift, wharfinger
146 Mrs Sarah Wilson
150 C V Price, Co Judge
156 O S Strange, M D

Union st intersects

160 J Brokenshire, pumpmaker
162 E Adams, steamboat insp'r

166 Rev A N Cooke
168 Miss H Martin, teacher
172 J M Strange, merchant

Gore st intersects

190 F Reeves, merchant
196 Lawlor & Dartnell, fancy goods
198 Mrs E H Parker
202 Vacant
204 Mrs John Craig
208 Alex Duncan, driller
212 Mrs Mary Ferris

Earl st intersects

218 John Neill, traveller
220 Edward Amond
222 Vacant
224 Mrs Swift
226 Mrs Samuel Muckleston
232 R F Davis, photographer
238 C A Irwin, M D

William st intersects

244 H J Saunders, M D
246 Mrs Jane Saunders
254 John Thompson
258 Miss E Gleeson, dressmaker
r258 Mrs James Prince
r258 R Murray, teamster
r258 Alfred Elliott, mail carrier
260 George McMahon, weigh-master
264 Miss L Gildersleeve

Johnston st intersects

St George's Cathedral
Custom House

Clarence st intersects

298 John Shanahan, saloon
302 R H Toye, baker

304 John McIntyre, barrister
312 Mrs M Quinn, grocer
314 Michael Walsh, butcher
316 Ford Bros, tanners
318 W H Carnovsky, fruiterer
Masonic Hall
320 B J Leahy, grocer
322 Waddingham Bros, butchr's
324 T Doolan, hotel
326 P J Lawless, news dealer
328 Thos Grahen, hide dealer
W H Reid, butcher

Brock st intersects

Henry Wade, druggist
332 Robert Shaw, barrister
332 W Newlands, architect
334 Sheldon & Davis, photo-graphers
336 *British Whig* Office
342 Donald Fraser, private banker
344 W Brophy, gents' furnisher
346 John Cunningham, sewing machines
350 C A Vanarnam, confection'r
352 W Reeves, gents' furnisher
354 Thomas Moore, tailor
356 Thos McAuley, bookseller
358 McNaughton & Co, clothiers

Princess st intersects

360 Hon M Sullivan, M D
374 John Bushell, mariner
John F McDermott, car-riages

Queen st intersects

Victoria foundry
414 Alex McQuisten, bookkeeper
416 Chas Carson, stove fitter

Barrack st intersects

Bookbinding at McAuley's Bookstore.

420 T M Fenwick, M D
428 Robt Kidd, laborer
r428 Charles Christmas, laborer
434 Mrs Ann Free ·
434 Wm Stigney, laborer
438 Thos Sands, shoveller
  Edward Williams, coal
  dealer

King st West (north side) from Barrie to Portsmouth

 R C Carter
13 Sir Richard Cartwright, M P
17 W J Strethern, clerk

George st intersects

25 Richard Varney, mechanic
27 Robt Robinson, boatbuilder
29 Thos Crawford, fireman
31 Thos McKenzie, coachman
35 James Sherwood, cabman
37 Mrs McCullough
39 Wm Roach, fireman
41 Miles Sinnott, cabman
43 John Collins, letter carrier
45 Vacant
55 John Campbell, laborer
59 J R Smeaton, grocer

O'Kill st intersects

83 Wm Cunningham, finisher
89 John Waters
99 John Willis
101 M B Staley, carpenter
103 Josiah Abrams, car driver
105 Matthew Campbell, laborer
107 Norman Davy, grocer

Gordon st intersects

117 Joseph Daunt
123 John Gleeson, ice dealer

125 J Hewton, manufacturer
143 Col John Campbell
165 S H Paine

St Lawrence ave intersects

Rev C E Cartwright
Edward Ferris, farmer

Albert and Collingwood sts intersect

Pipes' ice house

Newman's Cottages.
{ Geo Wilson, boiler maker
{ Wm Newman, guard K P
{ Mrs Jackson
{ Patrick Ryan, laborer
{ R McCormack, guard K P
{ Robt Evans, keeper K P

Beverley st intersects

303 John Wright, city foreman
 John B Murphy, " Edge Hill "
 Thos Turnbull, engineer

Baker Cottages.
{ 5 Mrs M Bates
{ 4 Miss Stoughton
{ 3 Vacant
{ 2 Frank Dobbs
{ 1 Mathew Paterson, mariner

Centre st intersects

St Mary of the Lake
Fenton Green, laborer
Henry Bowley, tool dresser
Chas Macaway, engineer

Ellerbeck ave intersects

Michael Doran, manuf'r

Livingston ave, Pembroke st and Alwington ave intersect

King st west (south side)

Geo Robinson, boat builder
Kingston Knob Factory
Kingston Paint Works
Geo Davy, carpenter
John Gleeson's ice house
Kingston Hosiery Co
118 Grand Trunk brewery
300 The Rathbun Co
302 John F Wilson, manager
    Bay of Quinte Malt House
    Lt-Col H R Smith, "Ringwood"
    Thos Jones, coachman
    J A Allen

Livingston ave (east side) from King w to Union

Edward Geary, shoemaker
A Simmons, candle manufacturer
J G Valdock, guard K P
Herbert Lyon, student

Livingston ave (west side)

39 Edward Burke, laborer
44 Nicholas Hugo, keeper K P

Macdonnell st north from Union to Princess

John McColl, butcher

Mack st west from Alfred to Nelson

1 Capt N D Moore, miner
7 W D Carmichael, traveller
11 Mrs Daniel McGuin
13 Geo Williams, sec Y M C A

15 Mrs David English
17 Vacant

Frontenac st intersects

23 Prof C Harris, R M C
31 Geo Mills, laborer

Main st (north side) from n Bagot to Division

Picard st intersects

27 Wm Mitchell, baker
29 D Nesbitt, carpenter
31 John Steel, carpenter
33 James Hartrey
35 ——Walker
41 Vacant

Main st (south side)

14 Geo Creggan, tailor

Picard st intersects

28 Geo Pogue, mason
36 John Suddard, laborer
38 Thos Daly, laborer

Maitland st from the water to King e

Miss Gertrude Dunlop

Market Square, south side City Hall

Ontario st intersects

Stanley House
6 John Kavanagh, grocer
8 Michael Conroy, grocer
10 Hinds Bros, soda water

7

12 W F Baker, flour and feed
14 C Lyons, saloon
16 Inland Revenue office
18 Henry Hughes, implements
18 C D Franklin, flour and feed
20 E R Martin, auctioneer
22-4 Albermarle Hotel
    J G King & Co, druggists

King st intersects

Markland st, also called Centre, (north side) from Montreal to Patrick

Vacants
John Higgins, tailor
John Whitehead, laborer
John O'Brien, laborer
Joseph Aiken, carter
James Aiken, laborer
Vacant

Markland st (south side)

A Forster, bartender
Daniel Gurney, engineer
John King
John Farmer, salesman
' Mrs James Simpson

Miller's Lane, from Bagot to Montreal

Robt Henderson, laborer
John Woods, laborer
Wm Hamilton, shoemaker

Montreal st (east side) from Brock north to limits

7 Thos R Dupuis, M D
9 Mrs Dunbar

11 C H Otto, bookbinder
11 John Mundell, M D
13 Major King
15 Mrs James McCammon
19 G W Clerihew, commission
21 Mechanics' Institute
21 Art School
21 Odd-Fellows' Hall
25 H H Curtis & Co, druggists

Princess st intersects

A Strachan, hardware
35 Hall Bros, portrait painters
39 N Wilmot, blacksmith
41-3 T W Milo, painter
47 Mrs Sarah Holder

Queen st intersects

St Paul's Church
Artillery Barracks

Ordnance st intersects

117 Robert Newman, contractor
118 Vacant
119 Alex Carr, machinist
120 Wm Hill, blacksmith
121 Mrs E Knifeton
122 James Suddard, carter
123 Anthony Lake, sawyer
124 John Maloney, blacksmith
125 Philip Mackay, moulder
127 Mrs Charles Lafrance
r127 Mrs Mary Spotten
129 Wm Edgar, painter
131 Robert Nugent, laborer
133 Mrs Robert Clark
135 Vacant
137 John McGlinn, shoemaker
141 S Donnelly, machinist
143 Alex Barton, engineer
145 Wm Simmonds, mariner
147 Philip Haffner, grocer

Bay st intersects

149 Wm Strainge, grocer
151 Charles Crane, miller
153 James Hamilton, machinist
153 Wm H McGuire, traveller
157 Wm Erwin, roadmaster K P R
159 John A McDonald, mariner

North st intersects

167 Michael Sullivan, carpenter
169 Mrs Catherine Sullivan
173 Vacant
175 A F Roney, clothier

Miller's Lane intersects

185 Thos Bailie, shoemaker
187 John Keough, laborer
189 Jas Murphy, carpenter
195 John McIlroy, laborer
209 Chas Diamond, laborer
211 Vacant

Picard st intersects

F X Lachance, grocer
217 John Pringle, moulder
217a Napoleon Parent, paymaster K P R
219 Michael Doyle, bartender
221 John Bell, baker
223 John Cowdy, quarry owner
225 N H Perry, carter
243 J Snider, carpenter
245-7 Vacant

John st intersects

275 Timothy O'Brien, shoemaker
277 Samuel Kirkpatrick, laborer
279 Jos Griffin, laborer

281a Charles Brown, sailor
281 Daniel Reeves, engineer
283 Colin Stewart, telegrapher
293 Alex Sloan, laborer
299 Wm Parker, engineer
301 Thos Frost, laborer
303 Walter Gow, watchman

Charles st intersects

305 Jos Groves, laborer
307 James Riley, spinner
309 Robt Frizzell, tailor
315 Mrs Wm Marion
321 Samuel Greer, engineer
322 John Greer, engineer
325 Thos Dehaney, carter
329 Lewis Robinson, salesman
331 Vacant

James and Rideau sts intersect

Edward Holmes, laborer
Jos Baxter, laborer
Vacant
St Patrick's Separate school
675 John Fallon, section boss
681 Alexander Darragh
689 Geo Darragh, carpenter
693 Patrick Lawler, carpenter
Methodist Church
765 Alfred Laidley, telegrapher
775 Thos McDermott, baggageman
777 Patrick Delaney, laborer
798 Mrs John Gamble
Star Hotel
John Druse, laborer
Alex Campbell, grocer
Robt Brignall, car inspector
Robt Hunter, pumpman
Mrs Jas McKay
Thos Sweetman, laborer
Wm Upham, conductor

Montreal st (west side)

Third Methodist Church
12 Vacant
   Shore Loynes & Co, grocers

Princess st intersects

   Odd-Fellows' Relief Association
   Public School Board Office
36 Merriman Bros, implements
46 Albion Hotel

Queen st intersects

   Mrs John Power

VICTORIA TERRACE.
1 Miss A Telgmann, teacher
2 Miss M A Doyle, teacher
3 B D Noxon, merchant
4 Alex Sutherland
5 Geo W Amey, manuf'r
6 E D Mundell, M D
7 Mrs Hester Chamberlain
   Major Wm King

WELLINGTON TERRACE.
5 Thos Meagher, customs
4 Thos Hurst, blacksmith
4 John McIntyre, carpenter
4 Walter Jones, painter
3 John Ryan, laborer
3 Wm Millard, carpenter
2 Vacant
1 Arch Urquhart, traveller

Ordnance st intersects

Convent grounds

Bay st intersects

140 John Irwin, grocer
144 Henry Sands, hide buyer
146 Mrs John Brady
148 Vacant

North st intersects

176 James Randall, sawyer
200 David Jones, carpenter
202 Felix O'Reilly, laborer
206 Mrs Ellen Scanlan
210 Geo W Walsh, loom fixer
212 Henry Shook, grocer

Picard st intersects

216 Jas Mahoney, grocer
220 John Branigan, grocer
228 Vacant
230 J J Gallagher, painter

Markland st intersects

240 Jas Soward's hotel
246 Samuel Rowcroft
248 Mrs John Mann
250 Mrs Daniel Stinson
252 Conway Millane, butcher

John st intersects

   B Halligan, boilermaker
284 Samuel Hornibrook, shoemaker
290 Mrs Jane Spencer
292 Mrs Patrick Nugent
294 Charles Keeler, carpenter
298 Edward Creamer, laborer
304 Vacant
308 Robert Allan, grocer

Charles st intersects

312 Thos Tooher, grocer
326 S McCormack, manufact'r
330 Mrs N Palmer, boarding
332 Thos G Ockley, grocer
334 Manuel Sturgess, carter
338 Mrs Anna Sherratt

James st intersects

356 Stephen Tyo, mariner
358 Robert Tilson, fireman

362 House of Industry
390 Robert Glasgow, currier
398 Marcus Walker, laborer
    Mrs Bridget McDonald

Stephen st intersects

460 Jas Kennedy, laborer
466 Walter Shufflebottom, quarry owner
468 Robert Agnew, carpenter
480 A Skelton, laborer

John st North intersects

    Patrick Gorman, carpenter
    Frontenac Public School
    K & P R car works
    Wm Hughes, carter
    Mrs Catharine Mills
680 J W Boakes, conductor
    J Cuddeford, stone cutter
    John Hoag, switchman
    David Funnell, carpenter
    W H Harmer, carpenter
770 John Kerr
772 Mrs John Donald

Park st intersects

    Jas Quigley, Depot House
    G T R station

Nelson st (east side) north from Johnston

    Mrs Fenwick
123 Vacant

Mack st intersects

141 John Graham, gardener
149 W Dempster, stone cutter
155 Henry Brouse, machinist
157 C Goodman, laborer
159 Alfred Howells, contractor

161 Wm Bennett
163 John Newlands, mason
171 Wm R Davy, carpenter
173 Jas McIlquham, plasterer

Princess st intersects

    Daniel Gunn, laborer
    Wm Langdon, contractor
    Bryce Douglas, bricklayer
    Capt Jos Dix, mariner
    John Orr, caretaker

Nelson st (west side)

138 John Bates, laborer
140 John Carver, carpenter
170 Wm Follast, laborer

Princess st intersects

    Robt Reynolds, mason
    N Langdon, mason

North st (north side) runs west from water's edge

Rideau st intersects

    Oil & Enamel Cloth Co

Bagot and Montreal sts intersect

North st (south side)

    John D Page, car inspector

Rideau st intersects

50 Mrs Donovan
52 Jas Whalen, mariner
56 Michael Garvin, laborer
62 Daniel Campbell, carter
64 Mrs Mary Ann Glancey
68 James Vance, laborer

54   CITY OF KINGSTON.

Bagot st intersects

Thomas Tucker, laborer
Patrick Corrigan, laborer

Montreal st intersects

O'Kill st (north side) west from Barrie to King w

5 Mrs George Dodd
15 James Barrigan, laborer
17-19 Vacant
21 Michael Donoghue, carpenter

George st intersects

O'Kill st (south side)

10 Patrick O'Donnell, storekeeper K P

George st intersects

40 Alex McClymont
42 James Gallivan, engineer
44 George Creighton, bookkeeper
48 George Murray, mariner
50 John Dunn, laborer
52 Mrs John Regan
62 Wm Milroy, laborer
60 Mrs J B Rogers

Ontario st (east side) from West to the River

13 Felix Lennon, fireman
 Pump house
19 Wm Vince, engineer
23 Henry Yeddo, engineer
23a Patrick, O'Hern, plumber
25 John Purtell, laborer

25a R McIlgorne, blacksmith
27 Mrs Martin Staley
r27 John Dyer, laborer
31 Thos Furlong, laborer
 Kingston Foundry

Union st intersects

(RAILWAY COTTAGES.)
2-3 Vacant
4 Mrs D B Grant
5 Mrs E Sullivan, grocer
6 Edward Garry, barber
7 Geo Grath, laborer
8 Francis Knott, laborer
9 W Thompson, carpenter
10 Vacant
11 J St Thomas, laborer
12 —— Orr
13 Dennis Pelow, laborer
14 Edward Jackson, laborer
15 Michael Riley, laborer

Gore st intersects

Canadian Engine and Locomotive Co
111 John Corrigan, storeman
113 Thos Corrigan, storeman
121 Thos Clancy, laborer
 A Gunn & Co., wholesale grocers

William st intersects

Grand Trunk Station

Johnston st intersects

Vacant
175 Jas Brown & Co., wholesale grocers
183 George Robertson & Son, wholesale grocers
189 Fenwick, Hendry & Co, wh. grocers
195 Vacant

Clarence st intersects

Kingston & Pembroke Railway Station

Brock st intersects

Union Hotel
K & P Railway stables
Fire station
J Gaskin, manager M T Co

Princess st intersects

Ottawa Hotel
259 F X Lachance, grocer
261 James Tierney, grocer
263 Oldrieve & Horn, sailmakers
265 Jas McParland, bottler
267 B McCarey, grocer
269 Vacant
273 J Cockburn, steam fitter
277 Wm Cockburn, blacksmith

Queen st intersects

Vacant
Henry Lafrance, pilot
F F Cole, grain merchant
Vacant
Mrs Catharine Donoghue
M Mallen, wood dealer

Barrack st intersects

Tete du Pont barracks
M T Co's shipyard
Mrs Mary A Knapp
A C Knapp, boat builder
Cataraqui Bridge

Ontario st (west side)

8 Rev Wm Bain, D D
10 Vacant
22 Augustus Thibodeau

---

52 W G Craig, merchant
The Shedden Co stables

Union st intersects

56½ Goudrea, grocer
58 Vacant
60 G Donaldson, engine fitter
62 A A Macdonald, laborer
64 Mrs Andrew Sharp
68 Mrs Fred Dewsberry
70 Philip Dine, boiler maker
72 John Bejean, carpenter
72a Jas Scott, laborer
74 Alex Watson, laborer
    P McArdle, engineer
    Fred Rail, mariner
78 Wm Torkington, turnkey
    John Sproule, laborer
    John Kane, fitter
    Wm Henderson, laborer

Gore st intersects

84 Mrs Patrick Smith
90 H M Lacey, shoemaker
90a Alex Rushford, mariner
92 M McGoldrick, boilermaker
94 Mrs Daniel Magnet
96 James Bulger, grain shoveller
96 Pierce Kelly, harness maker
100 Wm Hinds, laborer
102 Mrs David Fitzgerald
106 Henry Paladeau
106a John Milne, laborer

Earl st intersects

Vacant
128 Vacant
130-32 A Haaz, vinegar manuf'r
136 Thos Nicholson
136 Thos McConville

William st intersects

City lumber yard
144 Edward Sanders, hotel
148 Wm Christmas, mariner
r148 Fred Beebe, mariner
150 Jas Fullen, foreman
152 Wm H Maguire, boarding
154 John McCummiskey, pilot
156 John Hackett, hide dealer
166 Owen McGinnis, hotel
168 John O'Connor, shoemaker

Johnston st intersects

Anglo-American Hotel
176 John Milne, fruiterer
178-84 Hotel Frontenac
186 Bell Telephone office
188 Custom Examining Warehouse
190 D S Robertson, broker
192 Smythe, Smith & Lyon, barristers
194 Kirkpatrick & Rogers, barristers
196 United States Consulate
198 Breck & Booth, coal and wood

Clarence st intersects

200 T L Snook, barrister
202-3 Stanley House

Market Square intersects

Bank of British North America
City Buildings

Brock st intersects

228 Owen Kennedy, hotel
234 Vacant
236 Mrs David Lafreniere, boarding
238-40 John Braddon, hotel

242 Benj White, hotel
248 Wm McRossie, lumber
250 Wm S West, auctioneer
252 Jas Gowdy, butcher

Princess st intersects

Stevenson's piano factory
268 Patrick McDermott
270 Richard Booth, fireman
272 Andrew Maclean, grocer
274 Henry Jennings, shoemak'r
276 Mrs M Corrier, second hand dealer
282 Manley Williams, hotel

Queen st intersects

286 Arch Simpson, hotel
288 Dennis Millane, butcher
290 Jos R Donaldson, grocer
294 Mrs Patrick Carroll
298-300 Globe Hotel
306 John Dickson, shoemaker
312 Hogan House

Barrack st intersects

Campbell's wood yard

Place d' Armes intersects

Soward's wood yard

Orchard st north from Cataraqui

Frank Lalonde, blacksmith
Z Glazier, carter
Edmund Scrutton, laborer
Robt Stevenson, tinsmith
T Sands, grain shoveller

River st intersects

J. B. PAGE & Co. Fashionable Hatters & Furriers
138 Princess Street.

STREET DIRECTORY. 57

Montreal Lead Mining and
Smelting Co
Jas Keenan, caretaker

Alma st intersects

187 J Sharman, boat builder

Ordnance st (north side) from 287 Wellington

Rideau st intersects

39 D McEwen, machinist
41 J F McEwen, machinist
43 Patrick Burns, baker
45 James Collins, engineer
47 Vacant
49 Andrew McAvey, laborer

Bagot st intersects

Joseph Elmer, barber
J F Martin, sign painter
Joseph Shaw, laborer

Montreal st intersects

House of Providence
107 Edward Rousseau, laborer
109 James Ausem, laborer
111 Mrs James Pratt
115 S Burton, upholsterer
117 N Vanwinkle, carpenter
119 M McMillan, sailor
121 A H Knapp, carpenter
123 Wm McNeill, merchant
125 H McDonald, shoemaker

Sydenham st intersects

135 Lewis Gourdier, carver
139 Edward Ball, clerk
141 Mrs Elliott
143 J H Kilpatrick, stonecutter
145 Jas Graham, mechanic
147 Daniel Eves, carter
149 Patrick Aiken, carter
Burial ground

Ordnance st (south side)

Rideau st intersects

John Cooke, engineer
Samuel Lafleur, laborer
Philip Bajus, shoemaker
46 P McCormack, laborer
48 M J Leaden, clerk
Thos Keats, laborer

Montreal st intersects

110 C W Crowley, laborer
112 Peter Wafer
114-116 Vacant
118 Fred Williamson
122 Patrick Flanagan, engineer

Sydenham st intersects

134 Patrick Healey, laborer
142 A Simmonds, merchant
146 Patrick Lyons, hide dealer
154 Mrs Jane Hogan
162 Mrs Ralph King

Clergy st intersects

178 Wm Abernethy, machinist
184 Isaac Newlands, contractor
188 James Gardiner
190 A McBride, engineer
192 S McBride, carpenter
194 Wm Abernethy

Park st, G T R Station, Montreal st

John Fleming
Mrs Dorah McDermott

Edward Doyle, carpenter
Jos Dennis, tel repairer
Patrick Smith, engineer
Joseph Cully, laborer
Thos Kent, laborer
Samuel Wood, laborer
Wm Lappage, signalman
Mrs Hugh Cleary
D Mulrooney, laborer
S Lambert, bridge inspect'r
F Jeffers, signalman
Lawrence Mallon, laborer
Francis Gates
Henry Marshall, laborer
Michael Delaney, trackman
F W Clarke, carpenter

Patrick st (north side) from junction of Balaclava and Alma to James

15 Patrick Hart, laborer
17 John Behan, clerk

Picard st intersects

23 Chas Bailey, laborer

Markland and John sts intersect

Vacant
M Fallen, carter

Charles st intersects

Patrick st (south side)

James Dew, laborer
16 Vacant
18 Luke Joyce, carter

Picard st intersects

Vacant

John st intersects

Luke Whalen, mariner
Chas Clarke, blacksmith

Quebec st intersects

John Ryder, laborer
Mrs E Sears
Jas Shaver, laborer

Pine st intersects

Pembroke st (east side) from King w to Union

7 Allen Macdonald
29 R McDonald, manuf'r
Thos Davidson, instructor K P

Pembroke st (west side)

5 Chas Bostridge, guard K P
7 Jas Rutherford, guard K P
9 Jos Fisher, merchant
11 James Doyle, guard K P

Picard st (north side) from Rideau west

Edward Maddigan, fireman
Thos Gallagher, laborer
John Riley, laborer
Patrick Flanagan, laborer
Patrick Maloney

Bagot st intersects

Samuel Sawberry, laborer
Adam Lees, spinner
John Seale, carpenter

Montreal st intersects

40 Charles Smeaton, currier
48 Michael Galvin, carter
95 Edwd J Taylor, machinist
97 Richard Randalls, laborer
103 Chas Powell, carpenter
105 Mrs Powell
111 Thos Newton, cab driver
123 John Stewart, watchman

Patrick st intersects

149 Vacant

Barrie st intersects

155 Wm Massie, contractor
157 Wm Massie, jr, contractor

York and Main sts intersect

Patrick Lennon, laborer

Picard st (south side)

Vacant

Bagot and Montreal sts intersect

John Tetlock, carpenter

Sydenham st intersects

100 Wm Ferguson, laborer

Redan st intersects

114 Robt Rollinson, blacksmith
118 John Smilie, watchman
124 Isaac David

Patrick st intersects

150 Alfred Dougal, carpenter
152 Lewis Dougal, teamster
154 Mrs Catharine Morris

Barrie st intersects

James McGlone, mason

York, Main and Vine sts intersect

Pine st (north side) from Patrick to Alfred

5 W Campsall, carpenter
7 H Peters, mason
9 Jas Campsall, mechanic

Catharine st intersects

13 Vacant
21 D Walker, blacksmith

Cowdy st intersects

25 Geo Ball, mason
27 Frank Pollitt, baker
29 Thos Pollitt, baker
31 Thos Graham, painter
33 J S Donaldson, carpenter
35 Vacant
37 John Babcock, carpenter
39-41 Vacant
45 George Brown

Cherry st intersects

85 Willard Stephens, mariner
89 Wm Joyce, painter
101 W H Godwin, ins agent
103 Benj Lane, driver

Division st intersects

145 Wm Bloomfield, sailor
147 Wm Osser, laborer
153 Wm Campbell, plasterer

Albert st intersects

169 Mrs Robert Morrison
175 John Howell, mason
189 John Allan, mechanic

J. B. PAGE & Co. WHOLESALE AND RETAIL HATS, CAPS AND FURS, 138 Princess St.

60 CITY OF KINGSTON

Pine st (south side)

4 Thos Hanley, laborer
6 Jas Ilett, clerk
8 John Bell, carpenter
10 Wm McIlroy, laborer
12 Patrick Mallen, laborer
14 John Free, brakeman
16 H Potter, engineer
20-22 Vacant
24 Robt Bushey, carpenter
46 Vacant
50 John McCabe, tailor

Cherry st intersects

Mrs M McDonald, grocer
86 John Morrison, moulder
98 H Saunders, carpenter
100 H Yeatman, engineer
102 C David
104 W D Derry, mason

Division st intersects

136-8 Vacant
140 Richard Lake, painter
142 John H McMaster, laborer
144 Henry Stratford, carpenter
146 Wm Coburn, laborer
152 Levy Scouten, carpenter

Place d'Armes (north side) from Ontario to Wellington

James Sowards, wood merchant
A Caldwell & Son, lumber
Jos Mercier, carpenter
Chas Beach, teamster

King st intersects

Hay Market

Jas Dunlop, hay dealer
J McLeod, sash and doors

Wellington st intersects

Place d'Armes (south side)

C H Leclair, brakeman
16 Thos Daley, trader
22 Benj Stokes, teamster
22 Joseph Paradis, carpenter
26 Peter Lamoreux, cooper
28 Wm Lawler, laborer
34 Jas McGowan, hotel

King st intersects

48 Richard Brown, laborer
48 Henry Conley, clerk
54 Thos Woodhead, laborer
Thos Worth, caretaker
Riding School

Wellington st intersects

Plum st (east side) from James

John McKee, carpenter
Vacant

Plum st (west side)

J Turcott

Princess st (north side) from harbor to limits

H Mooers & Co, grain
Ottawa Hotel

Ontario st intersects

Stevenson & Co, pianos
35-7 J L Orr, blacksmith

39 B Barney & Co, metals
41 Vacant
43 Jos Fisher, flour
45 M Julian, dealer
47 — Hall, blacksmith
49 A Fields, barber
51 T Palmer, confectioner
53 H Wells, harness maker
55 L W Murphy, grocer

King st intersects

65 Hon M Sullivan, M D
67 *News* Office
69 Jackson & Co, bottlers
71-3 J Muckleston & Co, hardware
75 W M Drennan, furniture
77 Elliott Bros, plumbers
79-81 R White, dyer
83 D A Waddell, harness mk'r
85-7 McMahon Bros, hardware
89 S Oberndorffer, cigar manfr
91 A McCormick, liquors
93 Benj Silver, clothier
95 John Corbett, hardware

Wellington st intersects

101 L M Woods, fancy goods
103-5 Alex Sutherland, boots
107 Geo Sarsfield, boots
109 Stroud Bros, teas
111 Jos Dillon & Son, boots
113 W J Mahood, fancy goods
115-17 Vincent Ockley & Sons, grocers
121 J Hiscock, grocer
123 Young Men's Christian Association
125 S Weaver, fancy goods
127 Geo Offord, sr, boots
131 John Tweddell, tailor
129 City Hotel
r129 G J Hutton, livery

139 Wm Mundell, barrister
141 D F Armstrong, boots
143 Dalton & Strange, hardware
145 Noxon & Rockwell, boots

Bagot st intersects

155 G S Hobart, druggist
157 N T Greenwood, fruiterer
159 M Kirkpatrick, fancy goods
161 R H Elmer, barber
165 J W Powell, photographer
167 H A Liffiton, watchmaker
171 H Skinner & Co, druggists
173 W K Routley, tobacconist
175 S P Fraser, tailor
177 Rees Bros, confectioners
185 W J Wilson, druggist
187 Robertson Bros, crockery
189 R M Horsey & Co, hardware
191 J Laidlaw & Son, dry goods
193 A Strachan, hardware

Montreal st intersects

201 Vacant
203-7 Windsor Hotel
209 R D Baker, tobacconist
211 J Franklin, flour and feed
213 Singer Manuf'g Co
215 J Granger, carpenter
217 E J Fokes, barber
219 M Dolan, saddler
223 W C Loiseau, hairdresser
225 J M Sherlock, tailor
227 Hop Lee, laundry
225 R Montgomery, dyer
227 Miss Weller, fancy goods
229-31 Wm Dunn, stoves
233-5 G W Robinson, carriages
241 F C Marshall, cabinetmaker
243 Chadwick & Clark, marble

Sydenham st intersects

251 H Brame, undertaker
261 Wm Pipe, bottler
263 W L Richardson, cabinet maker
265 Alex O'Brien, tailor
267 Thos Cunningham, boots
269 James Davis, shoemaker
271 Mrs J Gray, dressmaker
273 Wm Cannon, tailor
279 B B Carnovsky, cabinet maker
281 J M Sherlock, pianos
285 Wm Pipe, manufacturer
289 James Boyd, baker
291 Hugh Morgan, piano agent
293 James Macdonald, dealer
295 Miss Sullivan, dressmaker
297 Mrs R Pigion, ladies' furnisher

Clergy st intersects

St Andrew's Church
333 Mrs M A Cliff, crockery
335 Richard Campion, painter
341-43 John Ward & Co, grocers
345 David Gibson, grocer
347 Owen Jones, printer
349 John Laird, paper hanger
351 B Harris, barber
353 Mrs Mary Toland
355 Henry Laughan, grocer
357 Geo Dick, carriage trimmer
359 J S Babcook, grocer

Barrie st intersects

367 Charles Milford
371 Mrs Roland Benedict
375 C Jenkin, blacksmith
383 Mrs Patrick King
385 Mrs Jane Minnes
387 W J Arneil, watchmaker
389 Wm Drury, tinsmith
393 Wm Drury, sr

395 Robt Graham, shoemaker
405 S H Fee, M D
407 Thomas Campbell, carriage maker
411 Wm Corbett, tinsmith
413 Miss Rebecca Lee
421 Fred Welsh, marble cutter

Division st intersects

435 Wm Pillar
437 Henry P Wells, livery
443 T A Caswell, carriage mk'r
445 Sidney Orser, carpenter
449 Duncan Cays, real estate
451 Thos Prittie, rope maker
453 H A Miller, laborer
455 W J Livingston, merchant
457 Wm Miller, bookkeeper
459 Richard Gilbert, traveller
461 D Gibson, grocer
473 R J McDowall, merchant
475 Vacant
477 T W McCrea, carriage manufacturer
479 Mrs Henry Burns
483 Kingston Street Railway Offices
487 Alex Ely, bartender
495 Thos D Minnes, merchant
497 Peter Bates
499 Henry A Lacroix, cabinet maker
501 Wm Gibson, agent
503 John Thornton, grocer

Chatham st intersects

521 Thos Galloway, tailor
523 Richard Elliott, shoemaker
525 Wm Jarvis, carpenter
527 Wm Murray, clerk

Alfred st intersects

563 Jos McBride, carpenter
569 Vacant
571 Thomas D Carscallen, carpenter
573 Wm D Graves, carriage trimmer

Frontenac st intersects

601 D J Patterson, carpenter

Albert st intersects

619 Henry Bailey, grocer
621 Stephen Graver, clerk
623 Francis Moorland, laborer
627 Jos Gates, driver
629 William Pillar
631 J Nelson Armstrong, printer
635 Thomas Carter, grocer

Nelson st intersects

639 Wm Reid, clerk
641 James Allen, laborer
Mrs J Peters, grocer

Victoria st intersects

Walter Wiltshire, baker
Mrs Wm Bryant
Jas Doyle, butcher
Vacant
Wm Lee, laborer
Charles Jones, laborer,
Patrick Doyle, grocer
Geo Adsit, carpenter

Smith st intersects

T F Vanluven, co treasurer
Robt Reeves, carter
Vacant
Geo Patterson, moulder
769 Robt Hyland
798 John Hyland, carpenter
801 Mrs John Jones

Joseph Moore
A McGuire, drover
Robt Saunders, laborer
Vacant
Wm Murphy, laborer
Wm Green, butcher
John Green, butcher
Wm Pickering, milk dealer
Wm Carson
City limits

Princess st (south side)

J Richardson & Sons, grain
N D Moore, mining engineer

Ontario st intersects

Wm McRossie, lumber
36 H P Wells, livery
38 C M Percival, horseshoer
44-8 R S Patterson, commission
52 McBroom Bros, grocers

King st intersects

62 McNaughton & Co, clothiers
66 George McDonald, harness maker
66 P O Carnovsky, tobacconist
66 Mrs H Fahey, confectioner
70 R Newlands, tobacconist
70 Thos McGowan, boarding
72 A E Elmer, barber
76 Wm Shanahan, hotel
78-80 Cousineau, Quinn & Corrigan, dry goods
82 Kingston Business College Comp'y
82 Victoria Hall
84 Jas Galloway, sen, hatter
86 J Henderson & Co, booksellers

88 J C Hardy & Co, dry goods
90 Henry Henderson, photographer
90 A M Brock, watchmaker
92 Vacant

Wellington st intersects

100 John Dunbar, tailor
102 A J McMahon, dry goods
106-8 Walsh & Steacy, dry goods
108 Miss M Richardson, hair works
108 Miss R McNamee, dressmaker
110 Lambert & Walsh, tailors
114 Federal Warehouse
116 Haines & Lockett, boots
118-120 Richmond, Orr & Co, dry goods
122 Grand Union Clothing Co
124 Chown & Mitchell, druggists
124½ W G Ashley, gents' furnisher
126 B Doran & Co, milliners
128-30 Alex Ross, dry goods
132-34 Spence & Crumley, dry goods
136 Rigney & Hickey, grocers
138 J B Page & Co, hatters
140 Minnes & Burns, dry goods

Bagot st intersects

156 T Mills & Co, hatters
158 A J Lee, barber
162 John McKay, leather
164 M Hickey & Co, milliners
166 Vacant
168 W J Dick & Son, boots
170 Vacant
174 F Shaw & Co, dry goods
176 Murray & Taylor, dry goods
178 Jas Redden, grocer

180 R McFaul, dry goods
182 Jas Crawford, grocer
184 Vacant
186 H H Curtis & Co, druggists

Montreal st intersects

200 Shore Loynes & Co, grocers
202 A Sine, fancy goods
204 Bowes & Bisonette, dry goods
206 J R Rattenbury, gents' furnisher
208 A D Simmonds, bookseller
210 Mrs M C Elmer, saloon
212 W H Carnovsky, fruiterer
214 A G Flett, tailor
216 W C Martin, saddlery hardware
218 Martin's Opera House
220 R J McDowall, pianos
222 John McLaughlin, confectioner
224 W P Bell & Son, photogr's
226 Vacant
228 W J Merriman, organs
230 Dr Alice McGillivray
230 R E Sparks, dentist
232 N C Polson & Co, druggists
232 J S R McCann, accountant
236 Wood Bros, watchmakers
238 Robt Wood, tobacconist
240 John Haffner, butcher
242 N E Runians, grocer
240a Vacant
244 Geo Carruthers, grocer
254-56 Jas Reid, furniture
258 Mrs Branigan
260 J Abernethy & Co, boots
262 B A Booth & Co, woollens
264 John Green, butcher
266 H M Hawley, salesman
268 Vacant
270 T H Johns, grocer

270½ Herbert Day, boarding
272 A McDonald, baker
274 J A Greenwood, confectioner
280 Mrs Ellen Jones, fancy goods
282 S J Kelly, painter
284 Mrs H Stratford, grocer
286 H Sharpe, grocer
286 Alex Robinson, carpenter
288 Joseph Salter, auctioneer
290 James Boyd, livery
292 Jas Robbs, butcher
296 Robt Campbell, saloon
298 M Campbell, grocer
300 E R Welch & Son, marble cutters

Clergy st intersects

312 Vacant
314 Jos Freeman, restaurant
316 Thos James, butcher
320 John Carson, merchant
322 Carson Bros, grocers
324 R J Carson, wh grocer
326 Vacant
338 John Saunders, butchers
340 Samuel Harkness, hotel
344 Vacant
348-50 R J Brown, hotel
352 W J Kemp, grocer
354 Henry Stratford, taxidermist
356-58 A Swanston, baker

Barrie st intersects

366 J W Brown, carriagemaker
368 Miss Lemon, dressmaker
370 Jas Schofield, baker
378 Vacant
380 Samuel Mason, mariner
382 Wm Lapage, plasterer
384 Patrick O'Brien, laborer

386 A B Gordon, miner
388 Samuel Jenkins, contractor
390-92 J Laturney, carriage maker
394 George Brown
396 O V Bartells, deputy city treas
400 Mrs McPherson
412 Mrs John Wiley

Division st intersects

424 Dr Edwin Hemsted

VAUGHN TERRACE {
426 M D Price
428 George Smith
430 James Johnston
432 Vacant
434 John Mills, teacher
436 John Dunbar, merchant
}
450 Col John Duff

Gordon st intersects

G M Weber factory
500 George Mooers
502 Chas Livingston, merchant
506 George Newlands, architect
518 Rev Thos G Smith
522 James Ferguson, salesman
524 Patrick Hammond, lumberman
526 James Hinds, soda water manuf'r

Alfred st intersects

Jas Adams, grocer
Mrs Hentig

Frontenac and Albert sts intersect

Rev W Sparling
622 Vacant
624 Michael Walsh, butcher
628 Elijah Veal, baker
630 Joseph Stewart, carpenter

Nelson st intersects

Public School
668-70 Thos Carnovsky, baker

Victoria st intersects

Jos McConnell, hotel
680 Vacant
716 Wm Spankie
720 Wm Hamilton, mason
730 John Saunders, butcher

Macdonnell st intersects

768 Wm Doyle, butcher
772 Mrs Cooper
776 Daniel Cooper, merchant
826 Jas H Metcalfe, M L A
834 Robt Middleton, laborer
836 Wm Townsend, carpenter
840 Alfred Blakey, butcher
842 E Haffner, butcher
844 W J Daley, grocer
848 Perry Lake, horse dealer
852 Richard Cooper, butcher
868 Mrs Lasher

Regent st intersects

914 D Fallon, hotel

Bath Road intersects

Quebec st (north side) from Patrick to Division

John Jenkins

Cherry st intersects

Geo Turcott, car builder

Quebec st (south side)

2 John Ryan, carpenter
4 Jas Delph, laborer

6 Jas Smith, mason
8 Jas Scruton, teamster

Cherry st intersects

32 Mrs Catharine Beven
34-6-8 Vacant

Queen st (north side) from the Harbor to Division

Montreal Transportation Co

Ontario st intersects

Simpson's Hotel
Albert Lemay, blacksmith
19 Gas Works and coal yard
19 S Hobbs, laborer

King st intersects

Victoria Foundry
57 Vance Burton, foreman
63 Wm O'Neill, laborer
65 Alex Rushford, engineer
67 F J Gallagher, laborer
69 H Angrove, shoemaker

Wellington st intersects

73 Thos Dunn, grocer
75 Mrs Julia Blair
77 Thos Welch, teamster
79 John Maloney
81 Mrs Elizabeth Elliott
85 John McLellan, baker
87 Alex Begg, carter
89 Capt A H Miller, mariner
91 Miss Ellen Patterson
93 Thos E Hughes, teamster
95 M Strachan, planing mills
97 Capt S Fraser, mariner
101 Miss Sarah Coy
103 Mrs Ann Manion
103 Wm Bushell, carpenter

105 Mrs Daniel Hagarty
107 John Hume, cutter
Salvation Army Barracks

Bagot st intersects

Greenwood & McGuire,
marble
125 Daniel Doran, laborer
131 J G Porter, painter
133 Richard Seaton, laborer
St Paul's Church

Montreal st intersects

199 John Hopkirk, P O clerk
163 Thos Driver, custom officer
165 G M Wilkinson
167 John Cornelius, sailor
167 David Milne, sailmaker
177 Mrs M McQuaig
179 Miss Rosanna McFadden
185 Donald Ross, professor

Sydenham st intersects

201 Robt Sellars, J P
211 Wm Ford, merchant
213 Rev W B Carey
219 W J Mahood, merchant
223 Queen St Methodist Church

Clergy st intersects

235 Andrew Davidson, contractor
237 Chas T G Patton, agent
241 Capt Taylor
245 Richard Roy, tailor
247 G W Robinson, carriage
manufacturer
249 Miss J C Ferns
251 John Saunders, mariner
253 James Marshall, carter
257 H Lacey, shoemaker
259 James Brown, painter

263 Adam Jacob, shoemaker
267 Miss E Crook, dressmaker
269 R McFaul, merchant
271 Robt McFaul, sen

Barrie st intersects

273 Wm Fee
275 Wm Sangster, baker
281 Wm Shannon
285 Catholic Apostolic Church
287 Arthur Chown
289 Bailie Bros, broom manfrs
309 Geo Armstrong, traveller
311 S A Aykroyd, dental stud't
319 Public School
329 Wm McCammon, butcher
331 John Maynard, carpenter
333 Mrs James McCammon
335 Mrs Henry Turpin
337 E F Chapman, grocer

Division st intersects

Queen st (south side)

R Crawford & Co, coal
The Rathbun Co

Ontario st intersects

Coal yards
St Lawrence Hotel

King st intersects

McDermott's carriage works
D McEwen & Son, machin-
ists
D Kane, carriagemaker

Wellington st intersects

72 Wm Hastings, laborer
82 H Staley, painter
84 Miss Mary McQuaid

Horseshoe Island. Boats twice a day each way. Liquor prohibited from being sold.

86 John Tierney, grocer
88 S Oberndorffer, cigar manfr
92 Isaac Knight
94 Hiram Henderson
102 John Tweddell, merchant
102½ Mrs Wm Baxter, teacher
104 Mrs Thos McGrath, board-
    ing
108 Thos D Robinson, painter
114 James Barry, tailor

Bagot st intersects

124 Peter Lenea
128 John Lemon, tinsmith
130 Wm Leadbeater, laborer
132 Thos Graham, teamster
136 Solomon Weaver, merchant
138 Mrs Alex Fraser
140 James Pappa
144 Miss Eliza Jarvis
148 Mrs Charles Lansing

Montreal st intersects

Albion Hotel
164 R M Horsey, merchant
170 R A Spence, carpenter
182 Jos Kidd, customs officer
184 Mrs Dr James Meagher
186 Rev A Spencer

Sydenham st intersects

196 Allan J Rees, traveller
198 William Wilson
200 Edwin Plant, bookkeeper
202 T C Wilson, livery
210 Jos R Payne, laborer
212 Jas Robinson, machinist
216 B Bailey, broom manufr
220 J S Walker, clerk
226 Wm Chrisley, cab driver
228 Wm Darby, bookkeeper

Clergy st intersects

250 Wm Deeks, laborer
254 J M Sherlock, merchant
256 Jas Dumphy
258 David Hinton, shoemaker
260 Wm J Pynter, machinist
262 John Pynter, engineer
266 Robert Besson, blacksmith
272 Samuel Thomas, plasterer

Barrie st intersects

282 James Marshall, clerk
286 George Barron, engineer
288 Fletcher Switzer, boarding
290 Rev J E Gillmore
294-6-8 Vacant
300 John Marshall, clerk
302 Vacant
304 John Ilett, clerk
306 J M Anderson, tinsmith
308 Vacant
310 Charles Woods, printer
312 Mrs John Lytle
316 Wm Lake, carpenter
318 H Dupont, manufacturer
320 Thos McGuire, fisherman
328 Owen McQuaid, laborer
338 W J Moore, machinist

Division st intersects

**Redan st (east side) from
Balaclava to Picard**

9 Samuel Gray, clerk
13 Wm Nicholson, blacksmith
15 John Cavanagh, pattern-
    maker
21 Patrick Fallon, laborer

Redan st (west side)

8 Mrs Robert Spencer
10 James Ellis, laborer

J. B. PAGE & Co. Fashionable Hatters & Furriers
138 Princess Street.

STREET DIRECTORY. 69

12 Alfred Maxam, painter
14 Stephen Tyo, mariner
16 Vacant

Regent st, runs south from Princess

Mrs Lindsay
Thos England, gardener
Frank Berry, gardener

Rideau st (east side) from Barrack to Cataraqui

1 Mrs Geo Jenman
11 Mrs James Ennis
15 Thomas Halligan, mariner
17 Frank Malefant, diver
21 Andrew Rankin, carter
23 Patrick O'Connor, miller
25 Mars Simmons, carpenter
27 Jas Campbell, wood dealer
29 Benj Allen, carpenter
33 John Waters, baker
35 Thos Murphy, mariner

Ordnance st intersects

41 Chas Chambers, mariner
47 Philip Bajus, brewer
57 Capt Wm Bajus, mariner
59 Capt Daniel Noonan, mariner
63 Jacob Bajus, brewer
65 John Macdonald, journalist
Joyce's wood yard

Bay st intersects

Vacant
Richard Wilson, laborer
91 Miss Mary Ann Shanahan
Joseph Burke, laborer
Patrick Burke, pensioner

99 Mrs Daniel Lynch
101 John Doyle, mariner
Owen Aldred, machinist

North st intersects

Martin Holland
Wm Wilson, sr, manager cotton mill

Cataraqui st intersects

Rideau st (west side)

Barrack st intersects

Mrs Chas Mead, grocer
2 Mrs Robert Newell
4 B Simpson, carpenter
6 L Spencer, boiler maker
8 Mrs John Marchand
10 Chas Goyett, engineer
12 Francis Murray, laborer
14 Wm Little, carpenter
16 M Mallen, wood dealer
18 M Madden, engineer
20 Jos Murray, mariner
24 Wm Carey, music dealer
38 J M Dunlop, hay dealer

Ordnance st intersects

50 Mrs Mary Shannessy
52 Matthew Donnelly
54 James Daly
56 Mrs Jas R Burke
58 Wm Cannon, carpenter
Cataraqui Public School

Bay st intersects

94 Jeremiah Doolan, laborer
96 Andrew Dunlop, mariner
100 James Austin, shoemaker
102 Patrick Doyle, laborer
116 M J Neville, accountant

North st intersects

Oil Cloth Factory
142 Patrick O'Neill, laborer
144 D J Funnell, engineer
148 Patrick Keating, laborer
150 John Nelson, jr, carter
152 John Nelson, sen
154 Jos Siddall, mariner
156 Robert Hughes, merchant
158 W R Moore, marble cutter
160-62 Peter McGlade, grocer

Picard st intersects

168 Vacant
John Weir, laborer
172 Mrs Francis Laidley
176 Thos Harrison, bricklayer

Corrigan st intersects

180 Robt Davis, prop dry dock
182 Leon Verbeck, electrician
186 Geo Baker, carpenter
188 Bedoe Wright, currier
Jas Hickson, confectioner
Baptiste Bourdeau, laborer
Zephrew King, shoemaker
Geo Gruber, cigar maker
Wm Swindlehurst, weaver
Stephen Young, tanner

Dufferin st intersects

200 Victory Sykes, tanner
202 Maitland Emmett, engineer
204 Thos Funnell, conductor

Charles st intersects

258 Chas H Hubbard, carpenter
Vacant

River st, west from Orchard

I Jamieson, engineer
John Spence, currier
David Leslie, engineer
J J Carrington, tanner

Grove st intersects

St Catharine st (east side) from Pine

1 James Munroe, miner
5 ——Asselstine, mechanic
11-13 Vacant

St Catharine st (west side)

4 John Hughes, laborer
10 to 14 Vacant

St Lawrence ave, n from King w to Stuart

Capt Jas Allen, mariner

Simcoe st (north side) from the water to King e

7 Lewis Francis, ladder manufacturer

Simcoe st (south side)
T N Sharman, boat builder
22 Capt E A Booth, jr, mariner
34 Mrs Marian Cameron

Sixth st, w from Division

9 Thos Hall, moulder
Wm Coleman, basket mak'r

Chatham and Alfred sts inter-
sect

Smith st from Princess n

No houses

Stephen st (north side) from Montreal west

Thos Huddars, foreman
W H Clark, tanner

Stephen st (south side)

Samuel Smith, spinner
Thos White, laborer
David Vick, carpenter
—— Markee, tailor
S Pelletier, tailor
John Robertson, tailor
Samuel Costello, laborer
John Hanlon, laborer
John Burtch, laborer

Stuart st (north side) from Barrie to Albert

Queen's University

Gordon st intersects

103 John Henderson, carter
107 John Little, policeman
115 S S Phippen, sec'y School
     Board
119 Wm Coffey, guard K P

St Lawrence ave intersects

Stuart st (south side)

10 Robt Carroll, manufact'r
18 R McColl, stone cutter

20 Thos Mooney, raftsman
26 Samuel Taylor, machinist

George st intersects

Kingston Hospital
100 Jas Richardson, merchant
102 H Richardson, merchant

Gordon st intersects

106 W A Webster
108 Capt T F Allen, mariner

St Lawrence ave intersects

122 W K Kerby, carter

Sydenham st west, (north side) from West to Johnston

3 B M Britton, Q C
13 Mrs Laura Folger
15 Fred A Folger
17 Jos Franklin, merchant
19 W H Macnee, merchant
23 J T McMahon, merchant

Earl st intersects

39 J B Carruthers, banker

William st intersects

John McKay, merchant
63 H F Wilmot, clerk P O
65 Miss Eliza Nelson, teacher
67 J Cooke, salesman
69 Miss Harriet Rice

Sydenham st west (south side)

16 Rev James Brock
28 John McIntyre, Q C

30 T R Casey, traveller
32 Vacant
34 W G Kidd, public school inspector
36 Mrs Mary A Davis

Earl st intersects

Mrs George Robertson

William st intersects

First Methodist Church
72 J N Power, architect
72 Miss Annie Baxter
76 John C Jones. C E
78 Mrs Colin McNab

Sydenham st (east side) from Princess to Picard

147 Alex Armstrong, blacksmith
151 John Rockwell, merchant
153 Wm Burk, grocer
159 N Gatfield, traveller

Queen st intersects

161 Mrs Catharine Rose
163 D Callaghan, accountant
171 R McFarlane, shoemaker
173 Mrs Adam Thomson
177-79 Vacant
       Central School
209 M Fitzpatrick, laborer
211 Thos Percy, boiler maker

Ordnance st intersects

225 Mrs Andrew Guild
227 Mrs Henry Myers
237 J McCutcheon, mariner

Bay st intersects

Patrick Conley

North st intersects

263 Arthur O'Neil, laborer
269 Geo Gray, laborer
271 Wm Gray, laborer
    John Nolan, laborer
275 Alex Middleton, laborer
279 A Thompson, carpenter
281 Chas O'Toole, engineer
283 Harvey Campbell, sailor
285 John Sharp, student
287 John Anderson, fitter

Picard st intersects

Sydenham st (west side)

H Brame, undertaker
146-48 Vacant
150 Wm G Fraser, carriage maker
152 J A Charles, bookkeeper
160 Jas Gowdy, butcher

Queen st intersects

166 W C Martin, merchant

Colborne st intersects

188 David Martin, grocer
190 F Thompson, mariner
192 C Hermiston, carpenter
194 Alex Mavety, M D
196 B Wilson, agent
198 C S Davidson, fireman
200 M Miller, traveller
212 Miss Twinkler

Ordnance st intersects

214 Wm Hales, grocer
216 D O'Connor, laborer
218 L Martinelli, laborer
220 Robt Lowers, mail carrier

222 Vacant
224 James Garrigan, shoemaker
226 Michael Goodman, laborer
228 John Geach, laborer
230 Wm Morrison, tinsmith
232 Mrs Robert Walker
242-44 Vacant

Bay st intersects

252 Vacant

North st intersects

256 Geo Beecher, sailor
258 Wm McKenny, laborer
260 Mrs Catharine Armstrong
262 Jas Mullen, weighman
264 Hiler Belanger, painter
266 Mrs Michael Collins
270 Mrs Rosette St John
272 J McIntyre, stove moulder
278 Thos Quigley, laborer
280 Thos Regan, foreman
282 Vacant
284 Patrick Rooney

Picard st intersects

Union st (north side) from Barrie to limits

15 Vacant
19 Chas McKay, bookkeeper
21 Thos Barlow, machinist
23 Jas A Skinner, finisher
23 Wm McClennand, laborer

Arch st intersects

29 F W Holder, engineer
31 P W Derry, moulder
35 Paul Reid, carpenter
51 Alex Sharpe, store keeper

Division st intersects

63 Hugh Crumley, carpenter
65 Rev C A Jones
67 L O'Brien, engineer
75 H W Wilson, chemist
Orphans' Home

Gordon st intersects

121 Prof Jas Fowler
123 Prof A B Nicholson
125 S Hamilton, blacksmith
127 Vacant
129 Robt Creighton, clerk
131 John Reyner, merchant
133 ——Rice
135 C J Graham, baker
137-39 Vacant

Alfred and Frontenac sts intersect

163 Capt F Patterson, mariner

Albert st intersects

169 Miss W B Anglin

Nelson and Beverley sts intersect

I A Breck

Macdonnell and Centre sts intersect

J D McKenzie, M D

Livingston ave, College and Pembroke sts intersect

W A Haskell, jr

Alwington ave intersects

Union st (south side)

St James' Church

Arch st intersects

30-32 Vacant
34 Thos Burns, engineer
38 Michael Toban, dyer
46 John Manson, carpenter
48 J Hanover, pattern maker
50 F Davis, lumberman
52 Wm Nobbs, carpenter
56 Wm Dunlop, cutter
60 James Coulson, diver
64 Alfred Perry, caretaker
    Drill Shed

Gordon st intersects

122 Jas Gibson
126 Major E B Wilson
128 Rev C Cameron
130 Jas Fitzgerald, laborer
136 Rev T G Porter
138 Wm Keeley, engraver
140 Rev A B Wilkes
142 John Graham
144 R D Auglin, customs

Alfred, Frontenac, Albert, Nelson, Beverley, Macdonnell, Centre, Livingston ave, College, Pembroke and Alwington ave intersect

Union st East (north side)
from the water to Bagot

1 Thos O'Brien, carpenter

Ontario st intersects

Wm Muckler, moulder
Geo Titus, mariner
Birkett's planing mills

King st intersects

69 Mrs Chas Crysler
75 Mrs Ann Amos
81 Chas Illsey
85 D McElhern, boiler maker
89 Mrs Ann Begg

Wellington st intersects

101 Mrs M McMahon
105 J J Campbell, watchman
107 A A McKenzie, mariner
109 Samuel Gaw
r109 Henry McIntosh, coachm'n
    Jas Redden, grocer
    Mrs Jas Macnee

Union st East (south side)

Dry dock
Kingston Foundry

Ontario st intersects

30 Dry dock office
32 Vacant
34 G Stitt, blacksmith
36 George Henderson, brass
    moulder
38 Isaac Jaquith, carpenter
40 Wm Forest, carpenter
42 Mrs James Lovett

King st intersects

68 O S Strange, M D
74 J McManus, storekeeper
    Asylum
82 T McK Robertson, merch't
84 J Kinghorn, sec K C M Co
86 J S Patch, agent Can Ex Co

Wellington st intersects

Victoria st (east side) north from Johnston to city limits

Edward Law, ropemaker
Edwin Rescorla, laborer
James Kavanagh
Cornelius Williams
Hiram Stover, laborer
Mrs Waudell
Mrs Day

Princess st intersects

J W Tenny, laborer
Wm Gavine, laborer
G E Theobald, painter
W H Townsend, bricklayer
Mrs Michael Conley
Alfred Langdon, mason
249 Philip Brickwood
251 Miss E Talbot
261 N Langdon, mason
321 Mrs Samuel Reynolds
329 S Reynolds, broom maker
City limits

Victoria st (west side)

John Scrivens, carpenter
J J Lawson, fireman
David Harris, ropemaker
Isaac Smith, carpenter
Robt Robinson, painter
Mrs Rendle
Chas Selby, blacksmith
134 Henry Ward, painter
132 Geo Ward, lumberman
J J Harpelle, farmer

Durham st intersects

Benj Salsbury, laborer
Jas McKnight, laborer
E Gray, laborer
Thos Cooper, laborer

Princess st intersects

Henry Wilson
Wm Watts, gardener
James Ramsay
Geo Watkins
John Lauder
Vacant
N Timmerman, policeman
Jas Brickwood, traveller
Wm Mercer
Vacant
Mrs John Burgess
John Reynolds, moulder
City limits

Victoria st (Upper) west from Division to Alfred

Thos King, carpenter

Albert st intersects

John Strachan
Wm Miller, laborer
Wm King, carpenter
Vacant
Jas Howell, mason

Vine st (east side) from Ellice to Picard

11 Wm J Murray, carpenter

Vine st (west side)

6 Jas Gordon, laborer
8 Vacant
10 Wm Crewlin, laborer
18 W J Savage, painter
24 Mrs Jane Jones
34 Jas Arthurs, cabinet maker

Wade's Lane (east side) n from Union to Young

11 Geo Hess, laborer
21 John Jones, gardener
23 Albert Piper, checker
25 W F Ryan, laborer

Wade's Lane (west side)

14 P Ward, blacksmith
20 Daniel Anderson, laborer
22 Wm J Ryan, fitter
24 Napoleon LaRose, laborer

Wellington st (east side) from the Park to the River

7 G S Oldrieve, merchant
9 Wm Skinner, merchant

Union st intersects

Thomas V Wade, cabinet maker
Mrs Jeremiah Meagher
27 G G Meagher, clerk P O
29 George Macdonald, harness maker
35 Mrs Jane Oldham
r35 Geo Thompson, carpenter
37 Michael Tetro, laborer

Gore st intersects

49 Dennis Driscoll, mason
Public School
Mrs Wm Brophy

Earl st intersects

79 J Henderson, grocer
81 J P Hanley, ticket agent
r81 John Hurst, laborer

r81 Terrence O'Neill, laborer
r81 Mrs Daniel Egan
85 Thomas Conley, instructor K P
87 Mrs Jane D'Arcy, dressmaker
87 Mrs Jas Abraham
89 Wm H Woodrow, engineer
91 David Downey, teamster
Dr Henderson

William st intersects

97 Mrs Robert Smith
103 Mrs Turner
105 Mrs Samuel McMillan
107 Mrs M A Robb
111 Andrew Waldie, insurance agent

Johnston st intersects

St George's Hall
Ontario Diocesan Book Depository
Clerical Secretary's office
Post Office

Clarence st intersects

Bon Ton saloon
151 Wm Kelly, photographer
153 John Smith, printer
157 J B Johnson, barber

Brock st intersects

F Nisbet, bookseller
167 J M Theobald, barber
171 J S Sands & Son, tailors
173 C Anglin, milliner
175 Slavin & Mackin, tailors
177 M Henley, fancy goods
179 J Walsh, tobacconist
181 W E Dorland, tailor
183 Nugent & Taylor, tinsmiths

185 C Robinson, tailor
187 Vacant

Princess st intersects

197-9 M A Moore, boots and
   shoes
201 Miss Emma Greaza, milliner
203-5 Albert McVety, M D
207-9 H & W J Crothers, biscuit
   manufacturers
213 D Kane, waggon maker

Queen st intersects

221 Henry Angrove, shoemaker
223 Miss Bridget Curtis, dressmaker
225 Chas Nicolls, laborer
227 Jas Christmas, laborer
229 Mrs Mary Gallagher
231 Mrs Jas Murray
235 Bernard Sheridan, grocer
   Jubilee House

Barrack st intersects

Riding School

Place d'Armes intersects

283 Capt Wm Scott, mariner
285 Patrick Daley, publisher
287 David A Waddell, harness
   maker
289 John Spooner, carpenter
293 John Gratton, laborer
295 Capt A Milligan, mariner
297 John Bullis, hay dealer
299 Delos Grimshaw, contractor

Bay st intersects

Robert Davis & Son's dry
   dock

Wellington st (west side)

W McRossie, lumber

Union st intersects

18 Jas Farrington
26 Col M H Twitchell, U S
   Consul
28 Jos George, manufacturer
32 John Gowdy
34 Mrs John Mackerras
36 F W Spangenburg, merch't
38 Capt A V Rivers
42 Jas Davis, engineer

Gore st intersects

Geo Pidgion, customs
Vacant
54 S Angrove, customs
56 Geo Leader, machinist
58 Chas Munro, engineer
60 Henry Youlden, machinist
62 Mrs Robt Hermiston
70 Prof Z DesRochers
72 Miss M Young, dressmaker

Earl st intersects

74 John McMahon, builder
78 Prof John Fletcher
80 Geo E Perley, C E
82 Robt Waddell
88 Herb Walker, machinist
r88 Mrs Robt Kent
90 L Hansen, fish dealer
98 James Morahan

William st intersects

Joseph Paradis, carpenter
Pat'k Ruberry, laborer
Wm Carson, laborer
Patrick Lavery, laborer
116 Y I C B A Hall

118 John Donnelly, wrecker
120 Francis Cicolari, publisher
122 Capt J Trowell, mariner

Johnston st intersects

Congregational Church
132 Mrs Jas Beal, boarding
136 C L Curtis, M D
138 Mrs Margaret Martin
142 L Clements, dentist
146 Miss Eliza Robertson

Clarence st intersects

GOLDEN LION BLOCK
Ontario Bank
Wm Carey, music
J Reyner, pianos
Power & Son, architects
Catholic Literary Society
I Mitchell, wh jeweller
W R McRae & Co, wh grocers
McRae Bros, grocers

Brock st intersects

.R Waldron, dry goods
170 Geo Mills & Co, hatters
176 Miss M S McTaggart, milliner
178 C Wright & Son, hatters
180 G M Wilkinson & Son, grocers
182-4 P Ohlke, art decorations
184 Miss M Smith, dressmaker
186 St Nicholas Club
188 R W Vanderwater, pianos
190 Baillie Bros, printers
190 J H Clark, dentist
190 R F F Rowan, laundry
192 A C Johnston, watchmaker
John Dunbar, tailor

Princess st intersects

208 Peter Devlin, bowling alley

212 Elder Bros, livery
216 W Harkness, butcher
218 Z Wolf, mariner
220 Mrs Alice McCummiskey, grocer

Queen st intersects

224 Wm Woods, laborer
226 Mrs Patrick Kearns
228 Vacant
228 Wm Anderson, laborer
230 John Watts, laborer
232 J J Mowat, pensioner
234 Jas Watts, shoemaker
236 John Nobes, carpenter

Barrack st intersects

262 Thos R Power, architect
264 F Macdonald, clerk P O
266 John Geoghegan, mariner
268 Mrs John Gallagher
270 P J Quinn, merchant
272 John Bajus, brewer
274 Peter Bajus, malster
276 John Smart, laborer
278 Joseph Hackett, carter
280 John Oldfin, gasfitter
282 Mrs M A Oldfin

Ordnance st intersects

288 W J Wells, clerk P O
290 Capt Edward Beaupre

Brewery Lane intersects

Kingston Brewery

Bay st intersects

Mrs Wm McCutcheon, potash manufacturer

West st, from the water to Earl

Breck & Booth's coal yard
A McCorkell, boat builder
13 Captain Thomas O'Connor, mariner
Mrs Mary Groves
15 Miss Eliza Hennessy
17 Jas McDivet, machinist
19 H B Watson, machinist
23 Thos McAdam, machinist
25 Vacant

King st intersects

55 M S Sutherland, grocer
57 J G King, druggist
59 Edward H Smythe, Q C
61 Mrs F W Kirkpatrick
63 Prof Adam Shortt
63 Mrs E Smith-Shortt, M D

Wellington, Bagot and Syden- ham sts intersect

165 Vacant

Earl st intersects

William st (north side) from the water to Barrie

The Shedden Co
Immigration Office

Ontario st intersects

R J Burns, carpenter
Merchants Bank

King st intersects

H J Saunders, M D
53 David Coulthart, machinist
55 Capt Jas Smith, mariner

59 John Cudmore, laborer
Frank Conway, K & P R'y

Wellington st intersects

87 Thomas Linaugh
89 Wm H Sullivan, barrister
91 Major S Davidson, R M C
Convent School

Bagot st intersects

109 Thos Flanigan, cab driver
113 Mrs Barrons
115 Thos Kinchlea, laborer
117 Jos Hiscock, merchant
119 Robert Wales
121 John Maguire, clerk
125 W H Morton, clerk
129 Thos McAuley, merchant
133 A D Taylor, merchant
135 Mrs John Shaw
137 Samuel Dyde, accountant
139 Mrs R M Moore
141 Jos Quigley, customs

Sydenham st intersects

First Methodist Church
183 Rev W W Carson
185 John Mitchell, contractor

Clergy st intersects

203 A P Knight
205 Mrs George Maloue
207 H C Rothwell, mariner
209 Vacant
213 Mrs James Abernethy
215 John Breden

William st (south side)

Gunn's wharf

Ontario st intersects

McConville & Nicholson,
 butchers
Peter Bureau, carter
Bank of Montreal

King st intersects

C A Irwin, M D
44 J F Swift, insurance agent
46 Rev Thos Hall
50 Geo Begg, baker
52 R McCammon, sen, baker
56 C F Smith, barrister
58 H S Stevenson, manufact'r
60 Miss Eliza Penner
64 Mrs Bessie Yates
 W H Henderson, M D

Wellington st intersects

70 J Morrissey, messenger P O
72 Wm Sullivan, engineer
76 H B Savage, painter
78 Savage Bros, painters
80 Thos Savage, painter
84 John Goodman, laborer
88 John Regan, guard K P
90 Michael Dwyer, laborer
92 Mrs Patrick Donoghue
94 Wm Duffey, moulder
96 Robt Miller, carter
98 Robt Miller, boiler maker
100 Miss Jane Bateson, grocer
104 Edward Conlan, grocer

Bagot st intersects

112 John Conlan, tailor
114 Cornelius Mullally, laborer
116 J Driscoll, guard K P
118 P R Henderson, manager
 M T Co

Sydenham and Clergy sts intersect

188 Mrs H Macarow
200 D J Garbutt, real estate
202 Robt Holding, engineer
204 John Barkell, carter
206 Wm Wallace, fireman
214 Miss M A McMahon

William (Upper) st (north side) west from Barrie to Division

7 Jas Lochead, agent
13 Jas Turner, laborer
15 John Paterson, laborer
17 Edward Hinton, laborer
19 Robert Clark, mason

Gray's Lane intersects

25 Samuel Gillmore, laborer
27 Peter Laurencell, carpenter
29 Jacob Hatten, laborer
31 James Bloomley, laborer
33 Wm McNamee, laborer
35 A Rochfort, carpenter
47 John Purdue, laborer

William (Upper) st (south side)

12 John Spence, laborer
14 Mrs B Donoghue
16 John Hanley, cabman
24 Vacant
26 James Paul, moulder
28-30 Vacant
32 Alex McMahon, laborer
34 Geo Taylor, barber

York st (north side) from Alma

1 Vacant
3 John Calvert, clerk

5 Edward Frost
7 Geo Reynolds, sailor
11 Mrs John Ryan
13 Wm E Chappell, carpenter
15 Mrs Robt McKee

Barrie st intersects

P J Burns, grocer
19 Edward Rikley, baker
21 John McKee, laborer
25 Mrs Hamilton
35 Chas Walker, bartender
37 Edward Chatterton, carpenter
43 Hugh Johnston, laborer

Picard st intersects

63 J E Jenkins, blacksmith
65 H Smith, laborer
67 William Morrison, carriage maker
79 John Savage
81 Stephen Burk, sailor
85 Edward Leach, laborer
87 R J Lee, tailor
89 Rev F Prime
91 J C Landeryou, contractor
93 Henry Young, mason
95 F R Scobell

Cherry st intersects

103 Wm Moxley, blacksmith
105 Vacant
109 Samuel Marshall, traveller
111 Geo O'Brien, mariner
113-15-17 Vacant

Division st intersects

147 John Appleton, blacksmith
168 John Jones, miner

Albert st intersects

York st (south side)

18 Andrew Mills, carpenter
20 Geo Menary, carpenter
22 Geo H Northmore, baker
24 T P Hillier, carpenter
26 Thos Singleton, laborer
30 John Davidson, laborer
36 Chas Acres, shoemaker
40 Stephen Richards, boilermaker
42 C F Lamham, laborer

Picard st intersects

68 John Roach, laborer
70 Alex Olsen, steward
72 A C Grant, painter
74 Robt Moxley, blacksmith
76 Wm Tweed, painter
78 Henry Staley, musician
86 Richard McConnell, carpenter
88 Mrs Emma Jamieson
90 Wm Atkin, baker
94 Benj Gage, driver
96 James Dumphy, packer
98 Samuel Richards, mason

Division st intersects

140 John C Swain, butcher
142 Mrs Wm Hodges
154 Geo Holder, carpenter
156 Alex McCabe, laborer
164 W Ravenscroft, carter
166 Geo Holder, carpenter
170 Chas Kingswell, laborer

Young st (north side) from Barrie to Gordon

1 Miss A McGarvey
3 John Pymer, laborer
11 Miss Jane Clancy
15 Mrs Margaret Hanley

Little's Lane intersects

15 Mrs Matilda Godwin
17 C Rourke, stove fitter
21 John O'Brien, laborer
25 Mrs Ellen O'Donald
27 M McQuaid, laborer
29 Henry Jordan
31 Simon Burns, laborer
35 John Turcott, laborer
37 Miss J Doyle
39 Wm Dean, printer
41 John Shanahan, laborer

Division st intersects

55 Wm Carter
57 Wm Hazlett, engineer
83 J A Craig, policeman

Young st (south side)

10 John Veal, baker
14 J McGuire, boiler maker
16 Joseph Redmond, laborer
18 William Maddocks, black-
    smith
20 John Laird, machinist
22 John O'Brien, machinist
24 John Armstrong, moulder

Wade's Lane intersects

40 Vacant
42 Frank Porter, gardener

*Division and Gordon sts inter-
sect*

ALPHABETICAL DIRECTORY.

Abbott Thomas, 378 Division

Abernethy Arch, manager G Offord, 213 William

Abernethy Mrs Jas, 213 William

Abernethy John, (John Abernethy & Co) 213 William

Abernethy John & Co, boots and shoes, 260 Princess

Abernethy W, contractor, 430 Brock

Abernethy William, machinist, 178 Ordnance

Abernethy Wm, 194 Ordnance

Abraham Mrs Mary (wid Jas), 87 Wellington

Abrams Josiah, car driver, 103 King w

Acres Charles, shoemaker, 36 York

Ada Wm, mariner, 49 Bagot n

Ada Wm jr, clerk, 49 Bagot n

Adair Mrs Alex, grocer, 248 Barrie

Adams Edward, Gov steamboat inspector, 162 King e

Adams James, chief trade instructor K P, cor Union and Alwington ave

Adams James, grocer, cor Princess and Alfred

Adams Wm, boots and shoes, 67 Brock, h 318 Gordon

Adams W J, shoe cutter, 318 Gordon

Adsit Geo, carpenter, Princess

Agnew Mrs Emma (wid John), 299 Gordon

Agnew James, city solicitor, 332 Barrie

Agnew Robert, carpenter, 468 Montreal

Agnew Robt, moulder, 239 Earl

Aiken Jas, laborer, Markland

Aiken James, laborer, bds 149 Ordnance

Aiken John, salesman, Markland

Aiken Joseph, carter, Markland

Aiken Patrick, carter, 149 Ordnance

Aiken R E, policeman, 176 Alfred

Ainslie D J, carpenter, 246 Earl

Ainslie Patrick, boiler maker, Gore

Albertson Mrs Jane (wid David), 6 George

Albion Hotel, Arch Spafford, prop, Montreal, cor Queen

Alderdice Hugh, painter, 236 Barrie

Aldred Owen, machinist, Cataraqui Cottage, Rideau

Alexander Mrs J (wid D), 306 Brock

Alexander James, com traveller, 306 Brock

Allen A G, M D, 268 Johnston

Allen Mrs Agnes (wid Silas), 133 Clergy

Allen Benj, carpenter, 29 Rideau

Allen C, guard K P, 462 Brock

Allen C J, telephone operator, 49 Colborne

Allen Mrs E, 183 Brock

Allen J A, King w

Allen Jas, engineer, 41 Balaclava

Allen Capt James, mariner, St Lawrence ave

Allen Jas, laborer, 641 Princess

Allan John, mechanic, 189 Pine

Allen Mrs Margaret (wid Lewis) 155 Division

Allan Robert, grocer, 308 Montreal

Allen Mrs Sarah E (wid Wm) 297 Division

Allen T C, salesman, 126 Bagot

Allen Capt T F, mariner, 108 Stuart

Allen Thos, engineer, 41 Balaclava

Allen Thos D, bookkeeper, 155 Division

Allen Wm, boots and shoes, 84 Brock, h 126 Bagot

Allen W H, clerk, 133 Clergy

Allinson William, boilermaker, Albert

Amber George, carpenter, 163 Clergy

American Express Co, J S Patch, local manager, King, cor Brock

American Hotel, W H Hunter, prop, 27-29 Brock

Amey George W, oil cloth manufacturer, 5 Victoria Terrace, Montreal

Amey Overton, oil cloth manufacturer, 5 Victoria Terrace, Montreal

Amond Ed, clerk Collender hotel, 220 King e

Amos Mrs Ann (wid Wm) 75 Union e

Anderson Chas, clerk, 81 Colborne

Anderson Daniel, laborer, 20 Wade's lane

Anderson David, 111 Bay

Anderson Mrs Jane, 222 Barrie

Anderson J M, tinsmith, 306 Queen

Anderson John, fitter, 287 Sydenham

Anderson Miss Mary Ann, dressmaker, 178 Bagot

Anderson Michael, 178 Bagot

Anderson William, laborer, 224 Wellington

Andrews Mrs G W, 8 Garratt

Andrews Peter, ship carpenter, Ontario

Anglin C, millinery, 178 Wellington

Anglin R D, customs, 144 Union

Anglin Samuel (W B & S Anglin) h 85 Barrack

Anglin Mrs W B, 169 Union

Anglin W B & S, lumber and coal dealers, Bay, cor Wellington

Anglin W G, M D, M R C S, Eng., 52 Earl

Anglin William, bursar Insane Asylum, 56 Earl

Anglo-American Hotel, Jos Little, prop, Ontario, cor Johnston

Angrove Henry, shoemaker, 221 Wellington

Angrove Henry, machinist, 53 Arch

Angrove Samuel, landing waiter, 54 Wellington

Angrove W J, salesman

Annett Geo, carpenter, 204 Colborne

Ausley John, carpenter, 381 Earl

Anson G, caretaker Cedar Island

Anthony Rev Bro, Christian Brothers' School, 89 Clergy

Appleton John, blacksmith, 147 York

Armstrong A H, salesman, 17 Colborne

Armstrong Alex, blacksmith, 353 Princess

Armstrong Alex, blacksmith, 147 Sydenham

Armstrong Mrs Catharine (wid Wm) 260 Sydenham

Armstrong D F, boots, shoes and trunks, 141 Princess, h 17 Colborne

Armstrong Francis, 260 Sydenham

Armstrong Francis, laborer, 127 Alfred

Armstrong Geo, com traveller, 309 Queen

Armstrong I (wid J) 304 Brock

Armstrong John, moulder, 24 Young

Armstrong Miss, 294 Barrie

Armstrong Nelson, printer, 631 Princess

Armstrong Robt, carpenter, 260 Sydenham

Arniel Thomas, carpenter, 324 Division

Arniel Wm, caretaker Wellington street School

Arniel W J, watchmaker, 387 Princess

Arniel Sam, mariner, 84 Johnston

Arnold Mrs Margaret (wid John) King e

Arntfield A, carder, 74 Arch

Arrata Michael, cutler, 87 Johnston

Arthurs Alex, baker, 430 Princess

Arthurs James, cabinet maker, 34 Vine

Ashley Edwin, student, Frontenac

Ashley W G, gents' furnishings, 124½ Princess

Asselstine Benj, carpenter, 168 Division

Asselstine Charles, laborer, 59 Upper Charles

Asselstine Charles, carpenter, 437 Alfred

Asselstine David P, student, 168 Division

Asselstine Daniel, 59 U Charles

Asselstine J, blacksmith, 284 Earl

Asselstine I, carpenter, 302 Johnston

Asselstine John, piano maker, 254 Alfred

Asselstine Mrs N (wid Isaac), 135 Alfred

Asselstine Peter, carpenter, 100 Division

Asselstine W H, carpenter, 220 Alfred

Asselstine ——, mechanic, 5 St Catharine

Atkin Wm, baker, 90 York

Atkinson Thomas, mason, Collingwood

Atkinson W, laborer, 224 Barrie

Atwood F, laborer, 439 Alfred

Atwood Horace, laborer, 91 Elm

Aubin Mrs Mary Jane (wid William) r 87 Johnston

Auchinvole Gilbert, grocer, 41 Colborne

Augustus Capt Webster, 163 Division

Auldwell Geo, laborer, Bagot

Ausem J, laborer, 109 Ordnance

Austin James, shoemaker, 100 Rideau

Aykroyd S A, dental student, 311 Queen

Aylesworth G A, manager B A Booth & Co, h 9 Colborne

Babcock James, carter, 392 Division

Babcock Jno, carpenter, 37 Pine

Babcock J S, grocer, 359 Princess

Babcock Wm, well digger, Bagot

Bailey Alex, carter, 84 James

Bailey B, broom manuf'r, 216 Queen

Baihe Bros (Isaac and Henry M) printers, 190 Wellington, h 267 Gordon

Bailey Bros, broom manuf'rs, 291 Queen

Bailey Chas, laborer, 23 Patrick

Bailey E B, biscuit maker, 338 Brock

Bailey Henry, grocer, 619 Princess

Bayly N, accountant, Bank B N A, bds British American hotel

Bailey Samuel, broom manuf'r, 326 Gordon

Bailie Thomas, shoemaker, 185 Montreal

Baillie William, book and job printer, 81 Brock, h 88 Barrie

Bailey William, broom manufacturer, 120 Colborne

Bain A U, law student, 8 Ontario

Bain Thos, laborer, 298 Earl

Bain Rev William, DD, 8 Ontario

Baird Alex, bookkeeper, 373 Brock

Baird J, stove fitter, 371 Brock

Baird Robt, 12 Upper Bagot

Baird Robt, jr, carpenter, 12 Upper Bagot

Bajus Jacob, 63 Rideau

Bajus John, brewer, 272 Wellington

Bajus Philip, prop Kingston Brewery, h 47 Rideau

Bajus Philip, sr, shoemaker, Ordnance

Bajus Peter, driver, 274 Wellington

Bajus Capt William, steamboat owner, 57 Rideau

Baker George, carpenter, 186 Rideau

Baker H W, clerk, 12 Market sq

Baker Jas, Frontenac

Baker John, laborer, 39 Upper Charles

Baker John F, com traveller, Alwington ave

Baker Mrs Mary (wid John) 83 Frontenac

Baker R D, tobacconist, 209 Princess, h 380 Earl

Baker Wm, 382 Earl

Baker W F, flour and feed, 12 Market sq

Baker W J, clerk, 382 Earl

Ball Edwd, clerk, 139 Ordnance

Ball Geo, mason, 25 Pine

Ball Sam'l, jeweller, 398 Barrie

Ballantyne J, policeman, 422 Johnston

Bank of British North America, F Brownfield, manager, City Hall

Bank of Montreal, C E L

J. B. PAGE & Co.
FINE FURS A SPECIALTY
138 Princess St.

ALPHABETICAL DIRECTORY. 87

Porteous, manager, King, cor William

Bannister John, guard K P, Alwington ave

Barber Charles F, carpenter, 132 Clarence

Barber & Johnson, carpenters, 124 Clarence

Barber T, carpenter, 426 Johnston

Barkell J, carter, 204 William

Barlow T, machinist, 21 Union

Barlow Thomas, contractor, 153 Bagot

Barnes Alex, blacksmith, 208 Colborne

Barnes Mrs, 14 Deacon

Barney Benj, broker, 224 Earl

Barney B & Co, metal dealers, 39 Princess

Barr Robert, telegraph repairer, 35 Upper Bagot

Barrett Dan, mason, 70 Cherry

Barrett Thos, mason, 24 Cowdy

Barrigan J, laborer, 15 O'Kill

Barron George, engineer, 286 Queen

Barron W J, clerk, 286 Queen

Barrons Mrs, 113 William

Barry Jas, tailor, 114 Queen

Barry Patrick, laborer, bds Montreal House, Ontario

Barry Robert, coppersmith, 18 Division

Bartells O V, deputy city treasurer, 396 Princess

Barter Mrs Mary (wid Benj), r 67 Bay

Barton Alexander, engineer, 143 Montreal

Bastow J, 182 Clergy

Bastow J G, plumber, 349 King e

Bates H C, clerk, 5 Hales' Cottages, King w

Bates Henry, ship carpenter, 40 James

Bates Capt Dan, mariner, Ontario

Bates John, laborer, 138 Nelson

Bates Mrs M, 5 Hales' Cottages, King w

Bates Peter, 497 Princess

Bates Samuel, carpenter, 388 Division

Bates W C, salesman, 5 Hales' Cottages, King w

Bateson Miss Jane, grocer, 100 William

Bateson M, driver Express Co, 100 William

Baubih I, sailor, 47 Colborne

Bawden Joseph, barrister, 81 Frontenac

Baxter Miss Annie, 74 Sydenham w

Baxter Mrs Catharine (wid William), music teacher, $102\frac{1}{4}$ Queen

Baxter H, laborer, 181 Clergy

Baxter Miss J, 74 Sydenham w

Baxter Joseph, laborer, end Montreal

Beach Charles, teamster, K & P Ry, n s Place d'Armes

Beal Mrs Elizabeth F (wid Jas) boarding house, 132 Wellington

Beamish Mrs Bridget (wid Thos) 67 Bay

Bean John, clerk, 14 Balaclava

Beattie Chas, 161 Bagot

Beauchamp John, machinist, 15 Deacon

Beaupre Capt Edward, sup't 1,000 Island S Co, 290 Wellington

Beaupre R, 286 Barrie

Beebe Frederic, mariner, r148 Ontario

Boecher George, sailor, 256 Sydenham

Begg Alex, carter, 87 Queen

Begg Mrs Anne (wid William) 89 Union e

Begg George, baker, 50 William

Behan J J, salesman, Patrick, cor George

Bejean John, carpenter, 72 Ontario

Belanger Hiler, painter, 264 Sydenham

Belch J, agent, 434 Brock

Belch J, M D, 434 Brock

Bell Rev George, LL D, registrar Queen's College, 100 Barrie

Bell John, baker, 221 Montreal

Bell John, carpenter, 8 Pine

Bell Robt, 176 Gordon

Bell Telephone Co'y, A T Smith, local manager, Ontario

Bell Thos, watchman M T Co, n side Dufferin

Bell W P & Son (W P and John H) photographers, 224 Princess, h 203 Colborne

Belt Wm, laborer, 765 Montreal

Bendall Mrs Caroline (wid John) r 87 Johnston

Bendigo W, laborer, Albert

Benedict Mrs Renia (wid Roland) 371 Princess

Bennett Alex, baker, 287 Division

Bennett Edw'd, shoveller, Bagot

Bennett Jas, laborer, Corrigan

Bennett Jas, shoemaker, 35 Elm

Bennett Jas, laborer, 9 Cherry

Bennett Robert James, printer, 287 Division

Bennett Thomas, laborer, 6 Anglin's Cottages, Bay

Bennett Wm, 161 Nelson

Bennett William, tinsmith, 411 Barrie

Benson Miss Mary Jane, 89 Barrack

Berry Frank, market gardener, Regent

Besson Robert, blacksmith, 266 Queen

Betts Mrs, 5 Hales' Cottages, King w

Beuse Joseph, tanner, Grove

Beven Mrs Catharine (wid Jos), 32 Quebec

Beven Joseph jr, moulder, 32 Quebec

Bewis Jas, mason, 13 Durham

Bibby Bros (Fred A, Herbert D) livery keepers, 129 Brock, h 203 Brock

Bibby H D, (Bibby & Virtue), h 203 Brock

Bibby Mrs S (wid J), 203 Brock

Bibby & Virtue (H D Bibby, W Virtue) hardware, stoves and tins, 335-337 King e

Bickley F A, comm'l traveller, King e

Bidell Chas, driver, end Division

Bilton Richard, sailor, 290 Johnston

Birch Frank A, clerk Brigade office, Artillery Park Barracks

Birch Geo, contractor, 68 George

Birch Samuel, (McKelvey & Birch) h 196 Bagot

Bird Langley, laborer, 240 Barrie

Birkett J H, sec-treas Canadian Locomotive and Engine Co, h Centre

Birkett J, laborer, 44 Johnston

Birkett's Planing Mill, Jacob VanWinckel foreman, Union e

Birmingham Mrs J, 190 Johnston

Birmingham John, laborer, Albert

Bisonette Geo H, [Bowes & Bisonette], h 4 Barnstable Terrace, Clergy

Black James, carpenter, 137 Alfred

Black Jas, laborer, 47 John

Black John, Bagot

Blair Mrs Julia [wid Augustus] 75 Queen

Blake Henry, salesman, 136 Colborne

Blakey Alfred, butcher, 840 Princess

Blakley John, carter, Beverley

Blakley Traver, carter, 65 Bay

Blanger Jas, grainer, 55 John

Blaney John, coal heaver, e side Grove

Bliss J J, blacksmith, 54 Bay

Blomley James, laborer, 31 Upper William

Bloomfield Wm, sailor, 145 Pine

Boakes Jas W, conductor K & P R'y, 680 Montreal

Boakes Mrs, 2 Brewery Lane

Boles Alexander, 8 Grove

Bolger T O, city engineer, 142 Johnston

Bolton Richard, laborer, r 31 Johnston

Bonnie Geo, foreman, 351 Alfred

Bonnie Geo jr, blacksmith, 153 Division

Bonnie Henry, moulder, 349 Alfred

Booth B A & Co, G A Aylesworth, manager, woollen goods, 262 Princess

Booth Charles, civil engineer, 73 Division

Booth E A, [Breck & Booth] h 146 Barrie

Booth Capt Edward A jr, mariner, 22 Simcoe

Booth Frank, gardener, 255 Division

Booth George, machinist, 302 Barrie

Booth Mrs Mary Anne, [wid Geo] 136 Colborne

Booth Richard, fireman K & P R'y, 270 Ontario

Booth William Henry, carpenter, John north

Boston Hat Store, Geo Mills & Co, props, 170 Wellington

Bostridge Charles, guard K P, 5 Pembroke

Boswell P, laborer, 79 Elm

Bourdeau Baptiste, laborer, Rideau

Bourne John, coal oil peddler,51 Balaclava

Boutillier Sergt A S, A Battery, 2 Dunn Terrace, Bay

Bowen Jas, tailor, 100 Chatham

Bowen Jno, carter,100 Chatham

Bowen Mrs Mary [wid George] 326 Alfred

Bowen Robert, butcher, 100 Chatham

Bowen Wm, teamster, K P, 27 Gordon

Bower John, 86 Barrie

Bowes & Bisonette, [R J Bowes, G H Bisonette], dry goods, 204 Princess

Bowes Richard J, [Bowes & Bisonette], h 120 Earl

Bowley Henry, tool dresser, King w

Boyce Mrs Margret [wid Caleb] 296 Johnston

Boyce Richard, salesman, 296 Johnston

Boyd G, engineer, 309 Johnston

Boyd I, engineer, 398 Brock

Boyd J, mariner, 357 Brock

Boyd J, baker, 167 Clergy

Boyd James, livery, 290 Princess, h 397 Barrie

Boyd Jas, baker, 289 Princess

Boyd John, painter, bds 238 Ontario

Boyd Richard, cabman, 7 Colborne

Boyd Solomon, Albert

Brabant Aug F, J L Rattray manager, needles and needle cases, 43 Brock

Braddon John, prop Waterford House, 238-240 Ontario

Bradley Patrick, watchman, 182 Bagot

Bradley Peter, laborer, n s Place d' Armes

Brady Jno, salesman, 52 Rideau

Brady John, 139 Durham

Brady John, laborer, Bagot

Brady Mrs Margaret [wid John] 146 Montreal

Brame Henry, cabinet maker and undertaker, 251 Princess

Branch Jos, engineer, 84 Arch

Braniff Hugh, storeman, 267 Earl

Branigan Dennis, clerk, 258 Princess

Branigan Jno, grocer, 220 Montreal

Branigan Mrs, 258 Princess

Breck & Booth, [L W Breck, E A Booth], coal and wood dealers, and vessel agents, 28 Clarence, cor Ontario

Breck I A, Sunnyside, Union

Breck L W, [Breck & Booth], h 193 Brock

Breden John, Beverly

Breden John, 215 William

Brennan M E, bookkeeper, 288 Johnston

Brennan Michael, keeper K P, 288 Johnston

Brick Mrs Margaret, [wid Bryan], [old 69] Bagot

Brickwood H P, salesman, 249 Victoria

Brickwood Jas, com traveller, Victoria

Brickwood Philip, 249 Victoria

Briden G S, bookkeeper, 122 Colborne

Brider George, bookkeeper, 122 Colborne

Bridge ——, 78 Colborne

Bridgeford James, asst gunnery instructor R S G

Briggs Mrs, Albert

Briggs Thomas, Manager of Frontenac Loan and Investment Society, h 167 King e

Brightman Thos, gardener, 94 Arch

Brignall Robert, car inspector G T R, G T R station, Montreal

British American Hotel, J E Dunham prop, Clarence, cor King

Britton B M, Q C, [Britton & Whiting] h 9 Sydenham w

Britton & Whiting, [B M Britton, Q C, J L Whiting, B A] barristers, 69 Clarence

Brock A M, watchmaker, 90 Princess, 16 Sydenham w

Brock Rev Jas, 16 Sydenham w

Brockett Atwater E, com traveller, 48 Clergy

Brokenshire John, pumpmaker, 160 King e

Brooks Miss, 190 Barrie

BROOKES, THOMAS S., Joiner and Builder. Alterations and Repairs promptly attended to. Albert, between Johnston and Earl.

Brophy Mrs Margaret [wid William] Wellington

Brophy W, gents' furnisher, 344 King e

Brouse Henry, machinist, 155 Nelson

Brouse Edw'd, salesman, Alfred

Brouse Edwin, clerk, Albert

Brown Charles, sailor, 281 a Montreal

Brown David, moulder, 45 Division

Brown George, 45 Pine

Brown George, 394 Princess

Browne Geo W, inland revenue officer, 297 Gordon

Brown Henry, restaurant, City buildings

Browne J & Co (Jas and Patrick Browne) wholesale grocers, 175 Ontario

Brown Jas, painter, 259 Queen

Browne Jas (J Browne & Co) bds British American

Brown Johnston, Stanley House, Ontario, cor Market square

Brown J W, carriage maker, 366 Princess

Brown J W & Co, carriage makers, Barrie

Brown Mrs, 132 Clarence

Browne Patrick (J Browne & Co) h 138 Gordon

Brown Richard, laborer, 48 Place d'Armes

Brown R J, hotel keeper, 348 Princess

Brownfield F, manager Bank B N A, h Johnston, cor Barrie

Bruce John, moulder, 20 Chatham

Bruce William, carpenter, 20 Chatham

Bryan Mrs, 33 Albert

Bryant Mrs C (wid William) n side Princess

Bryant Fred, mason, 6 Adelaide

Bryant James, laborer (old 54) Bagot

Bryant Price, mechanic, 240 Montreal

Bryant Reuben, moulder, 215 Colborne

Bryant Robert, carriage maker, 9 Deacon

Bryson James, guard K P, 210 Gordon

Buckley John, Frontenac

Bulger James, grain shoveller, 96 Ontario

Bullis John, hay dealer, 297 Wellington

Bunt John, boiler maker, 172 Bagot

Bunt Richard, jr, blacksmith, (old 66) Bagot

Bunt Wm, blacksmith, 260 Earl

Bureau Peter, carter, foot of William

Burgess Mrs Anne E (wid John) Victoria

Burgess Mrs Eliza (wid James) 129 Colborne

Burk Edward, laborer, 39 Livingston ave

Burke Mrs Jane (wid Patrick) Ontario

Burke Joseph, laborer (off Bay, below Rideau)

Burke Patrick, pensioner, Rideau
Burk R, machinist, 153 Sydenham
Burke Mrs Sarah (wid Jas R) 56 Rideau
Burk Stephen, sailor, 81 York
Burk T H, chief operator C P R T Co, Ontario
Burke William, carpenter, 214 Colborne
Burk William, grocer, 153 Sydenham
Burnett M S, canvasser, 229 Gordon
Burnett Orlando, policeman, Frontenac
Burns Mrs A (wid G) 295 Johnston
Burnes Mrs Catharine, 11 Young
Burns Frank L, bookkeeper, 232 Johnston
Burns John, carpenter, 42 John
Burns Patrick, baker, 43 Ordnance
Burns R, laborer, 377 Johnston
Burns Mrs Rachael (wid Henry) 479 Princess
Burns R E, bookkeeper, Union, cor Alfred
Burns R J, carpenter, foot of William
Burns Robert, carpenter, Bagot
Burns Robert T, deputy postmaster, 232 Johnston
Burns Simon, laborer, 31 Young
Burns Thomas, engineer, 34 Union
Burns W, laborer, 116 Barrack
Burrows Wm, collector canal tolls, h 274 Gordon
Bartch Enoch, carpenter, 49 James
Bartch John, laborer, Stephen

Burton John, grocer, cor Division and Brock
Burns P J, grocer, cor York and Barrie
Burton Samuel, upholsterer, 115 Ordnance
Burton Vallance, foreman Victoria Foundry, 57 Queen
Bush John, laborer, 277 King e
Bushell Jno, mariner, 374 King e
Bushell William, carpenter, 103 Queen
Bushy Charles E, carpenter, 487 Alfred
Bushy Francis, carpenter, 487 Alfred
Bushy Robt, carpenter, 24 Pine
Busso Mrs Agatha [wid Anthony], 22 Alma
Byers Rev Henry, 104 Queen
Bryant J W, butcher, 82 Colborne
Bryant Wesley, butcher, 387 Division
Cable Harry, painter, 217 Earl
Cairns Sam, laborer, 429 King e
Caldback John H, carpenter, 66 Chatham
Caldback Mrs Martha [wid Jas] end Colborne
Caldwell A & Son, lumber dealers, V G Hooper manager, n s Place d' Armes
Callaghan Arthur W H, clerk, 163 Sydenham
Callaghan Daniel, accountant Frontenac Loan, 163 Sydenham n
Callaghan Harcourt V, bookkeeper, 163 Sydenham n
Callaghan J, cabinetmaker, 424 Johnston
Callaghan Thomas, engineer, 53 Colborne

Calvert Geo, bookkeeper, 3 York

Calvert John, clerk, 3 York

Calvert Wm, tinsmith, 3 York

Calvin Co [Limited] wharfingers, foot Brock

Cambridge Thomas, laborer, 8 Anglin's Cottages, Bay

Cameron Archibald, tanner, 330 Montreal

Cameron Rev C, Presbyterian, 128 Union

Cameron Major-Gen D R, R A, C M G, commandant R M C, King, cor Union

Cameron K A, clerk, 34 Simcoe

Cameron Mrs Marian, [wid Angus], 34 Simcoe

Campbell Alexander, grocer, Kingston station, Montreal

Campbell C, laborer, 12 James

Campbell Dan'l, carter, 62 North

Campbell Harvey, sailor, 283 Sydenham

Campbell J G & Son, flour mills, foot Brock

Campbell J M, manager of Kingston Electric Light Co, foot Brock

Campbell James, mason, 391 Division

Campbell James, mariner, Beverley, Newman's Cottages

Campbell Jas, wood merchant, 27 Rideau

Campbell John, laborer, 55 King w

Campbell Col John, 143 King w

Campbell John, carpenter, Albert

Campbell John J, watchman, 105 Union e

Campbell Martha, grocer, 298 Princess

Campbell Mathew, laborer, 105 King w

Campbell Michael, cotton operative, 13 Upper Charles

Campbell Robert, saloon, 296 Princess

Campbell Thos, carriage maker, 407 Princess

Campbell William, plasterer, 153 Pine

Campion Richard, painter, 335 Princess

Campion Wm, blacksmith, 298 Johnston

Campsall Jas, mechanic, 9 Pine

Campsall Wallace, carpenter, 5 Pine

Canadian Express Co, J S Patch, local manager, King, cor Brock

Canadian Freeman, Cicolari & Daley, props, 119 Brock

Canadian Locomotive and Engine Co [limited] F J Leigh, sup't, J H Birkett, sec-treas, Ontario

Canadian Pacific Railway Co's Telegraph, R J Wilson, manager, 30 Clarence

Cannem Sam, sailor, 35 Cherry

Cannon Mrs Jane (wid James) 396 Division

Cannon Wm, merchant tailor, 273 Princess

Cannon Wm, jr, bookkeeper, 19 Charles

Cannan Wm, ship carpenter, 58 Rideau

Cappon Prof, bds British American hotel

Carey John, moulder, 282 Johnston

Carey T C, trumpet major, RSG

Carey Rev Thomas, Roman Catholic, 225 Johnston

Carey Rev W B, Rector St Paul's Church, 213 Queen

Carey Wm, music dealer, Golden Lion block, Wellington, h 24 Rideau

Carey Wm, clerk, 24 Rideau

Cardwell Mrs Mary (wid Gilbert) Bay

Cardwell Miss, 301 Barrie, Maple Row

Carleton F, grocer, cor Division and Young

Carmichael W D, com traveller, 7 Mack

Carnegie Miss Nellie, grocer, 258 Johnston

Carnovsky B H, cabinet maker, 279 Princess

Carnovsky C F, cabinet maker, 279 Princess

Carnovsky Thomas, baker, 668-70 Princess

Carnovsky P O, tobacconist, 66 Princess, h 111 Princess

Carnovsky Walter, draughtsman, Bagot, cor Brock

Carnovsky W H, fruiterer, 212 Princess and King e

Caron F, repairer Bell tel Co, American Hotel

Carr Alex, machinist, 119 Montreal

Carrington Jos J, prop tannery, River

Carroll Mrs Henrietta [wid Patrick], Carroll House, 291 Ontario

Carroll Robert, 10 Stuart

Carruthers George, grocer, 214 Princess

Carruthers J B, financial agent, King, over King's drug store, h 99 Sydenham w

Carruthers Mrs Mary, [wid John] 67 Chatham

Carruthers Wm C, 99 Sydenham w

Carscallen Thos D, carpenter, 571 Princess

Carson Rev Alex, Roman Catholic, 225 Johnston

Carson Bros, grocers, 322 Princess

Carson Charles, stovefitter, 416 King e

Carson John, merchant, 320 Princess

Carson R J, wholesale grocer, 324 Princess, h 279 Brock

Carson Robert, sergt police, 220 Gordon

Carson Thos A, merchant, 320 Princess, residence

Carson Wm, head Princess

Carson Wm, laborer, Wellington

Carson Rev W W, Methodist, 183 William

Carswell Robert, boiler maker, Beverley

Carter Daniel, quarryman, Durham

Carter R C, Rathbun Co, Barrie cor King w

Carter Thomas, grocer, cor Princess and Nelson

Cartmell Miss Catharine, 203 Alfred

Cartwright Rev C E, chaplain K P, King w, Willow Bank

Cartwright H, clerk Bank B N A, 13 King w

Cartwright Sir Richard, M P, 13 King w

Carver John, carpenter, 140 Nelson

Casey Miss Ellen, 212 Bagot

Casey H W, 214 Division

Casey Thos R, com traveller, 30 Sydenham w

Cassidy Mrs Nancy (wid Wm H) 210 Alfred

Cassidy Mrs Sarah, [wid Andrew] 51 John

Caswell John D, carpenter, 443 Princess

Caswell Thos A, carriagemaker, 443 Princess

Caulfield Thomas, grocer, 206 Bagot

Cays Duncan, real estate agent, 449 Princess

Chadwick Allan, bookkeeper, 106 Bagot

Chadwick & Clark [W M Chadwick, C H Clark], marble cutters, 249 Princess

Chadwick W M, [Chadwick & Clark], 42 Albert

Chamberlain Mrs Hester, [wid John], 7 Victoria Terrace, Montreal

Chambers Charles, mariner, 41 Rideau

Chance E, barber, 159 Brock

Chapman E F, grocer, Queen, cor Division

Chapman H, 277 Albert

Chapman Miss, Maple row, 305 Barrie

Chapman S, contractor, 375 Brock

Chapman W J, contractor, 124 Colborne

Chappell William E, carpenter, 19 York

Charles Augustus, mechanic, bds American Hotel

Charles Edwin, carpenter, 41 Division

Charles John A, bookkeeper, 152 Sydenham

Charlton Robert, foreman boiler maker, 163 Bagot

Chatterton Edwd, carpenter, 37 York

Chestnut Miss H H, Bible woman Y W C A, 128 Clarence

Chown A, 287 Queen

Chown A & Co, hardware, 252 Bagot

Chown A F [A Chown & Co] h 126 Gordon

Chown A P [Chown & Mitclell] h 341 Barrie

Chown Charles D [Chown & Cunningham] h 110 Bagot

CHOWN & CUNNING-HAM (Limited), manufacturers of Stoves, Ranges, Iron Railing, Job Castings, etc., King, corner of Queen

Chown Edwin [Edwin Chown & Son] h 187 Brock

Chown Edwin & Son [Edwin & Geo Y] stoves and tinware, 248-250 Bagot

Chown Geo Y [Edwin Chown & Son] h 257 Brock

Chown & Mitchell [A P Chown, E C Mitchell] chemists & druggists, 124 Princess

Chown Oliver [A Chown & Co] h 397 Queen

Chown Robert J, agent, 220 Johnston

Chown S T, student, 187 Brock

Chrisley Edward, hostler, 16 Alma

Christian Brothers' School, Rev Bro Halward, director, 89 Clergy

Christmas Charles, laborer, r428 King

Christmas James, laborer, 227 Wellington

Christmas William, mariner, 148 Ontario

Christmas Wm J, laborer, 25 Ontario

Christo Thos, bookbinder, Bagot

Chronicle & News, (weekly) L W Shannon, prop, 67 Princess

Church A & L D, hotel, 298 Ontario

Cairns Samuel, carpenter, e s Grove

City Hotel, Sloan Bros, 129 Princess

Cicolari & Daley, [Francis A Cicolari, P J Daley], props *Canadian Freeman*, 119 Brock

Cicolari F A, Cicolari & Daley, h 120 Wellington

Clanahan Mrs Susan, 81 Clarence

Clanahan Thomas, baker, 36 Bagot n

Clanahan William, laborer, 79 Clarence

Clancy Miss Jane, 11 Young

Clancy Thos, laborer, 121 Ontario

Clarke Charles, blacksmith, Patrick

Clark Charles H, prop Bay of Quinte House, 230 Bagot

Clarke Edmund, boiler maker, 201 Colborne

Clark Edward G, accountant O B & S Society, 40 Clergy

Clarke Francis, laborer, 63 Bay

Clarke Frederick W, carpenter, w s lane off Park, GTR station

Clarke Frederick W, machinist, 36 Grove

Clark James W, currier, 50 Bay

Clarke J H, M D, D D S, L D S, dentist, 190 Wellington, h 191 Princess

Clark Joseph E, accountant, 40 Clergy

Clarke Mrs M A (wid Robert) 133 Montreal

Clarke Mrs Mary [wid Lawrence] 63 Queen

Clark Mrs Mary [wid William] 149 Division

Clark Percy, com traveller, 293 Alfred

Clark Robert, mason, 19 Upper William

Clarke Mrs Sarah (wid Wm) 125 Division

Clark Thomas, laborer, 14 John

Clark W H, tanner, end Stephen

Clark Wm, engineer, bds 238 Ontario

Clark Wm J, carter, Charles

Clark —, carter, 8 James

Clare Miss M, dressmaker, 133 Colborne

Claxton Mathew, tinsmith, 27 Charles

Clayton Martin, ship carpenter, 187 Bagot

Cleary Mrs Catharine [wid H] Park, G T R station

Cleary Right Rev James Vincent, S T D, Bishop of Kingston, the Palace, 225 Johnston

Clements Leonard, L D S, dentist, 142 Wellington

Clerihew Geo W, commission, 19 Montreal, h 255 Brock

Cliff Geo, real estate agent, 95 Clarence, h 164 Barrie

Cliff Mrs Mary Ann [wid John] crockery, 333 Princess

Clint Pat'k, hotel, foot Johnston

Clugston R, contractor, 396 Brock

Clugston T, mason, 396 Brock

Clugston W, mason, 396 Brock

Coates E W, salesman, Division, cor Princess

Coburn Wm, laborer, 146 Pine

Cochrane Mrs C [wid William], 164 Frontenac

Cochran Jas, sailor, 294 Gordon

Cochrane John, mason, Albert

Cochrane Capt John B, R M C, 122 Earl

Cochran Mrs Mary, [wid Geo] Barrack, cor King

Cochrane Mrs, dressmaker, 215 Princess

Cochrane Wm, clerk Asylum, bds City Hotel

Cochran Wm, grocer, 377 King e

Cockade Wm, blacksmith, 55 Division

Cockburn John, plumber and steam fitter, 273 Ontario

Cockburn William, general blacksmith, 277 Ontario, h 271 Ontario

Coffee Thos, laborer, 174 Barrie

Coffee Thomas, laborer, 54 Division

Coffey Wm, guard K P, 119 Stuart

Coggan Jesse A, pattern maker, 6 Grove

Cole F F, grain merchant, Ontario

Coleman William, basketmaker, cor Sixth and Chatham

Collins Dewitt C, engineer K & P Ry, Barrack

Collins Henry, laborer, 92 Arch

Collins J, hatter, 421 Brock

Collins James, engineer K & P Ry, 45 Ordnance

Collins John, letter carrier, 48 King w

Collins Mrs Margaret, [wid Michael] 266 Sydenham

Collins P, carter, r102 Barrack

Collins Thomas, mariner, 438 Division

Comber Mrs M [wid J], 307 Brock

Comeau Jos, laborer, up 74 Ontario

Comer George, purser, 80 Division

Comerford Joseph, salesman, 286 Queen

Comper John, carpenter, Frontenac

Conlan Edward, grocer, 104 William

Conlan Jno, tailor, 112 William

Conley E B, farmer, 426 Brock

Conley Henry, clerk military store department, 48 Place d'Armes

Conley John, plumber, 368 Division

Conley Mrs Mary [wid Michael] Victoria

Conley Patrick, cor Sydenham and Bay

Conley Mrs Rebecca, [wid William], 368 Division

Conley Thos, trade instructor K P, 85 Wellington

Connell J C, M A, M D C M, 279 King, h King cor West

Connolly James, laborer, Bagot

Connolly Patrick, laborer, old No 52, Bagot

Connor J, cabinet maker, 354 Brock

Connor John, mechanic, bds Albermarle House

Connors Jno, laborer, up 89 Earl

Horseshoe Island. Boats twice a day each way. Liquor prohibited from being sold.

13

Conroy Michael, grocer, 8 Market square, h 26 Ellice
Conroy Patrick, 26 Ellice
Conway F, assistant freight and passenger agent, William, cor Wellington
Cooke Rev Arthur W, assistant St George's Church, 166 King E
Cook Chas, laborer, 16 Ann
Cooke F W, bookkeeper, 82 Bagot
Cook Jervis, salesman, 67 Sydenham w
Cook John, engineer, Ordnance
Cook Wm, blacksmith, 9 Cherry
Coombs W H, clerk, Alwington ave
Coon D A, B A, medical student, 95 Wellington
Cooper D, merchant, 364 Brock
Couper Daniel, merchant, 776 Princess
Cooper John, 80 Arch
Cooper Mrs, 772 Princess
Cooper Richard, butcher, 825 Princess
Cooper Thos, laborer, Victoria
Copeland Philip, flagman G T Ry, 793 Montreal
Copley Wm, trader, 180 Cherry
Corbett C H, governor jail, res jail
Corbett John, hardware, 95 Princess, h 5 Barnstaple Terrace, Clergy
Corbett S S, salesman, 413 Princess
Corbett William, tinsmith, 411 Princess
Corby Mrs G B (wid Henry), Frontenac
Corien Mrs Mattie, second hand dealer, 276 Ontario

Cornelius John, sailor, 167 Queen
Corrigan Daniel (old 58 Bagot)
Corrigan John, storeman, 111 Ontario
Corrigan Patrick, laborer, North
Corrigan Richard, waggon mkr, 355 Division
Corrigan Thos, storeman, 113 Ontario
Corrigan Wm, pilot, foot Gore
Crosby C S, shoemaker, 237 Earl
Crosby Frederick, barber, 237 Earl
Costello Alex, moulder, Stephen
Costello Sam'l, laborer, Stephen
Cotton John, tanner, 240 Montreal
Cotton Lt-Col W H, Commandant R S G, Tete du Pont Barracks
Coughlin Mrs J, 321 Brock
Coughlin ——, laboratory foreman R S G
Coulson James, diver, 60 Union
Coulson James, carpenter, 93 Queen
Coulthart David, machinist, 53 William
Counter Charles A, laborer, 81 Queen
Counter George, truck builder, 105 Colborne
Cousineau, Quinn & Corrigan, dry goods, clothing and gent's furnishings, 78 and 80 Princess
Coward Geo, painter, 325 Brock
Coward M W, clerk, 325 Brock
Coward Wm, baker K P, 227 Gordon
Cowdy John, quarry owner, 223 Montreal

Cowdy William, contractor, 67 Cherry

Cowie Robt, carpenter, 21 John

Cowie Thomas, stone mason, 23 John

Cowman Richard, mechanic, 10

Coy Miss Sarah, 101 Queen

Coyle Edwd, clerk, 23 Balaclava

Coyle Henry, clerk, 23 Balaclava

Coyle J, clerk, bds Windsor Hotel

Coyle John, cabdriver, 23 Balaclava

Coyle Mrs Rose [wid Henry] 23 Balaclava

Coyne Sergt M, Fort Frederick

Craig Adam, porter, Alfred

Craig Mrs Agnes, [wid John], 204 K e

Craig J A, policeman, 83 Young

Craig James, coppersmith, r85 Gore

Craig John, conductor, 59 Colborne

Craig Miss Sarah, 23 Arch

Craig Wm G, [A Gunn & Co] h 82 Ontario

Craik Mrs Mary, [wid Andrew] 66 Arch

Crane Charles, miller, 151 Montreal

Crate Thos, clerk British American Hotel

Crawford Anthony, 124 Division

Crawford George, mariner, 329 Division

Crawford James, grocer, 182 Princess, h 327 Division

Crawford J J, cutter, 6 Garratt

Crawford R & Co, coal and wood, foot Queen

Crawford Robert [R Crawford & Co] 2 Barnstaple Terrace, Clergy

Crawford Samuel, coal merch't, 124 Division

Crawford Thomas, fireman, 29 King w

Creamer Edward, laborer, 298 Montreal

Creeggan Geo, tailor, 14 Main

Creighton Geo, bookkeeper, 44 O'Kill

Creighton Robt, clerk, 129 Union

Crellian Edward, boiler maker, 51 Upper Charles

Crewlin Wm, laborer, 10 Vine

Criddiford John, hair dresser, 73 Clarence

Crisley J, laborer, 320 Johnston

Crisley William, cab driver, 226 Queen

Crothers H & W J, wholesale biscuit and confectionery manufacturers, 207-209 Wellington

Crothers Hutchison [H & W J Crothers] bds City hotel

Crothers W J [H & W J Crothers], Earl, cor Clergy

Crook Miss E, dressmaker, 267 Queen

Crowley Charles W, laborer, 110 Ordnance

Crowley Frank, salesman, Alfred and Johnston

Crowley J, carter, 373 Johnston

Crowley John, sailor, 69 Bay

Crowley Peter, laborer, 298 Montreal

Crozier Mrs Mary [wid Thos], 235 Colborne

Crumley Alexander, baker, Bagot

Crumley E, [Spence & Crumley], h 63 Union

Crumley Hugh, carpenter, 63 Union

Crumley W H, salesman, 63 Union

Cruse Thomas, 328 Gordon

Cruse W H, shoemaker, Albert

Crysler Mrs Eunice [wid Chas] 69 Union e

Cuddeford John, stonecutter, Montreal

Cudmore John, laborer, 59 William

Culle Patrick, laborer, 16 James

Cullen Wm, engineer, 31 James

Culley Joseph, laborer, Park, G T R station

Culpack Mrs B, 252 Earl

Colville H, printer, 323 Brock

Cumming Mrs C, [wid G], 312 Brock

Cummins M C, laborer, 384 Brock

Cunningham Mrs C, [wid R], 291 Johnson

Cunningham Charles, confectioner, 358 Barrie

Cunningham Daniel, ship carpenter, 51 Bay

Cunningham David, trade instructor K P, 318 Earl

Cunningham David, cabman, 180 Bagot

Cunningham Henry [Chown & Cunningham] h 163 Earl

Cunningham John, sewing machine dealer, 348 King e

Cunningham Samuel, carpenter, 18 Deacon

Cunningham Thomas, boots and shoes, 267 Princess

Cunningham Wm, finisher, 85 King w

Cunningham Wm, currier, 48 Grove

Currie James, machinist, 117 Barrack

Curtis Miss Bridget, dressmaker, 223 Wellington

Curtis C Loomis, M D, 136 Wellington

Curtis Fred, plasterer, 16 Cherry

Curtis Henry H, druggist, 327 Barrie

Curtis H H & Co, druggists, 186 Princess

Curtis Patrick, shoemaker, 105 Gore

Cushion Thos, laborer, 28 Alma

Daily and Weekly British Whig, E J B Pense, proprietor, 336-340 King e

Daily News, Lewis W Shannon, proprietor, 67 Princess

Dalton & Strange [W B Dalton, J M Strange] hardware, 143 Princess

Dalton W B [Dalton & Strange] h 138 Johnston

Daly C B, civil engineer, 298 Gordon

Daly James, 54 Rideau

Daly James, printer, Bagot

Daly Justus, 288 Gordon

Daley P J, [Cicolari & Daley] h 285 Wellington

Daley Thomas, laborer, 98 Main

Daley Thomas, trader, 16 Place d' Armes

Daley W J, grocer, 844 Princess

Darby William, bookkeeper, 228 Queen

D'Arcy Mrs Jane [wid Robt], dressmaker, 87 Wellington

D'Arcy Robert J, clerk P O, 87 Wellington

Darragh Alex, 681 Montreal

Darragh George, carpenter, 689 Montreal

Darragh John, guard K P, 204 Alfred

Dartnell Miss Ellen, [Lawlor & Dartnell], 196 King e

Dartnell Miss Jane, [Lawlor & Dartnell, 196 King e

Daunt Jos, brewer, 117 King w

David C, 102 Pine

David Daniel, 94 York

David Isaac, 124 Picard

Davidson Miss Ann, Principal Cataraqui Public School

Davidson Andrew, contractor, 285 Queen

Davidson Bryce, clerk, 347 Alfred

Davidson, Doran & Co, founders, Ontario, cor Union

Davidson Douglas, clerk, 347 Alfred

Davidson Duncan A, law student, 347 Alfred

Davidson John, supervisor Regiopolis branch Asylum for Insane

Davidson John, laborer, 30 York

Davidson Robert, carpenter, 197 Colborne

Davidson Major S, R E, R M C, 91 William

Davidson Thos, trade instructor K P, Pembroke

Davis Ebenezer, lumberman, 50 Union

Davis Francis, contractor, bds (old 82) Bagot

Davis James, engineer, 42 Wellington

Davis James, shoemaker, 269 Princess

Davis John, carpenter, 106 Barrack

Davis John, bds (old 66) Bagot

Davis Louis, laborer, Ontario

Davis Mrs Mary A (wid James) 36 Sydenham w

Davis Richard F, photographer, 232 King e

Davis Robert & Son, prop dry dock and ship yard, n e end Wellington

Davis Robert (Robert Davis & Son) h 180 Rideau

Davis Mathew R, ship builder, Corrigan

Davies Wm, carpenter, 12 Upper Charles

Davidson C S, fireman, 198 Sydenham

Davy Albert, grain shoveller, 431 King e

Davy Benjamin, ship carpenter, 433 King e

Davy George, carpenter, King w

Davy George, carpenter, 28 Chatham

Davy John, carpenter, old No 16, Bagot

Davy Norman, grocer, cor King w and Gordon

Davy Stuart, carpenter, Garratt

Davy W R, carpenter, 171 Nelson

Dawson Edward, machinist, 381 Division

Day Prof Fershaw, R C A, R M C, 181 Division

Day Mrs, Victoria

Day Herbert, boarding, 270½ Princess

Deacon Mrs Amanda, [wid R], 108 Bagot

Deacon Andrew, M O clerk, P O, bds 108 Bagot

Dean Ed C, clerk, 216 Barrie

Dean Mrs M, 216 Barrie

Dean William, printer, 39 Young

DeCarteret C, merchant, 393 Brock

Decharme L O, ass't gunnery instructor, R S G

Decker Remain, blacksmith, 44 Division

Decker Thomas R, laborer, 44 Division

Dee C H, salesman, bds 247 Brock

Deeks W A, carriage maker, 147 Brock, h 199 Brock

Deeks Wm, laborer, 250 Queen

Dehaney Thomas, carter, 325 Montreal

De Lacey Miss Nellie, dressmaker, 208 King e

Delaney James, John north

Delaney Martin, carpenter, John north

Delaney Michael, trackman, G T R, off Park, G T R station

Delaney Patrick, fireman, John north

Delaney Patrick, laborer, 777 Montreal

Delph Jas, laborer, 4 Quebec

Dempsey Miss M, 312 Johnston

Dempster Wm, stonecutter, 149 Nelson

Denn W, laborer, 320 Brock

Dennis Mrs Fanny (wid James) grocer, 83 Colborne, corner Barrie

Dennis Jos, tel repairer, Park, G T R station

Dennison James, stone cutter, 51 Division

Dennison J G, carpenter, Alwington ave

Dennison W, shoemaker, 367 Brock

Denny Jas, laborer, 238 Earl

Deputy Adjt Gen Office, Col Straubenzie commandant, Artillery Park Barracks

Derry Hugh, mason, 240 Colborne

Derry James, boiler maker, bds 271 Princess

Derry P W, moulder, 81 Union

Derry Thomas boilermaker, 234 Wellington

Derry W D, mason, 104 Pine

Derry William, engineer, 268 Gordon

DesRochers Prof Zephren, music teacher, 70 Wellington

De St Remy Miss Elizabeth, H D L L, private school teacher, 59 Gore

Devan Maurice, ship carpenter, 55 Colborne

Devine James, carter, 48 Albert

Devlin James, engineer, 218 Gordon

Devlin Patrick, cabman, Barrack

Devlin Patrick, porter, City Hotel

Devlin Peter, bowling alley, 203 Wellington

Dew James, laborer, cor Alma and Patrick

Dewsberry Mrs Jessie, [wid Frederick], 68 Ontario

Deyo Charles, conductor, 65 Charles

Diack Robert, miller, bds Union Hotel

Diamond Charles, laborer, 209 Montreal

Dick D J, (W J Dick & Son), h 252 Alfred

Dick George, carriage trimmer, 357 Princess

Dick W J (W J Dick & Son) h 360 Brock

Dick W J & Son (W J & D J) boots, shoes, trunks and valises, 168 Princess

Dickinson Robt, carpenter, 449 Division

Dickinson Solathiel, carpenter, 449 Division

Dickson Mrs Anne (wid John) 225 Wellington

Dickson C I, inspector of liquors, 314 Gordon

Dickson James, blacksmith, 116 Barrack

Dickson John, shoemaker, 306 Ontario

Dickson Mrs J R, 172 Johnston

Dickson John H, engineer, 32 Division

Dillon James E, h Brock

Dillon Joseph, h 111 Princess

Dillon Joseph & Son (Joseph & Jas Edward) boots and shoes, 111 Princess

Dine Mrs Maria (wid Charles) 90 Gore

Dine Philip, boiler maker, 70 Ontario

Dinsmore Charles, laborer, John north

Diplock Miss M, 23 Wade's lane

Dix Capt James, mariner, 227 Earl

Dix Capt Jos, mariner, Nelson

Dobbs Frank, 2 Hales' cottages, King w

Dobbs R S, civil engineer (retired) 195 Johnston

Dodd Mrs J, (wid Geo) 5 O'Kill

Dodd Jno, engineer, 415 King e

Dodd William, blacksmith, 47 James

Dodds Mrs Mary, (wid John) 10 George

Doherty Isaac, dyer, Bagot

Doherty John, laborer, 99 Elm

Doherty Mrs, 260 Johnston

Doherty Wm, laborer, 99 Elm

Dolan J F, clerk, 219 Princess

Dolan Martin, saddler, 219 Princess

Dolan Michael, saddler, 219 Princess

Dolphin John, 21 Gordon

Dominion Express Co, J F Swift, agent, King, cor Clarence

Donald Mrs Jane, (wid John), 772 Montreal

Donaldson George, tender Cataraqui Bridge

Donaldson George, engine fitter, Ontario

Donaldson Joseph R, grocer, 290 Ontario

Donaldson J S, carpenter, 33 Pine

Doney Luke, hotel, 33 Brock

Donnelly Capt Thos, 195 Gordon

Donnelly David, carpenter, 53 Division

Donnelly Capt John, wrecker & diver, 118 Wellington

Donnelly John, jr, engineer, bds City hotel

Donnelly J P, com traveller, 209 Colborne

Donnelly Sandford, machinist, 141 Montreal

Donnelly Mrs Sarah [wid Felix] 223 Gordon

Donnelly Mathew, moulder, 52 Rideau

Donoghue Mrs B, 14 Upper William

Donoghue Mrs Catharine [wid Daniel] end Ontario

Donoghue Daniel, baker, bds 223 Wellington

Donoghue Jas, bartander City hotel, 111 Barrack

Donoghue Michael, r 164 Bagot

Donoghue Michael, carpenter, 21 O'Kill

Donoghue Mrs Margaret [wid Patrick] 92 William

Donoghue Peter, clerk, 130 Division

Donoghue Timothy, commercial traveller, 107 Clergy

Donovan Cornelius, bricklayer, 50 North

Donovan Mrs, 50 North

Doolan Jeremiah, laborer, 94 Rideau

Doolan John, laborer, Bagot

Doolan T, Collender Hotel, 322-6 King c

Dooley James, shoemaker, 396 Barrie

Doran B, (B Doran & Co) h 64 Barrie

Doran B & Co, millinery and dry goods, 126 Princess

Doran Daniel, painter, 264 Gordon

Doran Dan, laborer, 125 Queen

Doran Jas, clerk, bds 70 Princess

Doran Michael, (Davidson, Doran & Co) h King w

Dorland W E, merchant tailor, 181 Wellington, h 239 Division

Dougal Alfred, carpenter, 150 Picard

Dougal Lewis, teamster, 152 Picard

Dougherty James, bookkeeper, The Rathbun Co

Douglass Brice, bricklayer, Nelson

Douglass James, mason, Albert

Douglass James, blacksmith, 92 Gore

Douglas Robert, storeman, head Princess

Dousley William, shoemaker, 8 George

Dow J W, n side Cataraqui

Downey David, teamster, 91 Wellington

Downey Mrs Hester (wid Robt), 103 Queen

Downey Robt, carpenter, Albert

Downey Timothy, shoemaker, Bagot

Downing James, Alice

Downing W, cashier, 356 Brock

Downs James, laborer, 20 Alma

Dowsley D H, M D, 218 Johnston

Doyle Edward, carpenter, Park, G T R station

Doyle Hugh, grocer, 296 Barrie

Doyle Miss J, 37 Young

Doyle Jas, butcher, n s Princess

Doyle James, guard K P, 11 Pembroke

Doyle John, mariner, 101 Rideau

Doyle Miss Mary Ann, school teacher, 2 Victoria Terrace, Montreal

Doyle Michael, clerk Albion Hotel, 221 Montreal

Doyle, Patrick, grocer, n s Princess

Doyle Patrick, laborer, 102 Rideau

Doyle Wm, hotel, 21 Brock

Doyle Wm, butcher, 768 Princess

Drennan Rev Alex, 222 Gordon

Night. 75 Princess, h
118 Earl.

Driscoll Dennis, stonemason, 49 Wellington

Driscoll J, guard K P, 116 William

Driscoll Patrick, painter, old No 86, Bagot

Driver John, bookkeeper, Bagot

Driver Thomas, appraiser, customs, 163 Queen

Druce John, laborer, Montreal

Drury William, tinsmith, 389 Princess

Drury Wm, sen, 393 Princess

Dry Dock Office, Public Works Dept, W O Strong, engineer in charge, 30 Union

Duff Col John, police magistrate, 450 Princess

Duffy Edward, laborer, r80 Earl

Duffy Francis, dyer, 46 Division

Duffy Patrick, pensioner, bds 238 Ontario

Duffey William, moulder, 94 William

Dunbar Henry, 168 Bagot

Dunbar Mrs Hester, 9 Montreal

Dunbar John, merchant tailor and gents' furnisher, 100 Princess, h 436 Princess, Vaughn Terrace

Duncan Alexander, driller, 208 King e

Dunham E H, prop Hotel Frontenac, Ontario

Dunham J E, prop British American Hotel, Clarence, cor King

Dunlop Andrew, mariner, 96 Rideau

Dunlop A W, bookkeeper, 48 Colborne

Dunlop Miss Gertrude, Maitland

Dunlop H A, clerk, 251 Division

Dunlop James M, hay dealer, n s Place d'Armes, h 38 Rideau

Dunlop Robt, tailor, 29 John

Dunlop W B, salesman, 56 Union

Dunlop Wm, cutter, 56 Union

Dunn John, laborer, 50 O'Kill

Dunn Thomas, grocer, Queen, cor Wellington

Dunn William, stoves and tinware, 229-231 Princess, h 309 Brock

Dunnett Wm, foreman of Shedden Co, 26 Barrie

Dunnill, T D, shooting gallery, 31 Brock

Dunning Philo, pork butcher 84 Brock

Dunphy Edward, painter, 79 York

Dunphy James, 256 Queen

Dunphy James, packer, 96 York

Dunstar John, mariner, 20 Earl

Dupont Hippolyte, oil cloth mfr, 318 Queen

Dupuis D R, medical student, 7 Montreal

Dupuis N F, M A, F B S Edin, professor Queen's College, Gordon

Dupuis Thomas R, M D, M R C S Eng, fellow R C P & S, physician and surgeon, prof clinical surgery and surgeon Kingston Hospital, Montreal, cor Brock

Dupuy H S, accountant Bank of Montreal, 128 Barrie

Dutton Samuel, laborer, 437 Barrie

Duval Arthur D, M D, R M C, 331 King e

Dwyer Edward, salesman, Barrie, between O'Kill & Stuart

Dwyer John, laborer, r 27 Ontario

Dwyer Michael, laborer, 90 William

Dyde Samuel, bookkeeper, 137 William

Dyde W H, com traveller, 137 William

Edgar David, fireman, n side Cataraqui

Edgar Wm, painter, 129 Montreal

Edwards Charles, mason, 38 Ellice

Edwards Peter, laborer, bds 199 Colborne

Edwards R, grocer, 225 Division

Edwards Richard, grocer, 78 Division

Egan Daniel, Dom Exp messenger, bds r 81 Wellington

Egan John, moulder, 116 Johnston

Egan Mrs Mary Ann (wid Daniel) r 81 Wellington

Egan Miss, 88 Brock

Egan Morton, engineer, bds r 81 Wellington

Eggleton James, laborer [old 67] Bagot

Eilbeck Robt, 112 Clarence

Elder Bros, livery, 212 Wellington

Elder Geo, St Lawrence House, 418 King o

Elder James, livery, 281 Bagot

Eldridge Rev G S, Third Methodist Church, 242 Johnston

Elliott Alex M, driver, 366 Division

Elliott Alfred, mail carrier, r 258 King o

ELLIOTT BROS (Robt F, Mathew and J M), Hot Water Heating Engineers and dealers in Stoves, Ranges, Tinware, etc, ; Tinsmiths and Plumbers, Steam & Gas Fitters, 77 Princess, h 366 Division

Elliott Christopher, groom, 47 Bay

Elliott Mrs Elizabeth, boarding house, 81 Queen

Elliott Geo, traveller, 149 Brock

Elliott Mrs Jane (wid William) 19 Balaclava

Elliott J G, man'g editor *Whig*, 27 Colborne

Elliott John, bookkeeper, 366 Division

Elliott Mrs, 141 Ordnance

Elliott Otho, salesman, 47 Bay

Elliott Richard, shoemaker, 523 Princess

Elliott Robert, carpenter, 366 Division

Elliott William, cor Gordon and Johnston

Ellis Jas, laborer, 10 Redan

Elmer A E, barber, 72 Princess, h 28 Division

Elmer Mrs M C, saloon, 210 Princess

Elmer Jos, barber, Ordnance

Elmer R H, barber, 161 Princess

Elmer Thos, moulder, 229 Earl

Elsmere Alex, instructor K P, 228 Gordon

Ely Alex, bartender, 487 Princess

Ely Joel, foreman Knitting mill, 131 Alfred

Ely Samuel, 178 Alfred

Emmett Maitland, engineer K & P Ry, 202 Rideau

England Thomas, gardener, Regent

English Mrs C (wid David) 15 Mack

English Robt H, druggist, 250 Alfred

Ennis Mrs Jane (wid James) 11 Rideau

Enright Michael, salesman, Chatham, cor First

Enwright Thos, ship carpenter, 69 Chatham

Erwin Wm, roadmaster K P R, 157 Montreal

Evans Richard, carpenter, 177 Clergy

Evans Robt, keeper K P, King w

Everett Miss Harriett, 231 Bagot

Eves Daniel, carter, 147 Ordnance

Eves Jas, cab driver, Bagot, cor Bay

Eves Mark, bds 149 Ordnance

Eves William, painter, 142 Colborne

Eward F W, blacksmith, 258 Division

Eward Mrs Mary (wid Thos), 240 Division

Eward Robt, clerk, 207 Colborne

Fahey Edward, asst canal collector, 158 Bagot

Fahey Mrs H, confectioner, 68 Princess

Fairbanks Mrs, 215 Earl

Fallen M, carter, Patrick

Fallon Pat'k, laborer, 21 Redan

Fallon D, Prince Edward hotel, 914 Princess

Fanning Charles, sailor, bds 35 Brock

Fanning Mrs Elizabeth, (wid John) r31 Johnson

Fanning Patrick, carter, 34 Alma

Farley Mrs Emma, (wid Thos) 147 Colborne

Farley J, carter, 305 Johnston

Farmer John, salesman, Markland

Farrell Thomas, groceries and liquors, 41-45 Brock

Farrington Jas, 18 Wellington

FEDERAL WAREHOUSE. The Largest and Cheapest Dry Goods House in Kingston. Staple Goods a Specialty. 114 Princess.

Fee Samuel Henry, M D, 405 Princess

Fee William, 273 Queen

Fenwick G S, (Fenwick, Hendry & Co) h 176 Johnston

Fenwick Mrs H E, Nelson

Fenwick, Hendry & Co, wholesale grocers, 189 Ontario

Fenwick K N, M D, M A, M R C S, Eng, F O S, Edin, 141 King e

Fenwick Thomas M, M D, Barrie, cor King

Ferguson A, laborer, 138 Bay

Ferguson G D, Prof Queen's University, 195 Earl

Ferguson James, salesman, 522 Princess

Ferguson William, Sheriff Co Frontenac, King e, cor Gore

Ferguson William, laborer, 100 Picard

Ferns Mrs J C, 249 Queen

Ferris Edward, farmer, King w, Willow Cottage

Ferrier Geo, machinist, Bagot

Ferris Mrs Mary (wid John D) 212 King e

Fidler Edward, moulder, 81 Queen

Field Sergt S, R S G

Fields A, barber, 49 Princess

Fillion Edward, bailiff, 22 Chatham

Filtz Geo, cabinet maker, 387 Johnston

Filtz Wm, cigar maker, 387 Johnston

Filtz P, carpenter, 414 Johnston

Filtz R, mason, 405 Johnston

Finlay Alex, bricklayer, 87 Elm

Fisher John, contractor, 264 Johnston

Fisher John, carpenter, 120 Albert

Fisher Joseph, flour and feed, 43 Princess, h 9 Pembroke

Fischer M, cutter, 21 Frontenac

Fisk Ira, laborer, 63 U Charles

Fitzgerald Mrs Catharine, (wid David), 102 Ontario

Fitzgerald James, laborer, 130 Union

Fitzgibbon, James, laborer, 158 Clergy

Fitzpatrick Michael, laborer, 209 Sydenham

Fiveash Charles, laborer, end Fifth

Flaherty Thomas, pensioner, bds 238 Ontario

Flanigan Andrew J, 421 Princess

Flanagan John, cigarmaker, Rideau

Flanagan Michael, City Clerk 82 Barrie

Flanagan Pat'k, laborer, Picard

Flanagan Patrick, engineer, 122 Ordnance

Flanigan Thomas, cab driver, 109 William

Flanagan T J, barber, 223 Princess

Fleming Capt James, mariner, 214 Earl

Fleming John, Park, G T R station

Fletcher Prof John, Queen's University, 78 Wellington

Flett A G, merchant tailor, 214 Princess, h 74 Colborne

Flood James, laborer, bds Montreal house, Ontario

Foden James, fitter, 120 Bay

Fokes E J, hair dresser, 217 Princess

Foley Michael, carter, 97 Earl

Folger Bros, bankers, foot Brock

Folger B W [Folger Bros] King e, cor Earl

Folger F A [Folger Bros] 15 Sydenham w

Folger F A, jr, clerk, King, cor Earl

Folger Mrs Laura (wid Frederick) 13 Sydenham w

Folger M H [Folger Bros] Emily

Follast Albert, carpenter, 264 Earl

Follast William, laborer, 170 Nelson

Forbs Mrs Jane [wid William] 429 Barrie

Ford Bros [W G & R M] tanners, 316 King e, tannery Cataraqui

Ford R M [Ford Bros] h 84 Barrie

Ford William, merchant, 211 Queen

Ford W G [Ford Bros] h 7 Barnstaple Terrace, Clergy

Forder Geo, sailor, 146 Colborne

Forest William, carpenter, 40 Union e

Forster Augustus, bartender, Markland

Forsyth Francis A, mariner, Bagot

Forsyth Geo, carriage trimmer, 176 Clergy

Forsyth J B, 175 Clergy

Forsyth Jas M, bds 212 King e

Fowler F, M D, 249 Brock

Fowler Mrs J, (wid J), 321 Johnston

Fowler Prof James, Queen's University, 121 Union

Fowler Miss Mary, 130 King

Fowler Mrs, 307 Barrie

Fowler Thomas, salesman, bds American Hotel

Fox Frank, carpenter, centre McCormack Cottages

Fralick J W, 186 Gordon

Francis J, shoemaker, 369 Brock

Francis John, pressman, Beverly, Newman's Cottages

Francis Lewis, ladder manufacturer, 7 Simcoe

Francisco Edward, clerk American Hotel

Franklin C D, flour and feed, 18 Market Sq, h 94 Earl

Franklin Joseph, flour and feed, 211 Princess, h Sydenham

Fraser Mrs Ann, (wid Alex), 25 Earl

Fraser Mrs Annie, (wid Alex), 138 Queen

Fraser Mrs Catharine, (wid H), 133 King e

Fraser David, fitter, Beverly, Newman's Cottages

Fraser Donald, private banker, 342 King e, h King e

Fraser Fred, clerk, 50 Sydenham

Fraser Major John, R S G, res Barracks

Fraser N F, clerk, bds 132 Wellington

Fraser R, laborer, 148 Colborne

Fraser Capt Samuel, mariner, 97 Queen

Fraser S P, merchant tailor, 175 Princess, bds City hotel

Fraser Thos, laborer, Collingwood

Fraser Wm, carpenter, e side Grove

Fraser Wm G, carriage maker, 150 Sydenham

Fraser —, carpenter, 61 Elm

Free Mrs Ann [wid Thomas] 434 King e

Free John, brakesman, 14 Pine

Free Robt, mason, 94 Division

Frederick Rev Bro, Christian Brothers' School, 89 Clergy

Fressaw Jos, ice cream parlor, 314 Princess

Friendship Thos, gardener, 386 Division

Frizzell Robert, shoemaker, 309 Montreal

Frontenac Lead Mining and Smelting Co, limited, Orchard

Frontenac Loan and Investment Society, Thos Briggs, manager, 87 Clarence

Frost Arthur, painter, Frontenac

Frost Edward, 5 York

Frost Thos, laborer, 301 Montreal

Fullen James, foreman Water Works, 150 Ontario

Funnell David J, engine driver K & P R, 144 Rideau

Funnell David, carpenter, Montreal

Funnell R K, mechanic, 378 Barrie

Funnell Thos, conductor K & P R'y, 204 Rideau

Furlong Thomas, laborer, 31 Ontario

Gaffield Nathaniel, com traveller, 159 Sydenham

Gage Benj, driver, 94 York

Gallagher Mrs Ann (wid John), 268 Wellington

Gallagher Francis J, laborer, 67 Queen

Gallagher John J, painter, 280 Montreal

Gallagher Mrs Mary, (wid Emanuel) 229 Wellington

Gallagher Miss Mary E, dressmaker, 230 Montreal

Gallagher T, sailor, 84 Upper Charles

Gallagher Thos, cartage agent K & P R, 104 Barrack

Gallagher Thos, laborer, Picard

Gallagher Wm, carpenter, John north

Gallagher Wm, cab driver, 1 Dunn Terrace, Bay

Gallinger Alex, contractor, 332 Gordon

Gallivan Jas, engineer, 42 O'Kill

Gallivan John, engineer, 285 Alfred

Gallivan Miss Minnie, dressmaker, 258 King e

Gallivan Daniel, bds 238 Ontario

Galloway George, machinist, 17 Gordon

Galloway Jas, jr, bookkeeper, 84 Princess

Galloway James, sr, hatter and furrier, 84 Princess

Galloway Thomas, tailor, 521 Princess

Galvin J, 294 Division

Galvin Michael, carter, 48 Picard

Gamble Mrs Jennie [wid John] 793 Montreal

Garbutt D J, real estate agent, 200 William

Gardiner J A, bailiff 1st Div Court, 273 Bagot, h 307 Gordon

Gardiner Jas, 188 Ordnance

Gardiner Robt, merchant, 151 Earl

Garrett Mrs C [wid Robert] 12 Johnston

Garrett R W, M D, 52 Johnston

Garrigan Jas, shoemaker, 224 Sydenham

Garry Edward, barber, 6 Ontario

Garvin E, caretaker inland rev department, Clarence

Garvin Michael, laborer, 56 North

Gascoigne Joseph, engineer, 24 Ellice

Gaskin John, outside **Manager** Montreal Transportation Co, Ontario, cor Princess

Gaskin Robt A, law student, 244 Gordon

Gaskin Thos, **custom's clerk,** 244 Gordon

Gates Abel, laborer, 262 Earl

Gates Francis, off Park, G T R station

Gates Francis, mason, 51 Chatham

Gates Joseph, driver, 627 Princess

Gates W, carpenter, 322 Johnston

Gavine William, laborer, Victoria

Gaudier Lewis, carver, 135 Ordnance

Gautt W W, grocer, 148 Frontenac

Gaw Robert, contractor, 191 Gordon

Gaw Samuel, 109 Union c

Geach John, laborer, 228 Sydenham

Geale John, solicitor, 34 Frontenac

Geale John, 90 Division

Geary Edward, shoemaker, Livingston ave

Geary George, machinist, Livingston ave

Geary John, laborer, 16 George

Genau Francis, laborer, 11 John

Genge Mrs Mary Ann [wid Richard] 212 Alfred

Geoghegan John, mariner, 266 Wellington

George Joseph, organs, pianos and sewing machines, 112-14 Gore, h 28 Wellington

Germain Edmond, currier, Dufferin

Gibbs John, laborer, 3 Gray's Lane

Gibson D, grocer, 345 Princess, h 461 Princess

Gibson James, 122 Union

Gibson John, laborer, 43 James

Gibson Wm, clerk, bds (old 82) Bagot

Gibson Wm, piano agent, 501 Princess

Gilbert John, grocer, 194 Barrie

Gilbert Richard, com traveller, 459 Princess

Gilchrist Adam, man Loco & Engine Co, 84 Gore

Gilchrist Mrs E [wid John] 311 Earl

Gilchrist David, tinsmith, 311 Earl

Gildersleeve A M, ledger keeper Merchants Bank, 45 Gore

Gildersleeve C F, steamboat owner, 40 Clarence, h 45 King c

GILDERSLEEVE J P, General Insurance agent (Fire, Life, Marine, Accident & Guarantee), Railway Ticket Agent, Steamship Ticket Agent (Allan, Dominion, Cunard, Inman and other lines) ; Issuer of Marriage Licenses, Notary Public. 42 Clarence, h 45 Gore

Gildersleeve Miss Lucretia, 267 King c

Gill Mrs Catharine [wid Robt] 267 Gordon

•Gill Wm, clerk, 250 Barrie

Gillen E, [Gillen & Gillen], Bagot, cor Brock

Gillen Fred B, [Gillen & Gillen], Bagot, cor Brock

Gillen & Gillen, architects & appraisers, Bagot, cor Brock

Gillie James, engineer, 235 Earl

Gillespie James, keeper, Asylum, 45 Colborne

Gillmore Rev J E, rector Catholic Apostolic Church, 290 Queen

Gillmore Samuel, laborer, 25 Upper William

Gillmore Wallace, carriagemaker, 41 James

Gilmour Robt, letter carrier, 205 Gordon

Gissing Albert, grocer, 259 Gordon

Givins Charles, laborer, Beverly

Givens D A, barrister, 43 Brock, h cor Gordon and Brock

Givins Robert G. carpenter, 234 Barrie

Givens Mrs Susan, [wid Geo], 166 Bagot

Glaccon Mrs Lucy, 89 Elm

Glasgow Andrew, laborer, 390 Montreal

Glasgow Robert, currier, 390 Montreal

Glasgow Robert, telegrapher, 390 Montreal

Glazier Z, carter, w c rchard

Glancy Mrs Mary Ann, [wid Alexander], 64 North

Gleeson Mrs Ann, [wid James] Johnston

Gleeson Miss Elizabeth, dressmaker, 258 King e

Gleeson John, purveyor, 109 Brock, h 123 King w

Gleeson Mrs Mary, [wid John], r31 Johnston

Glenn Mrs M, [wid P] 259 Johnston

Globe Hotel, A & L D Church, proprietors, 298-300 Ontario

Godfrey Rev James, 156 Bagot.

Godfrey Wilson, 7 Pine

Godwin Enoch, insurance agent, 101 Pine

Godwin James T, 43 James

Godwin Mrs Matilda, 15 Young

Godwin W H, insurance agent, 101 Pine

Goodearle H, cabinetmaker, 249 Johnston

Goodearle H, machinist, 249 Johnston

Goodearle J A, clerk, 249 Johnston

Goodearle Capt John, watchman G T R, 157 Bagot

Goodell Mrs Priscilla, [wid Stephen] 399 Barrie

Goodfellow H G, mail clerk, 277 Alfred

Goodman C, laborer, 157 Nelson

Goodman John, laborer, 84 William

Goodman Michael, laborer, 226

Goodwin W L, prof, Queen's University, 191 Brock

Gordon A B, miner, 286 Princess

Gordon Jas, laborer, 6 Vine

Gordon John, mason, 278 Division

Gordon William, teamster, 54 John

Gordon W S, assessor, 152 Frontenac

Gorham Mrs Adelaide, ladies' furnishings, 73 Brock, h 13 Frontenac

Gormley James, mariner, 243 Colborne

Gormley James, laborer (old 48) Bagot

Gorman Patrick, carpenter, Montreal

Gorman Thomas, laborer, r 51 Barrack

Gorry Edward, barber, Ontario

Goudreau Zephyr, grocer, Ontario

Gould Charles S, engineer, 78 Gore

Gould Joseph, caretaker Sydenham St School, res school

Gourley David, boiler maker, 112 Barrie

Gow Walter, watchman, 303 Montreal

Gowan James, sailmaker, 43 Upper Bagot

Gowdy James, butcher, Ontario, cor Princess, h 150 Sydenham

Gowdy John, 32 Wellington

Goyette Chas, engineer, 10 Rideau

Grady Michael, 63 Earl

Graham C J, baker, 135 Union

Graham James, mechanic, 145 Ordnance

Graham John, 142 Union

Graham John, gardener, 141 Nelson

Graham Thomas, teamster, 132 Queen

Graham R, tailor, 6 Brewery Lane

Graham Robert, shoemaker, 395 Princess, h 39 Ellice

Graham Thos, porter, Wilkinson's

Graham Thos, painter, 31 Pine

Graham William, laborer, 38 Bagot n

Grahen Thomas, hide dealer, King, cor Brock, h 37 Charles

Grand Trunk Brewery, 118 King w

Grand Union Clothing Store, Roney & VanLuven proprietors, 122 Princess

Granger J, carpenter, 215 Princess

Grant Alex C, painter, 72 York

Grant Very Rev Geo Munro, M A, D D, principal and vice-chancellor Queen's College and University. Residence, College

Grant Mrs Isabella, [wid Daniel B] Ontario

Grant John, carpenter, bds 155 Division

Grant William, driver, 25 First

Grant Wm, salesman, Chatham

Grass John L, confectioner, 56 Brock

Grath George, laborer, Ontario

Gratton John, laborer, 293 Wellington

Gravell Oliver, salesman, College

Graver Stephen, clerk, 621 Princess

Greaves Mrs Ellen, (wid Joseph) bds 73 Division

Graves E J, bookkeeper, old No 82, Bagot

Graves Thomas R, blacksmith, 59 Chatham

Graves Wm D, carriage trimmer 573 Princess

Gray D G, salesman, 268 Sydenham n

Gray E, laborer, Victoria

Gray Geo, laborer, 269 Sydenham

Gray Mrs Isabella, dressmaker, 271 Princess

Gray J F, moulder, 271 Princess

Gray John, mariner, bds 238 Ontario

Gray John, contractor, Albert

Gray John, mariner, John n

Gray Samuel, clerk, 9 Redan

Grey William, laborer, 271 Sydenham

Great North-Western Telegraph Co'y, James Kearns, manager, 34 Clarence

Greaza Charles N, salesman, 104 Queen

Greaza Miss Emma, milliner, 201 Wellington

Green Charles, moulder, 255 Earl

Green Charles, laborer, 278 Sydenham

Green Fenton, laborer, King w

Green John, wholesale and retail butcher, Earl, cor Bagot (See advt.)

15

Green, John, butcher, 264 Princess, h head Princess

Green Lewis, 21 Upper Charles

Green Samuel, butcher, head Princess

Green William, laborer, 46-48 Upper Charles

Green William, butcher, head Princess

Greenizen Isaac, law student, 213 William

Greenwood Fred, clerk, 253 Division

Greenwood J A, confectioner, 274 Princess

Greenwood & McGuire, marble cutters, Bagot, cor Queen

Greenwood N T, fruiterer, 157 Princess

Greer John, engineer, 323 Montreal

Greer R, laborer, 327 Johnston

Greer Samuel, engineer, 321 Montreal

Greet T Y, manager Ontario Bank, h 98 Barrie

Greves Mrs Mary [wid Reuben] West

Griffin Gilbert, P O Inspector, 165 King e

Griffin Joseph, laborer, 279 Montreal

Grimshaw Delos, contractor, 299 Wellington

Grimshaw James, grain shoveller, Corrigan

Grimshaw Silas, carpenter, 284 Division

Grogan John, laborer, 20 Upper Charles

Groves Joseph, laborer, 305 Montreal

Gruber George, cigar maker, Rideau

Grundell Wm, carpenter, end Division

Grundy Wm, caretaker First Methodist Church, Sydenham

Guess Leighton, prop Bon Ton saloon, Wellington, cor Clarence

Guess —, 328 Johnston

Guild Mrs Castine (wid Andrew) 225 Sydenham

Guild John, grocer, 73 & 75 Bay

Guirey John, engine driver K & P Ry, s side Dufferin

Gunn A & Co [A Gunn, Samuel Harper, Wm G Craig], wholesale grocers, 125-27 Ontario

Gunn Alex [A Gunn & Co], h Johnston, cor Clergy

Gunn Daniel, laborer, Nelson

Gunn Mrs Sarah A [wid John], 12 John

Gunn Walter, laborer, Bagot

Gurney Daniel, engineer, Markland

Guy Mrs Diana (wid Z) 87 Division

Haaz Antoine, vinegar manufr, 130-32 Ontario

Hackett Jos, carter, 278 Wellington

Haffner Eckhart, butcher, 842 Princess

Haffner Jno, butcher, 240 Princess

Haffner Mrs, Albert

Haffner Philip, grocer, 147 Montreal

Haffner Philip, barber, 240 Princess

Hagerman Sylvester, teamster, 64 Upper Charles

Hagerty Mrs Helen, [wid Daniel], 105 Queen

The Most Stylish Dress Plaids in the City at Shaw's

Hagerty John, hide dealer, 156 Ontario

Hagerty Peter, laborer, 67 Queen

Hague G E, manager Merchants' Bank, res Bank

Haines & Lockett, W A Van-Tassel, manager, 116 Princess

Hales Mrs William, grocer, 214 Sydenham

Haley Thomas carpenter, bds cor Elm and Alfred

Haley William, shoemaker, 14 Colborne

Hall A W, agent, 277 Brock

Hall Bros [C M & R P], artists, Montreal, cor Princess

Hall David, plumber, 234 Alfred

Hall John, stoker fire dept, Ontario, cor Princess

Hall Samuel, carter, r51 Barrack

Hall Rev Thomas, sup't Home Mis Society, 46 William

Hall Thomas, moulder, 3 Sixth

Hall William, teamster, Barrack

Hallett Chas, laborer, 214 Alfred

Hallett John, laborer, King

Hallett Samuel, farmer, 216 Barrie

Halligan Bernard, boiler maker, Montreal

Halligan John, grocer, 53 Brock, h 395 Brock

Halligan Richard, grain shoveller, Grove

Halligan Thomas, mariner, 15 Rideau

Halward Rev Bro, director Christian Brothers, 89 Clergy

Hamer John, weighman, 35? Alfred

Hamilton C, Collector Customs, res Custom house

Hamilton C M, excise officer, Frontenac

Hamilton Edwd, tailor, 45 Arch

Hamilton Jas, laborer, 248 Earl

Hamilton Jas, machinist, Bagot

Hamilton John, laborer, 150 Colborne

Hamilton Mrs Margaret [wid John] 48 Division

Hamilton Mrs, 25 York

Hamilton Mrs, 300 Barrie

Hamilton Patrick, 244 Earl

Hamilton Robt M, mason, 56 Elm

Hamilton Samuel, blacksmith, 125 Union

Hamilton William, shoemaker, Miller's Lane

Hamilton William, mason, 720 Princess

Hamilton W L, inspector inland revenue, 78 Barrie

Hammond Edward, night clerk, British American hotel

Hammond Mrs L [wid W], 355 Johnston

Hammond Patrick, lumberman, 524 Princess

Hand Thos ,econd-hand dealer, 371 Kir , e

Harrett George, boiler maker, 379 Earl

Hanley Archibald, bookkeeper, inland rev dept, 75 Gore

Hanley A T, chief operator, G N W Tel Co, Earl

Hanley John, cabman, 16 Upper William

Hanley Joseph P, ticket agent, 81 Wellington

Hanley Mrs Margaret, 15 Young

Hanley Thos, laborer, 4 Pine

Hanley Thos A, city agent G T R, G T R station, h 65 Earl

Hanlon John, laborer, Stephen

Hannay Mrs Rachael [wid William], 70 Colborne

Hanscombe W, laborer, 311 Johnston

Hanscombe William, switchman G T R, e s Grove

Hansen Louis, fish dealer, 90 Wellington

Hansen Jas, carter, 2 Anglin's Cottages, Bay

Hanson John, blacksmith, 102 Barrie

Hardy John C, (Jno C Hardy & Co) 21 Colborne

HARDY J C & CO, importers of Staple and Fancy Dry Goods, Mantles, etc. Specialties — Fine Dress Goods and Mantles, 88 Princess

Hargraves Edward, moulder, 6 James

Harkess John, Sup't House of Industry, 362 Montreal

Harkness James, butcher, 40 Colborne

Harkness Mrs S J (wid Robert) 282 Earl

Harkness Samuel, hotel keeper, 340 Princess

Harkness W, butcher, 216 Wellington

Harkness J D, printer, 282 Earl

Harmer William H, carpenter, Montreal

Harold David, carpenter, 280 Bagot

Harold David A, carpenter, 218 Division

Harold Wm, pattern maker, 184 Gordon

Harpelle, J G, laborer, Frontenac

Harpelle John J, farmer, Victoria

Harper Mrs E A [wid W F S] 306 Johnston

Harper Samuel [A Gunn & Co] h 13 Maitland

Harper Samuel H, 153 Alfred

Harris B, barber, 351 Princess

Harris David, rope mkr, Victoria

Harris Hebron, lumber merch't, Bagot

Harris J, quartermaster R S G

Harris John, laborer, r 42 Johnston

Harris Lionel, polisher, 107 Ordnance

Harris R C, C E, R M C, 23 Mack

Harris Richard, broom maker, 76 Durham

Harrison Edward, laborer, old No 123, Bagot

Harrison Thos, bricklayer, 176 Rideau

Hartrey James, 33 Main

Hartrick James, fireman K & P R'y, Corrigan

Hartrick Mrs Martha [wid Geo] 256 Division

Harty Wm, 51 George

Harvey Mrs A, 327 Earl

Harvey Chas B S, clerk, Earl, cor Alfred

Harvey Edward, 327 Earl

Harvey P G W H, clerk, Bank of Montreal, Earl

Harvey R R F, ledger-keeper, Bank B N A, Earl, cor Alfred

Harvey W J C, accountant Ontario Bank, 327 Earl

Haskell W A jr, Rose Lawn, Union

Haskin Chas, laborer, Albert
Hastings Mrs, 192 Barrie
Hastings Wm, laborer, 72 Queen
Hatch Charles H, ticket agent, foot Johnston, h Bagot, cor Ordnance
Hattan Archibald, grain shoveller, Bagot
Hatten Jacob, laborer, 29 Upper William
Hawken E, boot & shoe maker, 357 Princess
Hawkes John, laborer, n side Dufferin
Hawley H M, salesman, 264 Princess
Hawley T B, manager Stroud Bros, h 109 Princess
Hawley Mrs, 314 Barrie
Hay David, laborer, 427 King e
Hay Robt, blacksmith, bds 62 Wellington
Hayward Mrs Christina [wid Wm] 90 Earl
Hayward Thomas, salesman, 90 Earl
Hayward Wm, blacksmith, 381 King e, h 303 Johnston
Hazlett G, engineer, 428 Brock
Hazlett J, boiler mkr, 496 Brock
Hazlett W, boiler mkr, 476 Brock
Hazlett Wm, engineer, 57 Young
Heaffren Miss Catharine, bds 32 Earl
Healey Thos, laborer, 46 Johnston
Healey Thos, brakeman K & P, Dufferin, cor Bagot
Healey Thos, clerk, 22 Deacon
Healey Patrick, laborer, 134 Ordnance
Healey —, Dufferin, cor Bagot
Heart Patrick, laborer, 15 Patrick

Hemley Geo, laborer, 1 Albert
Hemsted Edwin, M D, M C H, Q U I, M R C P & S, Ont, 424 Princess
Henderson Geo, blacksmith, 42 Elm
Henderson Geo, engineer, old No 70, Bagot
Henderson Geo, brass moulder, 36 Union e
Henderson H B, photographer, 313 Brock
Henderson Henry, photographer, 90 Princess, h 313 Brock
Henderson Hiram, 94 Queen
Henderson J A, Q C, master in chancery, 89 Clarence, h Johnston, cor Wellington
Henderson Mrs Jennie, [wid John], 45 Clergy
Henderson John, carter, 103 Stuart
Henderson John & Co, booksellers and stationers, wall paper and fancy goods, 86 Princess
Henderson J·R, manager, J S Henderson, 79 Wellington
Henderson J S, wholesale wines and liquors, 59 Brock, h 179 Queen
Henderson J S, groceries, provisions, etc, 61 Brock, h 179 Queen
Henderson P R, managing director Montreal Trans Co'y, h 118 William
Henderson Robert, laborer, Miller's Lane
Henderson, T F L, clerk, 33 George
Henderson W H, M D, 95 Wellington

Henderson Wm, laborer, Ontario

Henderson W W, salesman, 45 Clergy

Hendry Jomes A, King e

Hendry John, clerk, 309 Gordon

Hendry Robert, traveller, 122 Johnston

Hendrie Thos, mason, 93 York

Henley M, fancy goods, 177 Wellington

Hennessy Miss Eliza, 15 West

Hennessy Sergt Thomas J, 18 Rideau

Henower John, pattern maker, 48 Union

Hentig Geo Wm, tinsmith, 558 Princess

Hentig Mrs Sarah, 558 Princess

Herald John, M A, M D, 199 King e

Herbert S G, laborer, 14 James

Hermiston Charles, carpenter, 192 Sydenham

Hermiston Mrs Ellen (wid Robt) 62 Wellington

Hersey Mrs M G (wid S G) 275 Brock

Hess Geo, laborer, 11 Wade's Lane

Hewitt George, machinist, 85 Division

Hewitt Thos, foreman city water works, 96 Earl

Hewton John, manager knitting mill, 125 King w

Hewton John, machinist, 133 Alfred

Hewton Robt, chief keeper K P, Alwington ave

Hickey Mrs Catharine A (wid Edward), grocer, Bay, corner Bagot

Hickey D C, M D, 120 Barrie

Hickey Jas, engineer, 233 Earl

Hickey Mrs John, Chadwick's yard, Bagot

Hickey John (Rigney & Hickey) h 164 Princess

Hickey John, blacksmith, bds 33 Brock

Hickey M (M Hickey & Co), h 164 Princess

Hickey M & Co, milliners, 164 Princess

Hickson James, confectioner, Rideau

Higgins John, tailor, Markland

Hill E C, insurance agent, 43 Brock, h 304 Gordon

Hill William, blacksmith, 120 Montreal

Hill —, blacksmith, 47 Princess

Hillier N H, carpenter, 24 York

Hillier T P, carpenter, 24 York

Hilton T, saddler, 319 Brock

Hinds Bros [R W & J R], soda and mineral waters, 10 Market sq

Hinds J R [Hinds Bros], h Princess, cor Alfred

Hinds R W [Hinds Bros], h 10 Market sq

Hinds, William, laborer, 100 Ontario

Hinton David, shoemaker, 258 Queen

Hinton Edward, laborer, 17 Upper William

Hipson Joseph, boilermaker, 136 Division

Hirst Bannister, warehouseman Cotton Mill, Dufferin

Hiscock Edgar C, engineer, 104 Barrie

Hiscock J, grocer, 121 Princess, h 117 William

Hitchin Harry M, employee Immigration Office, foot William

Pure Teas. Shore Loynes & Co.

Hoag John, switchman G T R, Montreal

Hobart G F, stenographer, 247 Brock

Hobart G S, wholesale and retail druggist, depositor Kingston Auxiliary British and Foreign Bible Society, 155 Princess, h 247 Brock

Hobart S W, druggist, bds 247 Brock

Hobbs Sylvester, laborer, 29 Queen

Hodges Mrs Margaret, [wid William], 142 York

Hodgson Thos, stone yard, 306 Barrie, h 76 Arch

Hogan Mrs Deborah [wid Jas], prop Hogan House, 312 Ontario

Hogan George, laborer, 375 Division

Hogan Jas S, com traveller, 50 Colborne

Hogan Mrs Jane [wid Michael] 154 Ordnance

Hogan John, carpenter, 254 Division

Hogan Michael, laborer, r84 Bagot

Hogle James, drug clerk, 185 Princess

Holden J, laborer, 310 Johnston

Holden Robert, engineer, 202 William

Holder Edward, cabinet maker, 47 Montreal

Holder F W, engineer, 29 Union

Holder George, carpenter, 154 York

Holder J B, carpenter, 245 Colborne

Holder Mrs Sarah [wid Benj], 47 Montreal

Holland George, engineer, 40 Grove

Holland Jas, salesman, Alfred

Holland Martin, e side Rideau

Holland Wm, laborer, 60 Cherry

Holley J A, agent Singer Co

Hollowell Frank, laborer, 262 Johnston

Holman Albert E, tinsmith, 131 Queen

Holmes Edward, laborer, end Montreal

Hooper E, M D, medical supt hospital, res hospital

Hooper Richard, bookkeeper, bds 114 Clarence

Hooper Vere, manager A Caldwell & Co, 114 Clarence

Hop Lee, laundry, 227 Princess

Hopkins Edward, trader, 206 Barrie

Hopkirk John, clerk P O, 199 Queen

Hoppins A, agent The Rathbun Co'y, Barrack

Hoppins Densmore, 102 Barrack

Hoppins Harvey, weighman, McAuley's Cottages, Dufferin

Hopson J, caretaker Murney Tower

Horn Alex, sailmaker, 270 Gordon

Hornibrook Samuel, shoemaker, 284 Montreal

Hornsby Frederick, laborer, 65 Queen

Horsey E, chief of police, 151 Brock

Horsey Herbert Edward, student, 164 Queen

Horsey Richard M, [R M Horsey & Co] h 164 Queen

Horsey Edwin E, printer, 151 Brock

Notepaper & Envelopes
CHEAP AT McAULEY'S BOOKSTORE.

HORSEY R M & Co, Hardware, Stoves, Tinware, Refrigerators, Paints and Oils. House Furnishings our Specialty. 189 Princess

Horsey S J, [R M Horsey & Co], h 191 Clergy

Horsey T M, clerk, 151 Brock

Horton W C, fishmonger, 62 Brock

Houston Rev Samuel, pastor Cooke's Church, 98 Earl

Hotel Frontenac, E H Dunham prop, 178-184 Ontario

Howard T, foreman Graving Dock, foot Wellington

Howken Edward, shoemaker, 151 Clergy

Howell James, stonemason, end Upper Victoria

Howell John, mason, 175 Pine

Howells Alfred, contractor, 159 Nelson

Howes John, carpenter, 31 Division

Howland Thos, cab driver, 275 Alfred

Howlet Robt, carter, 277 Earl

Hubbard Chas H, carpenter, 258 Rideau

Hubbard E H, barber, 53 Colborne

Hubbard Lewis, carpenter, end Colborne

Hubbard William, carpenter, 50 Grove

Hubbell Mrs Eliza (wid Henry) 146 King e

Hudders Thos, foreman, Stephen

Huddy Wm, caretaker Frontenac School, Montreal

Hudon Lieut J A G, R S G, res Barracks

Hughes Henry, agri implements, 12 Market sq, h 18 do

Hughes Henry, carpenter, 810 Brock

Hughes John, laborer, 4 St Catharine

Hughes John, clerk, Wellington

Hughes Robert, flour merchant, 156 Rideau

Hughes Thos E, teamster, 93 Queen

Hughes W Booth, printer, bds 105 Wellington

Hughes Wm, carter, Montreal

Hughson Mrs Ann (wid Emos), 117 Alfred

Hugo Nicholas, keeper K P, 44 Livingston ave

Hull E, painter, 351 Johnston

Hume John S, cutter, 107 Queen

Hunt John, laborer, 18 Earl

Hunter Geo, carpenter, 118 Bay

Hunter G H, farmer, 117 Alfred

Hunter Henry, carpenter, 177 Clergy

Hunter Peter, printer, 16 Bagot

Hunter Robert, pumpman, G T R'y, G T R station, Montreal

Hunter W H, prop American hotel, 27-29 Brock

Hunter William, 23 Ontario

Hurley Jeremiah, laborer, 31 Johnston

Hurley Capt John G, mariner, 411 King e

Hurley Patrick, carter, 24 Johnston

Hurst Jas, carpenter, Beverly

Hurst John, laborer, r81 Wellington

Hurst Thomas, blacksmith, 4 Wellington Terrace, Montreal

Shaw's Tapestry and Brussels Carpets are Cheap.

Hurst Wm, mason, Beverly

Hurst Wm, guard K P, Alwington ave

Hutchison D, manager, S Neelon, h 295 Gordon

Hutcheson J E, com traveller, 275 Alfred

Hutchison John, salesman, 295 Gordon

Hutchinson Thomas, carpenter, Albert

Hutton G J, livery, r129 Princess

Hyett Wm, 27 Arch

Hyland John, carpenter, 793 Princess

Hyland Robt, 769 Princess

Hyland Samuel, carpenter, 429 Alfred

Hynds James, laborer, 244 Colborne

Hynds John, teamster, 26 Chatham

Hysop Miss Jennie, school teacher, G T R station, Montreal

Ilett Jas, clerk, 6 Pine

Ilett John, clerk, 304 Queen

Illsey Charles, 81 Union e

Inglis G W, draughtman, Maitland

Ingram Wm, painter, bds American Hotel

Innis Edward, laborer, Bajus' Brewery

Innes John C, civil engineer, 76 Sydenham w

Ireland F C, city treasurer, Alfred

Irwin Chamberlain A, M D, 238 K e

Irwin Capt John, grocer, 140 Montreal

Irwin William, machinist, 47 Earl

Irwin Wm, Grove House, cor King w and Beverly

Isaac William, carpenter, 28 Cherry

Jack Alex, clerk, Union

Jack H M, bookkeeper, 312 Gordon

Jack Hugh, city missionary, 312 Gordon

Jackson Chas, stove polisher, n side Dufferin

Jackson Edward, laborer, 14 Ontario

Jackson John M, ale bottler, 401 King e

Jackson Joseph, grocer, 45 Chatham

Jackson Mrs, Newman's Cottages, King w

Jackson Philip, carpenter (old 74) Bagot

Jackson Rev S N, First Congregational church, 193 Johnston

Jackson Mrs W (wid James) 26 Cowdy

Jackson Wm, printer, Newman's Cottages, King w

Jackson Wm, blacksmith, 65 Upper Charles

Jackson Wm, moulder, bds 45 Division

Jackson Wm, 93 Queen

Jacob Adam, shoemaker, 263 Queen

James Mrs Bridget [wid Wm] 131 Queen

James Martin, 189 Earl

James Richard, bartender, 76 Princess

James Thomas, butcher, 316 Princess

Jamieson Isaac, engineer, River

Jamieson Mrs Emma, laundress, 88 York

16

Jamieson Joseph, plumber, 42 Johnston

Jamieson Thomas, plumber, 85 Gore

Jamieson William, boiler maker, 258 Earl

Jaquitt Isaac, carpenter, 38 Union e

Jarrel Henry, laborer (old 72) Bagot

Jarrett Wm, laborer, cor Alma and Patrick

Jarvis Miss Eliza, 144 Queen

Jarvis William, carpenter, 525 Princess

Jeffers Francis, signal man G T R, Park, G T R station

Jenkin C, blacksmith, 375 Princess

Jenkin John, carpenter, 152 Division

Jenkin Walter, carriage maker, Quebec

Jenkin John, Quebec

Jenkins John E, blacksmith, 63 York

Jenkins Samuel, contractor, 388 Princess

Jenkins —, laborer, end Barrie

Jenman Mrs Ann Jane [wid G] 1 Rideau

Jennings Henry, shoemaker, 274 Ontario

JOHNS THOMAS H, Victoria Warehouse, Wholesale and Retail Dealer in Groceries, Flour & Feed, China, Glassware, etc., etc. Fine Teas a specialty. Tea imported direct from the place of growth. 270 Princess, h 330 Gordon

Johnston James, 430 Princess

Johnston A C, watchmaker and jeweller, 192 Wellington, h 269 Gordon

Johnston Arthur, laborer, 793 Montreal

Johnston Gilbert, engineer, 228 Bagot

Johnston Henry, laborer, 14 George

Johnston Hugh, laborer, 43 York

Johnston J, merchant, 330 Johnston

Johnston Mrs James, 185 Earl

Johnson James B, hairdresser, 155 Wellington, h 49 Earl

Johnston James W, carpenter, 41 James

Johnston John, salesman, 226 Earl

Johnston J S, watchmaker, 185 Earl·

Johnson Jos S, blacksmith, 53 Earl

Johnston Mrs, Collingwood

Johnston N B, gardener, 858 Johnston

Jolliff Mrs Mary [wid John] 390 Division

Jolley Mrs Sarah [wid Richard], 137 Clergy

Jones Rev C A, Methodist, 65 Union

Jones Charles, laborer, n s Princess

Jones Clarence, student, 192 Clergy

Jones Mrs Ellen, fancy goods, 280 Princess

Jones David, carpenter, 200 Montreal

Jones James H, hairdresser, 50 Clarence, h 192 Clergy

Jones Mrs Jane [wid John], 24 Vine

Jones John, miner, 163 York

Jones John, 24 Vine

Jones John, gardener, 21 Wade's Lane

Jones John, tailor, Montreal, cor Princess

Jones John Edward, trader, 110 Queen

Jones Mrs Margaret [wid John] 801 Princess

Jones Owen, printer, 347 Princess

Jones & Son [W I & W C], plasterers, 280 Princess

Jones Thos, coachman, King w

Jones Walter, 127 Colborne

Jones Walter, painter, 4 Wellington Terrace, Montreal

Jordan Henry, 29 Young

Jordan James, machinist, 29 Young

Joyce Mrs Ann [wid Robert], 260 Division

Joyce Mrs Honor [wid John], r31 Johnston

Joyce John, butcher, 373 King e

Joyce John L, coal and wood merchant, Bay, cor Rideau, h 4 Dunn Terrace, Bay

Joyce Luke, carter, 18 Patrick

Joyce William, painter, 89 Pine

Judson Jas, weaver, 240 Montreal

Julian M, dealer, 45 Princess

Kaillen Patrick, cab driver, John north

Kallaghur John, laborer (old 132) Bagot

Kane D, waggon maker, Wellington, cor Queen

Kane Jas, laborer, 67 Colborne

Kane John, fitter, Ontario

Kane Thomas M, telegrahist, Barrack

Kavanagh James, Victoria

Kavanagh James, salesman, 109 Clergy

Kavanagh John, grocer, 6 Market sq

Kavanagh John, pattern maker, 15 Redan

Kavanagh Mrs Mary, grocer, 246 Barrie

Keagen B, laborer, John north

Kean Geo, carpenter, 30 Ellice

Kearns James, manager G N-W Tel Co, h 53 Clergy

Kearns Mrs Mary Ann (wid Patrick) 226 Wellington

Kearns Robt, letter carrier, 33 George

Kearns Wm, coal heaver, n side Charles

Keates Thos, laborer, s s Ordnance

Keating Patrick, laborer, 148 Rideau

Keeler Charles, carpenter, 294 Montreal

Keeley W J, engraver & jeweller, 103 Brock, h 138 Union

Keeling Walter, laborer, 240 Earl

Keenan James, caretaker smelting works, e side Orchard

Keene Wm, fireman, 24 Elm

Keenan T J, salesman, 37 Charles

Kelaher Mrs Winnifred [wid Morris] Bagot

Kelly Isaac, carpenter, 87 Earl

Kelly Jas, salesman, 115 Bay

Kelly J J, school teacher, 218 Barrie

Kelly John, clerk P O, 240 Johnston

Kelly Mrs Mary [wid James] 18 Johnston

Kelly Pierce, harness maker, 98 Ontario

Kelly Samuel, machinist, Ellerbeck ave

Kelly S J, painter and paper hanger, 282 Princess

Kelly Rev Thomas, sec Diocese of Kingston, 225 Johnston

Kelly William, photographer, 151 Wellington

Kelly William A, engineer, 115 Bay

Kelly W A, salesman, 115 Bay

Kemp G J, clerk, 44 Clergy

Kemp W J, grocer, 352 Princess

Kennedy Miss Alice, bds 111 Gore

Kennedy James, laborer, 460 Montreal

Kennedy Capt James, mariner, 65 Arch

Kennedy Joseph, boiler maker, 13 Division

Kennedy John, machinist, 17 Deacon

Kennedy Owen, prop O K house, 228 Ontario

Kennedy Robert, ship carpenter, 92 Barrie

Kennedy Timothy, carter, r102 Barrack

Kennedy William, ship carpenter, 440 Barrie

Kennedy William, engineer, 65 Arch

Kenney Mrs Alice [wid Henry], 111 Gore

Kenny Patrick, hostler, Windsor Hotel

Kent Mrs Elizabeth, [wid Robert], r88 Wellington

Kent Noel, 161 King o

Kent R E, [Mills & Kent], h 132 Earl

Kent Rybert, Treasurer Can Exp Co, King o

Kent Thos, laborer, Park, GTR station

Kent W C, clerk, Merchants Bank, 85 King e

Keough John, laborer, 187 Montreal

Kerby Wm, carter, 122 Stuart

Kerr John, Manager Gas Co, h 155 Earl

Kerr John, 770 Montreal

Kessler Geo, cigar maker, 366 Barrie

Keys Andrew, boot and shoemaker, 320 Barrie

Keys Robert, 303 Earl

Kidd John, carpenter, 182 Queen

Kidd Joseph, customs officer, 182 Queen

Kidd Robt, laborer, 428 King e

Kidd W G, inspector of Public Schools, 34 Sydenham

Kilcauley Patrick, sr, engineer, 196 Bagot

Kilcauley Patrick, jr, compositor, 196 Bagot

Kilcauley William P, stenographer *Whig* office, 196 Bagot

Kilmurray Mrs Mary (wid Jos) 52 Division

Kilpatrick Fred A, telegrapher, 143 Ordnance

Kilpatrick John H, stone cutter, 143 Ordnance

Kilpatrick S J, stone mfr, 243 Brock, h 119 Colborne

Kincaid Mrs Mary, 77 Clarence

Kinchlea Thomas, laborer, 115 William

Kimpson Joseph, 142 Bay

King Mrs Ann (wid Ralph) 162 Ordnance

King Edward, laborer, 245 Earl

King J G [J G King & Co] h 57 West

King J G & Co, druggists, Market Square

King Mrs Annie (wid Patrick) 383 Princess

King Jno, oil maker, Markland

King John H, ship carpenter, Bagot

King Mrs Mary [wid John] old No 124 Bagot

King Robert, machinist, 174 Bagot

King Thomas, carpenter, cor Victoria and Albert

King William, Manager Federal Warehouse, bds City Hotel

King Major William, military storekeeper, Artillery Park, Montreal

King William, carpenter, Upper Victoria

King Zephren, shoemaker, Rideau

Kinghorn John, Sec'y Cotton Co, 84 Union e

Kingston Auxiliary British & Foreign Bible Society, G S Hobart, depositor, 155 Princess

Kingston Bottling Works, Wm Pipe, prop, 261 Princess

Kingston Brewery, Philip Bajus, prop, 308 Wellington

Kingston Business College Co, J B McKay, principal, 82 Princess

Kingston Cotton Manufacturing Co (Limited), Wm Wilson, sen, manager, s side Cataraqui

Kingston Electric Light Co, J M Campbell, manager, foot Brock

Kingston Knob Factory, King w

Kingston Gas Light Co, Jno Kerr, manager, E Moore, sectreas, 19 Queen

Kingston Hosiery Co, Jno Hewton, manager, King w

KINGSTON LAUNDRY, J R Rattenbury, prop, 206 Princess, opp Windsor Hotel. Work done on short notice. Travellers', Students', and Family work done promptly.— Telephone orders attended to. Number 22.

Kingston Paint Works, L B Spencer, prop, King w

Kingston Street Car Co, J E Jones, manager, 483 Princess

Kingswell Charles, laborer, 170 York

Kirk Mrs J, fancy goods, 83 Brock

Kirkpatrick Hon George A, Q C, M P [Kirkpatrick & Rogers] h Closeburn, Emily

Kirkpatrick Mrs Gertrude [wid Francis W] 61 West

Kirkpatrick M, fancy goods, 159 Princess

Kirkpatrick & Rogers [Hon Geo A Kirkpatrick, Q C, R V Rogers], barristers, 194 Ontario

Kirkpatrick Samuel, laborer, 277 Montreal

Kirkpatrick Thomas, foreman water works, 383 Princess

Kirkwood J, mariner, 412 Johnston

Koen Mrs H (wid Michael), Alwington ave

Knapp Mrs Mary A (wid Wm C), boat builder, Cataraqui bridge

KNAPP A C, Boat builder. Boats of all kinds for sale and built to order. Oars, Sails and all boat fittings supplied. All material and workmanship of the best quality and prices moderate. A first-class Boat Livery in connection. Cataraqui Bridge, foot of Ontario

Knapp A H, carpenter, 121 Ordnance

Knapp Dixon, carder, Albert

Knifeton Mrs E (wid Frank), 121 Montreal

Knight A P, M A, rector Collegiate Institute, 203 William

Knight Arthur, currier, Corrigan

Knight Isaac, 92 Queen

Knifton Frank, barber, 223 Princess

Knott Francois, laborer, Ontario

Knox W, butcher, 339 Johnston

Knies William, ship carpenter, 164 Clergy

Lacey Henry, shoemaker, 257 Queen

Lacey Henry M, shoemaker, 90 Ontario

Lachance F X, grocer, 218 Montreal and 259 Ontario, h 200 Bagot

Lacomb Samuel, engineer, bds 238 Ontario

Lacroix C A, plasterer, 499 Princess

Lacroix Henry A, cabinetmaker, 499 Princess

Laflour Samuel, laborer, Ordnance

Lafrance Mrs Cathrine [wid Charles], 127 Montreal

Lafrance Henry, river pilot, Ontario

Lafreniere Mrs Lucy [wid David], boarding house 236 Ontario

Lahey Michael, trade instructor K P, cor Alwington ave and King w

Laidlaw J & Son, [John & David G], dry goods, 191 Princess, h 216 Johnston

Laidley Alfred, tel operator, G T R, 765 Montreal

Laidley Mrs Francis, 172 Rideau

Laird John, machinist, 20 Young

Laird John, paper hanger, 340 Princess

Laishley J, manager Singer Man'g Co, h 213 Princess

Lake A K, barber, 202 Alfred

Lake Anthony, sawyer, 123 Montreal

Lake John, mechanic, 26 Elm

Lake Perry, horse dealer, 848 Princess

Lake Richard, painter, 140 Pine

Lake Simpson J, boarding, 115 Brock

Lake Wm, carpenter, 316 Queen

Lalonde Antoine J, machinist, Cataraqui

Lalonde Frank, blacksmith, Orchard

Lalonde Henry, cabinet maker, 19 Ellice

Lalonde Lewis, carpenter, 19 Ellice

Lamb Walter, lumberman, 129 Durham

Lambert Samuel, bridge inspector G T R, Park, G T R station

Lambert Thomas [Lambert & Walsh] h 116 Colborne

Lambert & Walsh [Thomas Lambert, Edwin Walsh] merchant tailors, 110 Princess
Lambert William, trackman G T R, e side Grove
Lamham C F, laborer, 42 York
Lamoureaux Peter, second hand dealer, 375 King e
Lamoureaux Peter, jr, cooper, 26 Place d'Armes
Landeryou J C, contractor, 91 York
Landeryou Joseph, 87 Colborne
Lane Benj, driver, 103 Pine
Lane Timothy, grocer, 89 Earl
Langdon Alfred, mason, Victoria
Langdon J, mason, 261 Victoria
Langdon Joseph, cabinetmaker, 261 Victoria
Langdon N, mason, end Nelson
Langdon Nathaniel, mason, 261 Victoria
Langdon William, contractor, Nelson
Langhan Henry, grocer, 355 Princess
Lanigan Andrew, caretaker City Hall, res city building
Lannon Thomas, blacksmith, 193 Colborne
Lansing Mrs Fanny [wid Charles], 148 Queen
Lapage William, plasterer, 382 Princess
Lappage William, signalman G T R, Park, G T R station
Lario Joseph, cooper, 8 Brewery Lane
Lark Mrs Mary Ann, [wid Edward] 171 Clergy
LaRose Napoleon, laborer, 24 Wade's Lane
LaRue D R, salesman, Johnston, cor Bagot

LaRue Mrs Ellen, Johnston, cor Bagot
Lasher Mrs, 868 Princess
Laturney George, carter, 26 Johnston
Laturney James, carriagemaker, 390-392 Princess
Lauder John, Victoria
Laurencell Jos, 45 Arch
Laurencell Peter, carpenter, 27 Upper William
Lavell H A, law student, Britton & Whiting, 69 Clarence
Lavery Patrick, laborer, Wellington
Law Edward, rope maker, Victoria
Lawless Jas, carter, 211 Gordon
Lawless Michael, carter, 222 Earl
Lawless P, carter, 319 Johnston
Lawless P J, news dealer, 326 King e, h 211 Gordon
Lawlor & Dartnell, fancy goods, 196 King e
Lawlor James, keeper, Asylum, 218 Alfred
Lawlor Joseph, baker, 309 Earl
Lawlor Miss Louisa [Lawlor & Dartnell] 196 King e
Lawlor Patrick, carpenter, 693 Montreal
Lawlor Wm, laborer, 28 Place d'Armes
Lawson Mrs Francis, 127 Bagot
Lawson J J, fireman, Victoria
Layton John G, printer, Centre
Leach Edward, laborer, 85 York
Leadbeater Wm, laborer, 130 Queen
Leaden Sergt-major M J, 48 Ordnance
Leader George, machinist, 56 Wellington

Horseshoe Island. Boats twice a day each way. Liquor prohibited from being sold.

Leahy B J, grocer, 320 King e, h 329 Barrie

Leahey R B, harnessmaker, 29 Wellington

Leahy T J, com traveller, 329 Barrie

Leclair Charles H, brakeman K & P Ry, Place d'Armes

Lee A J, barber, 158 Princess

Lee George, piano maker, 116 Earl

Lee James, carpenter, 386 Johnston

Lee John, laborer, 26 James

Lee Miss Rebecca, 413 Princess

Lee Robert G, shoemaker, 26 James

Lee Robert James, tailor, 87 York

Lee Samuel, moulder, end Frontenac

Lee Wm, laborer, n s Princess

Lees Adam, spinner, Picard

LeHeup A J, watchmaker, 335 Johnston

LeHeup Edward, saw sharpener, 89 Earl

LeHeup J A, watchmaker, jeweler and optician, 57 Brock, h 335 Johnson

Leheup, John, 27 First

Leigh F J, supt Canadian Locomotive & Engine Co, h Ontario

Lemay Albert, blacksmith, foot Queen

Lemon Charles, carpenter, 5 Division

Lemmon John, foreman fire department, Ontario

Lemmon John, tinsmith, 128 Queen

Lemon Mrs Margaret (wid Wm) 384 Division

Lemon Miss, dressmaker, 368 Princess

Lemon Miss, dressmaker, 295 Princess

Lemmon Samuel, laborer, 128 Queen

Lenea Peter, 124 Queen

Lennon Felix, fireman water works, 13 Ontario

Lennon Patrick, laborer, end Picard

Lennox Cooper, prop Bowen House, 421-25 King e

Lennox Wm, laborer, n Bay

Leslie Mrs Catharine (wid Wm) 81 Gore

Leslie David, engineer, River

Lesslie George, bookkeeper, 23 Union

Lesslie James F (James Swift & Co) h 39 George

Lesslie Wm, raftsman, 53 George

Lewers Robt, mail carrier, 220 Sydenham

Leyland Benj, shoemaker, Bagot

Liffiton Henry A, watchmaker and jeweller, branch office C P R Tel Co, 167 Princess

Light R H, artist, 317 Johnston

Lillie Jas, porter, Union Hotel

Linaugh Thomas, 87 William

Lindsay Mrs, Regent

Lindsay Patrick, 206 Colborne

Lingwood Wm, china riveter, bds 43 Earl

Linton C, blacksmith, 314 Brock

Linton James, grain shoveller, 42 Grove

Linton Mrs John J, 204 Bagot

Liston John, laborer, 216 Bagot

Little Joseph, prop Anglo-American Hotel, 208 Barrie

Little Joseph, laborer, 188 Colborne

Little Mrs, 213 Earl

Little William, carpenter, 14 Rideau

Litton John, grocer, 163 Alfred

Livingston Alex, carpenter, bds American Hotel

Livingston C & Bro, [Charles & Wm J] merchant tailors, clothiers and gents' furnishers, 75-77 Brock

Livingston Chas, [C Livingston & Bro] h 502 Princess

Livingston Mrs J [wid C], 189 Brock

Livingstone Marion, M D, 233 Bagot

Livingston W J, [C Livingston & Bro] 455 Princess

Loftus James, mariner, 88 Gore

Lochead James, agent, 7 Upper William

Locker Henry, baker, 387 Barrie

Lockhart John, colporteur, Albert

Loghran James, laborer, Chadwick's Yard, Bagot

Loiseau W C, hairdresser, 223 Princess

Loke Wm, laborer, 61 Bay

Lonergan Thomas, supervisor, Asylum, Centre

Long C E, sergt, R S G

Long Geo, machinist, 25 Arch

Loucks E B, com traveller, 226 King e

Lovett Mrs Ann [wid Thomas], 16 Earl

Lovick Andrew, salesman, 146 Gordon

Lovett Mrs Fanny [wid James] 42 Union e

Lovett Jeff, machinist, 16 Earl

Lovick John, blacksmith, 152 Gordon

Low E W, traveller, 114 Earl

Lowe Samuel, salesman, 400 Brock

Lowry Calvin, tanner, 330 Montreal

Lowry Mrs Mary, King e

Loynes Robertson, clerk, 146 Division

Loynes Shore, [Shore Loynes & Co], h 182 Barrie

Ludlow Richard, laborer, 278 Earl

Lum Richard, mechanic, 353 Johnston

Lynch Mrs Catharine J [wid Daniel], 99 Rideau

Lynch Mrs Ellen, 25 Johnston

Lynch M J, salesman, 99 Rideau

Lyon Herbert I, law student, Livingston ave

Lyon H V, B A, [Smythe, Smith & Lyon], h Livingston ave, cor Union

Lyons C, saloon, 14 Market Sq

Lyons Mrs E [wid M], 393 Johnston

Lyons John, laborer, 288 Division

Lyons M J, salesman, 286 Queen

Lyons Patrick, hide dealer, 146 Ordnance

Lyons Thomas, laborer, bds 97 Picard

Lyons William, laborer, bds 97 Picard

Lytle John, painter, 312 Queen

Lytle Mrs Alice [wid John], 312 Queen

McAdam James E, cleaner, 6 Dunn Terrace, Bay

McAdam Thomas, machinist, 23 West

Macalister Mrs Jane [wid Alex] 228 Johnston

Macalister Thomas, clerk, 228 Johnston

McArdle Patrick, engineer, Ontario

McArnen J, farmer, 293 Johnston

McArthur A, accountant, 397 Brock

McArthur J A, clerk Ontario Bank, Sydenham, cor Johnston

McArthur James, manager Ontario Building and Savings Society, h 93 Division

McArthur Jno, sailor, 9 Division

McAuley Thomas, bookseller, stationer, and bookbinder, 356 King e, h 129 William. *(See bottom lines.)*

McAvey Andrew, laborer, 49 Ordnance

McBratley Hugh, stone cutter, 137 Bay

McBride A, clerk, Macnee & Minnes

McBride Archibald, engineer, 190 Ordnance

McBride James, 96 Barrack

McBride J S, clerk, Ordnance

McBride Joseph, carpenter, 563 Princess

McBride Robert, engineer, 190 Ordnance

McBride S, ship carpenter, 192 Ordnance

McBride Mrs J, 202 Bagot

McBroom Bros [W F & Robt], King, corner Princess

McCabe Alexander, laborer, 156 York

McCabe John, tailor, 50 Pine

McCaig Neil, laborer, 334 Earl

McCallum John, stonecutter, 40 Elm

McCallum Mrs Margaret (wid James), grocer, 12 Grove

McCambridge Francis, laborer, 57 John

McCammon Bros [Wm & Jas], livery, Bagot, cor Brock

McCammon Mrs Jas, 333 Queen

McCammon Mrs Jas, 15 Montreal

McCammon John, butcher, 74 Brock, h 32 Upper Bagot

McCammon Robt, jr, baker, 162 Bagot

McCammon Robt, sr, baker, 152 William

McCammon Wm, butcher, 329 Queen

McCardless Wm, machinist, 85 Colborne

McCann J S R, insurance agent, 24 Montreal, h 474 Brock

McCann Mrs Mary, 29 First

McCardley Edward, laborer, 23 Upper Bagot

McCarey Bernard, grocer, 267 Ontario

McCarthy Thomas, mariner, bds 238 Ontario

McCarthy Timothy, mariner, bds 238 Ontario

McCartney Alex, mason, 248 Gordon

McCartney John, carter, 231 Gordon

McCartney Wm, contractor, 206 Gordon

McCartney Wm, mason, 238 Johnston

McClelland R J, clerk, 25 Union

McClemmand Wm, laborer, 27 Union

McCluskey Mrs Unity (wid Jas) (old 180) Bagot

McClymont Alex, 40 O'Kill

McColl E S, salesman, 132 Princess

MacColl Evan, customs officer, 266 Johnston

McColl J, butcher, Macdonnell

McColl Robert, stonecutter, 18 Stuart

McConville Bernard, mail carrier, 31 George

McConville John, butcher, cor Barrie and Earl

McConnell Jos, Farmers' Hotel, cor Princess and Victoria

McConville & Nicholson, butchers, William, cor Ontario

McConnell Richard, carpenter, 86 York

McConville Thomas [McConville & Nicholson, butchers], 138 Ontario

McCorkell Andrew, boat builder, foot of West

McCormick A, liquors, 91 Princess, h Centre

McCormick Chas, salesman, 236 Gordon

McCormack J, janitor Queen's College, 51 Arch

McCormack Patrick, laborer, 46 Ordnance

McCormack Robert, guard K P, Newman's Cottages, King w

McCormack Samuel, spring bed manufacturer, 326 Montreal

McCormick Thos, clerk, Centre

McCormack Thos, laborer, 46 Grove

McCormick Wm, guard K P, 236 Gordon

McCrath Mrs Annie, [wid Michael] 88 Arch

McCrea Thos W, carriagemaker, 477 Princess

McCuen Wm, teamster, 62 Upper Charles

McCullough G, cabman, 439 Brock

McCulla James, salesman, 46 Colborne

McCullough John, laborer, 60 Colborne

McCulla Jno, laborer, 23 Chatham

McCullough Mrs, 37 King w

McCullough Samuel, policeman, 390 Barrie

McCullaugh W G, mechanical engineer fire dept, Ontario

McCullough Wm, ship carpenter, 33 Bagot n

McCune Alex, carpenter, 225 Earl

McCummisky Mrs Alice, grocer, Wellington, cor Queen

McCummiskey John, river pilot, 154 Ontario

McCutcheon Mrs Anne [wid T], 95 Division

McCutcheon John, mariner, 237 Sydenham

McCutcheon Mrs, 404 Brock

McCutcheon Wm, baker, 292 Johnston

McCutcheon Mrs Wm, potash manufr, n end Wellington

McDermott Mrs Dorah(wid Lawrence), Park, G T R station

McDermott John F, carriage builder, &c, King e, cor Queen, h 380 King e

McDermott Patrick, 268 Ontario

McDermott Thos, baggageman G T R, 775 Montreal

McDivet Jas, machinist, 17 West

McDonald A, baker, 272 Princess

Macdonald Allan A, laborer, Ontario

McDonald **Amos**, teacher, Kingston Business College Co, 237 Division

McDonald Mrs A R, Collingwood

McDonald Mrs Bridget [wid Michael] Montreal, corner of Stephen

McDonald Mrs Catharine, 209 Gordon

McDonald Donald, boilermaker, 184 Division

McDonald Frank, laborer, 42 Upper Charles

Macdonald Francis,. clerk P O, 264 Wellington

McDonald G A, accountant, 247 Brock

McDonald Geo, harness maker, 66 Princess, h 29 Wellington

McDonald Hector, shoemaker, 125 Ordnance

McDonald Mrs Hannah [wid Hugh] 303 Alfred

McDonald J A, insp'r weights & measures, 69 Colborne

Macdonald James, second-hand dealer, 293 Princess

Macdonald John, reporter *News*, 65 Rideau

McDonald Capt John A, mariner, 159 Montreal

McDonald Martin, laborer, 144 Bay

McDonald Mrs Mary [wid Christopher], grocer, cor Pine and Cherry

McDonald R J, pilot, 144 Colborne

McDonald Roderick, manf Door Knobs, 29 Pembroke

McDonald —, carpenter, 69 Arch

Macdonnell Geo M, Q C, [Macdonnell & Mudie], Gordon, cor Stuart

Macdonnell & Mudie, [Geo M Macdonnell, Q C, John Mudie, B A], barristers, 38 Clarence

Macdonnell John, 80 Earl

Macdonald Allan, 27 Pembroke

McDowall Mrs H [wid James], 257 Earl

McDowall R J, pianos, organs and musical merchandise, sewing machines, wholesale and retail, and fire and burglar-proof safes, 220 Princess, h 473 Princess. *(See side lines.)*

McElhern Daniel, boiler maker, 85 Union e

McEwen Daniel, (D McEwen & Son], 39 Ordnance

McEwen Daniel & Son, machinists, 54-58 Queen

McEwen Geo, shoemaker, 282 Gordon

McEwen J, telegrapher, 258 Alfred

McEwen Jno, carter, 258 Alfred

McEwen John F (D McEwen & Son), 41 Ordnance

McFadden Jas, carter, 60 John

McFadden Edward, cab driver, 60 John

McFadden Miss Rosana, 179 Queen

McFarlane Mrs, College

McFarlane Robert, shoemaker, 171 Sydenham

McFaul John, machinist, 254 Barrie

McFaul R, dry goods, 180 Princess, h 269 Queen

McFaul Robt, sr, 271 Queen

McGarvy Miss A, 1 Young

McGill Arch, clerk, 21 Upper Bagot

McGill J, clerk, 385 Johnston

Handsome Beaded Goods at F. Shaw & Co's

McGill John, laborer, end Albert

McGill Lt-Col S C, Staff-Adjutant R M C, res College

McGillivray Alice, M D, 230 Princess

McGillivray Jas, engineer, 223 Earl

Macgillivray Rev Malcolm, pastor Chalmers Church, 121 Earl

McGillivray T S, M D, 230 Princess

McGinnis Francis, laborer, 45 James

McGinnis Mrs Margaret [wid Francis] 38 James

McGinnes Owen, prop Western House, 166 Ontario

McGlade Peter, grocer, 160-162 Rideau

McGlinn John, shoemaker, 137 Montreal

McGlone James, stonemason, Picard, between York and Barrie

McGoldrick Michael, boiler mkr, 92 Ontario

McGOWAN GEO A, Cigar Manufacturer. "La Flor de Frontenac," "She," "Bismarck," and "Old Judge." 43 Brock, cor King

McGowan J, hotel, 435 King e

McGowan Thomas, boarding, 70 Princess

McGrath Richard, carpenter, bds 62 Wellington

McGrath Mrs Sophia (wid Thos) boarding house, 104 Queen

McGrogan Miss Alice, 17 Division

McGuin Mrs A (wid Daniel) 11 Mack

McGuire A, drover, head Princess

McGuire Anthony, laborer, bds end Picard

Maguire John, clerk, 121 William

McGuire John, boiler maker, 14 Young

McGuire Jos, salesman, bds 70 Princess

McGuire Thos, fisherman, 320 Queen

McGuire Thomas H, butcher, head Princess

McGuire Wm H, com traveller, 155 Montreal

Maguire Wm H, boarding, 152 Ontario

McIlgorm Robert, blacksmith, 25 Ontario

McIlquham Andrew, traveller, Frontenac

McIlquham Jas, plasterer, 173 Nelson

McIlroy Jno, laborer, 195 Montreal

McIlroy John, clerk, 216 Colborne

McIlroy W, traveller, 216 Colborne

McIlroy William, laborer, 10 Pine

McIntosh Henry, coachman, r109 Union e

McIntyre Alex, shoemaker, 111 Ordnance

McIntyre Donald M, B A, barrister, 304 King e, h 231 Division

McIntyre John, Q C, barrister, 304 King e, h 28 Sydenham

McIntyre Neil, 231 Division

McIntyre John, stove moulder, 272 Sydenham

McIntyre John, carpenter, 4 Wellington Terrace, Montreal

McIntyre, Robert, laborer, 354 Division

McIver J B, accountant, 38 Clarence, h 162 Barrie and cor Union

McIver Kenneth, 2 Colborne

McKay Mrs Annie [wid James] G T R station, Montreal

McKay Charles, bookkeeper, 19 Union

McKay J B, principal Kingston Business College Co, h 4 Colborne

McKay John, leather, 162 Princess, h Sydenham w

McKay John jr, salesman, Sydenham w, cor William

Mackay Philip, moulder, 125 Montreal

McKee Andrew, mason, 204 Barrie

McKee John, carpenter, Plum

McKee John, laborer, 21 York

McKee Mrs Robt, 15 York

McKee Samuel, riveter, 244 Barrie

McKee Wm, moulder, Bagot

McKee William J, mariner, 256 Gordon

McKegney Patrick, laborer, 87 Barrack

McKelvey & Birch, (John McKelvey, Samuel Birch), plumbers, steam & gas-fitters, tinsmiths, hardware and house furnishings, 69-71 Brock

McKelvey John, (McKelvey & Birch), h 194 Bagot

McKenny Wm, laborer, 258 Sydenham

McKenna Mrs Bridget, (wid Bernard), McAuley's Cottages, Dufferin

McKenty J, 362 Johnston

McKenty J jr, student, 362 Johnston

McKenty Patrick, laborer, n John

McKenty R, clerk, 362 Johnston

McKenty Robert, salesman, 306 Gordon

McKenzie Alexander A, mariner, 107 Union e

MacKenzie J D, M D, Union

McKenzie John, coachman, 3 Division

McKenzie Malcolm, law student, 114 Johnston

McKenzie Thomas, coachman, 31 King w

McKillop Mrs Catharine (wid Alex) 21 Johnston

McKim J, 389 Johnston

McKim John, laborer, 61 Upper Charles

McKim Peter, hide inspector, 250 Alfred

McKnight Jas, laborer, Victoria

McLaren Mrs E (wid Rev P) 272 Gordon

McLaughlin John, confectioner, 222 Princess

McLaughlin P, prop Windsor Hotel, Princess, cor Montreal

Maclean Andrew, grocer, 272 Ontario, h King, cor Maitland

McLellan John, baker, 85 Queen

McLeod Mrs Ann (wid Samuel) Chadwick's Yard, off Bagot

McLeod James, machinist, 310 Gordon

McLeod John, prop sash, blind and door factory, n s Place d'Armes

McLeod John, laborer, 80 Johnston

McLeod Neil, 113 Alfred

McMahon A C, insurance agent, 230 Barrie

McMAHON A J, Dealer in Dry Goods, Carpets and Oilcloths and Gents' Furnishings, etc. 102 Princess, h 74 Wellington

McMahon Alex, laborer, 32 Upper William

McMahon Andrew (T McMahon & Co) h 81 Earl

McMahon Bros, hardware, 85-87 Princess

McMahon Edward, salesman, 101 Union e

McMahon George, weighmaster, 260 King e

McMahon John, builder, 74 Wellington

McMahon John T (McMahon Bros) h 23 Sydenham

McMahon Miss M A, 214 William

McMahon Mrs Margaret (wid Edward) 101 Union e

McMahon Robert, painter, 26 William

McMahon T & Co, painters and paper hangers, Brock, corner Bagot

McMahon Thos, 184 Bagot

McManus John, storekeeper Insane Asylum, 74 Union e

McMaster Mrs Jeanette (wid Peter) 357 Division

McMaster John H, laborer, 142 Pine

McMaster Wm, laborer, 34 Upper Bagot

McMillan A, storekeeper K P, 386 Brock

McMillen A, carpenter, 289 Brock

McMillan Mrs Agnes (wid Donald) 135 Clergy

McMillan C, auctioneer, 289 Brock

McMillan Mrs Hannah, hairworker, 70 Brock

McMillan M, sailor, 119 Ordnance

McMillan Richard, piano maker, 3 First

McMorine Rev J K, rector St James' Church, cor Barrie and Union

McMorran Wm, 120 Bay

McMullen James E, carpenter, Barrack

McMullen Mrs Jennie (wid Samuel), 195 Wellington

McMullen John E, 306 Gordon

McMullen Jos, blacksmith, 54 Wellington

McNab Francis, 78 Sydenham w

McNab Mrs Janet (wid Colin), 78 Sydenham w

McNamee James, laborer, 11 Ellice

McNamee Mrs Maggie (wid William), 116 Johnston

McNamee Miss Rosa, dressmaker, 108 Princess

McNamee Wm, laborer, 33 Upper William

McNamee James, printer, Upper William

McNaney Mrs Mary (wid Robt), 130 Queen

McNaughton & Co, clothiers, King, cor Princess

McNaughton John, (McNaughton & Co), h 49 Clergy

Maps Mounted at P. Ohlke's, 184 Wellington St.

McNaughton Wm, 11 Deacon
McNeil A W, plumber, 148 Johnston
McNeil Charles, laborer, 240 Montreal
McNeill Charles, guard K P, 280 Gordon
McNeill Charles, laborer, bds 123 Ordnance
McNeil John, foreman moulder, 76 Johnson
McNeil Neil, plumber and steam-fitter, 66 Brock, h 148 Johnston
McNeill W J, flour, feed and seed grains, 65 Brock, h 123 Ordnance
McNiven P C, draughtsman locomotive works, Wellington
Macpherson Alex F, clerk, 158 Earl
McPherson Mrs, 400 Princess
Macpherson Richard, Crown lands and Immigration agent, foot William, h 154 Johnston
Macpherson Miss Wilhelmina, bds 69 Union e
McParland James, wholesale liquors, ales and porters, 341 King e and 265 Ontario
McQuaid John, ship carpenter, John north
McQuaid Miss Mary, 84 Queen
McQuaid Owen, laborer, 328 Queen
McQuaid M, laborer, 27 Young
McQuaid Wm, carpenter, John north
McQuag Mrs Margaret, 177 Queen
McQuarrie G W, clerk Merchants Bank, Wellington
McQuisten Alex, bookkeeper, 414 King e

McRae Bros [David H, R W R & E J B], grocers and provision dealers, Golden Lion Block, Wellington, cor Brock
McRae D H (McRae Bros) h 254 Gordon
McRae E J B (McRae Bros) h Earl, cor Clergy
McRae R W R (McRae Bros)
McRea W D, traveller, 124 Barrie
McRae W R (W R McRae & Co) h Clergy, cor Earl
McRae W R & Co, wholesale grocers and wine dealers, Golden Lion block, Wellington
McRossie William, lumber merchant, 248 Ontario
McSurley Mrs Eliza (wid Edward), old No 76 Bagot
McTaggart Miss M S, milliner, 176 Wellington, h 219 Bagot
McVety Albert M D, 203-5 Wellington
McVety Robert, carpenter, 426 Division
McWaters James, carter, 210 Colborne
McWaters S J, engineer, 187 Colborne
McWilliams Capt Charles, mariner, 307 Bagot
Macarow Mrs H, 188 William
Macaway Charles, engineer K P King w
Machar J M, barrister, 38 Clarence, h 222 Johnson
Mackerras Mrs Margaret (wid John), 34 Wellington
Mackie Rev J, pastor St Andrew's Church, cor Clergy and Queen
Mackin Arthur, (Slavin & Mackin), Gore

Macnee F H, clerk, Bagot, cor Union

Macnee & Minnes, [James Minnes, W H Macnee, W T Minnes], wholesale dry goods, 249 Bagot

Macnee Mrs Sarah E (wid Jas), Union, e cor Bagot

Macnee W H, (Macnee & Minnes) Sydenham w

Madden James, engineer, 298 Barrie

Madden Jas W, varnish manf'r, 324 Alfred

Madden Michael, engineer, 18 Rideau

Madden Patrick, engineer, 93 Bay

Maddocks Wm, blacksmith, 18 Young

Madigan Edward, fireman K & P Ry, Picard

Madigan Michael, blacksmith, Bagot

Madill J A, com traveller, 15 Colborne

Madill Wm Henry, keeper Asylum, 285 Division

Madran Octave, butcher, 72 Brock

Magee Robt J, moulder, Artillery Park barracks

Maguet Mrs Josephine (wid D) 94 Ontario

Maher James, master gunner, R S G

Mahew Mrs Jessie (wid Alex) 140 Chatham

Mahoney James, grocer, 216 Montreal

Mahood W J, fancy goods, 113 Princess, h 219 Queen

Maiden Mrs Catharine (wid R) 25 Upper Bagot

Main Miss Helen, bds 89 Union

Mair Mrs Ester (wid John, M D) 79 Arch

Makins Wm, grain buyer, 231 Barrie

Mallefant Frank, marine diver, 17 Rideau

Malloch Mrs Cynthia (wid F) bds 146 King e

Mallen James, wood merchant, Cataraqui, h 17 Charles

Mallon Lawrence, laborer, Park GTR station

Mallen Michael, wood merchant, Ontario, cor Barrack, h 16 Rideau

Mallen Patrick, laborer, 12 Pine

Mallen Peter, laborer, Bagot

Malone A, mariner, 480 Brock

Malone Mrs S [wid G], 205 William

Malone Thomas, upholsterer, 51 Barrack

Maloney John, 79 Queen

Maloney John, blacksmith, 124 Montreal

Maloney Patrick, Picard

Manahan D, laborer, 307 Johnston

Manion Mrs Ann [wid James], 103 Queen

Mann Mrs Mary [wid John] 248 Montreal

Manning Edward J, saddler, 28 Johnston

Manson John, carpenter, 46 Union

March J, caretaker Shoal Tower

Marchand Chas, laborer, 22 Earl

Marchand Edward, engineer, 3 Dunn Terrace, Bay

Marchand Jno, laborer, 8 Rideau

Marchand Mrs Mary [wid John] 8 Rideau

Mark Rev Bro, Christian Brothers' School, 89 Clergy
Markee O, tailor, Stephen
Marriott G, farmer, 337 Brock
Marsh Alex, laborer, 60 Elm
Marsh Hy Jas, laborer, 60 Elm
Marsh John, laborer, 60 Elm
Marsh John W, storeman, 64 Elm
Marsh W, driver, 123 Princess
Marshall C A, traveller, 247 Brock
Marshall Prof D H, Queen's University, Centre
Marshall F C, cabinet maker, 241 Princess
Marshall Henry, laborer, e side lane off Park, G T R station
Marshall J, caretaker West ditch
Marshall Jas, clerk, 282 Queen
Marshall Jas, carter, 253 Queen
Marshall John, clerk, 300 Queen
Marshall John, mariner, Albert
Marshall Robert, engineer, 176 Bagot
Marshall Robt, salesman, Queen, cor Barrie
Marshall S, accountant, 466 Brock
Marshall Samuel, traveller, 109 York
Marshall Wm, salesman, Queen, cor Barrie
Marshall Wm, 68 Colborne
Martin A R, real estate agent, 278 Brock
Martin Mrs Catharine (wid Jas), 53 Upper Charles
Martin C H, insurance agent, 86 Brock, h 321 Gordon
Martin Chas, mariner, 21 Balaclava
Martin David, grocer, 188 Sydenham

Martin Edward, laborer, 236 Earl
Martin Mrs Emma [wid Peter], 63 Queen
Martin E R, auctioneer and com merchant, 20 market sq, h 460 Brock
Martin Miss Harriet, school teacher, 168 King e
Martin Jas, mariner, 17 Ellice
Martin John F, sign painter, Ordnance
Martin Miss Julia J, school teacher, 168 King
Martin J W, carpenter, 349 Brock
Martin Mrs Margaret T [wid Wm], 138 Wellington
Martin's Opera House, W C Martin, prop, 218 Princess
Martin Robert, laborer, 141 Durham
Martin W C, saddlery hardware and leather, 216 Princess, h 166 Sydenham
Martin W H, clerk, 125 William
Martin W H, salesman, 460 Brock
Martinelli Luciano, laborer, 218 Sydenham
Marvin Mrs Mary [wid Wm] 315 Montreal
Mason Henry, ship carpenter, 129 Bagot
Mason Samuel, mariner, 380 Princess
Massie James, V S, 237 Bagot
Massey John, machinist, 86 Colborne
Massie John R, pattern maker, 81 Colborne
Massy Mrs Martha (wid Michael) 87 Johnston
Massie William, contractor, 155 Picard

Massie Wm, jr, contractor, 157 Picard

Mathews Miss Kate, dressmaker, 82 Johnston

Mathews Thos, 40 Ellice

Matthews Wm, 210 Division

Mandeville Jos, ship carpenter, Ontario

Maund C F, wharfinger, 165 Bagot

Mavety Alex, M D, 194 Sydenham

Maxam Alfred, painter, 12 Redan

Maxam Geo, grinder, 51 John

Maxwell G W, clerk, 56 Rideau

Maxwell James, foreman, 71 Division

Mayell John, tailor, 76 Brock

Maynard John, carpenter, 331 Queen

Mayne Major C B, R E, R M C, res College

Mead Mrs Almira (wid Charles), grocer, Rideau, cor Barrack

Meadows Miss, 154 Gordon

Meagher Mrs Catharine [wid Dr James], 184 Queen

Meagher Gerald G, clerk P O, 27 Wellington

Meagher James G, trader, 28 Ellice

Meagher Martin, laborer, old No 79, Bagot

Meagher Mrs Sarah [wid Jeremiah], Wellington

Meagher Thos, customs officer, 5 Wellington terrace, Montreal

Medley Wm H, drug clerk, Barriefield

Meek Robert, Sec'y Odd-Fellows' R A, "Truevale," 50 Earl

Meek William, 48 Elm

Meek William, mechanical sup't, *Whig* office, 884 Gordon

Megarry James, policeman, 420 Johnston

Megill A E, salesman, 247 Brock

Melville Mrs Elizabeth (wid Jno) 104 Gore

Menary George, ship carpenter, 20 York

Mendell, J, oculist, 15 Ellice

Mercier Joseph, ship carpenter, n s Place d'Armes

Mercer Wm, Victoria

Merchants Bank of Canada G E Hague, manager, King, cor William

Merritt Gilbert, ship carpenter, 85 Queen

Merrit Henry, moulder, 106 Barrie

Merrett T E, teller Merchants Bank, Brock

Merritt Capt Thos, fishery inspector, 73 Gore

Merriman Bros [Wesley & Wellington], agricultural implements, 36 Montreal

Merriman W J, organs & pianos, 228 Princess

Metcalfe James H, M L A, 826 Princess

Metcalfe J C, butcher, 406 Brock

Middleton Alex, laborer, 275 Sydenham

Middleton Henry L, salesman, 55 Clergy

Middleton Miss Mary, hospital nurse, 55 Clergy

Middleton Robert, laborer, 884 Princess

Middleton Mrs Sophia [wid Capt Lewis] 55 Clergy

Middleton Wm [J Henderson & Co] h 55 Clergy

Milford Charles, 367 Princess

Milk Jos, tailor, 245 Colborne

Milk L, blacksmith,245 Colborne

Millan Conway, butcher, 252 Montreal, cor John

Millan Dennis, butcher, 289 Ontario

Millan Jeremiah, 91 Earl

Millan J T, salesman, old No 94 Bagot

Millard Wm, carpenter, 3 Wellington terrace, 108 Montreal

Miller A H, supt letter carriers, 157 Alfred

Miller Capt Andrew H, mariner, 89 Queen

Miller Charles, mariner, r428, King e

Miller Henry, blacksmith, 205 Alfred

Miller Henry A, laborer, 453 Princess

Miller Jno, engineer, 438 Barrie

Miller Matthew, traveller, 200 Sydenham

Miller Robt jr, boiler maker, 98 William

Miller Robt sen, carter, 96 William

Miller William, laborer, Upper Victoria

Miller William, bookkeeper, 457 Princess

Milligan Capt Alex, mariner,295 Wellington

Milne David, sail maker, 167 Queen

Milne John, fruiterer, 176 Ontario, h 106 Ontario

Milne John, laborer, 106 Ontario

Milne Robt, mariner, 221 Earl

Milne Thomas, engineer, 243 Earl

Milo E, carpenter, 365 Brock

Milo Thomas W, painter and dealer in wall paper, 41-43 Montreal

Milroy Wm, laborer, 62 O'Kill

Mills Andrew, carpenter,18 York

Mills Mrs Catharine (wid David) end Montreal

Mills Geo, laborer, 31 Mack

Mills George & Co, Boston Hat Store, 170 Wellington

Mills Geo, jr [Geo Mills & Co] 124 Gordon

Mills John, school teacher, 484 Princess

Mills & Kent [Thomas Mills, R E Kent], bankers and insurance, 91 Clarence

Mills Mrs Mary [wid James] 198 Bagot

Mills Robert, bookkeeper, 434 Princess

Mills T, trader, 386 Brock

Mills Thomas [Mills & Kent] h 122 Gordon

Mills Thos [Thos Mills & Co] h 120 Gordon

Mills Thomas & Co, hatters and furriers, 156 Princess

Minaker Leslie, 212 Division

Minnes & Burns, dry goods and Gents' Furnishers, 140 Princess

Minnes James [Macnee & Minnes] h 124 Bagot

Minnes James A, accountant, 124 Bagot

Minnes Mrs Jane [wid Thos] 385 Princess

Minnes T D (Minnes & Burns) h 495 Princess

Minnes W T, (Macnee & Minnes), h 124 Bagot

Minshull W, mechanic, 850 Brock

Mitchell Alex, laborer, Bagot

Mitchell C A, bookkeeper, 324 Brock

Mitchell E C, [Chown & Mitchell], 185 William

Mitchell Isaac, wholesale jeweller, Golden Lion Block, Wellington, h 167 Bagot

Mitchell Mrs I, 328 Brock

Mitchell James, 68 Arch

Mitchell J H, teller, Ontario Bank, Maitland

Mitchell John, printer, 74 Earl

Mitchell John, contractor, 185 William

Mitchell John, stone cutter, 22 Ellice

Mitchell P, ship builder, 28 . Barrie

Mitchell W A, salesman, 185 William

Mitchell Wm A, printer, 105 Bagot

Mitchell Wm, baker, 27 Main

Moffat Miss Elizabeth, 60 Arch

Moncoref Peter, guard K P, 100 Chatham

Monette Capt John, mariner, 409 King e

Monks Peter, laborer, 242 Earl

Monroe Jas, miner, 1 St Catharine

Montgomery R, dyer, 225 Princess

Montgomery Samuel, salesman, 225 Princess

Montreal Transportation Co, P R Henderson, managing director, foot Queen

Mooers George, 500 Princess

Mooers H (H Mooers & Co) h 90 Barrie

Mooers H & Co, grain, etc, foot Princess

Moon Robt, carpenter, 12 Alma

Mooney Robert, machinist, 19 Division

Mooney Thomas, raftsman, 20 Stuart

Moore Andrew, bookkeeper, 110 Earl

Moore Daniel, grain shoveller, Corrigan

Moore E, sec-treas Gas Co, h 211 Bagot

Moore John, engineer, Corrigan

Moore John, laborer, 217 Gordon

Moore Jos, head Princess

Moore Mrs M, 110 Earl

Moore M A, boots and shoes, 197 Wellington

Moore Nathaniel D, mining engineer, 357 King e, h 1 Mack

Moore Mrs R M, 139 William

Moore Thos, merchant tailor, 354 King e, h 148 Earl

Moore Thos, tailor, 406 Barrie

Moore T W, merchant, 399 Brock

Moore W B, clerk K P R, 139 William

Moore W J, machinist, 338 Queen

Moore Wm, real estate agent, 90 Brock, h Earl, cor Bagot

Moore Wm R, marble cutter, 158 Rideau

Moran Miss Bridget, 82 Earl

Moran Patrick, moulder, 79 Gore

Moreland A, grocer, 359 Division, cor Pine

Moreland Francis, laborer, 623 Princess

Morgan Hugh, piano agent, 291 Princess

Morham E, piano tuner, 180 Barrie

Bargains in Cottonades at F. Shaw & Co's

Morgan Mrs J, 255 Brock
Morhan James, 98 Wellington
Morris Mrs Catharine [wid Emmanuel], 154 Picard
Morrison Mrs Anne [wid Robt] 169 Pine
Morrison Mrs C [wid M] 199 Earl
Morrison F M, machinist, 340 Johnston
Morrison Francis, machinist, 56 Division
Morrison Jno, moulder, 86 Pine
Morrison Joseph, carpenter, 57 Bay
Morrison William, carriagemaker, 67 York
Morrison Wm, tinsmith, 230 Sydenham
Morrissey John, messenger P O, 70 William
Morton W H, clerk, 125 William
Mostyn Edward, clerk City Hotel, 202 Bagot
Moules Richard, laborer, 435 Barrie
Mowat J B, professor Queen's University, 188 Johnston
Mowat George, 226 Division
Mowat Henry, mason, 224 Division
Mowat John James, pensioner, 232 Wellington
Moxley Robert, blacksmith, 74 York
Moxley William, blacksmith, 103 York
Moyle Mrs, Centre
Moyle V, Centre
Muckler William, moulder, Union c
Muckleston J & Co, wholesale and retail hardware, 71-73 Princess

Muckleston Mrs Ann [wid Samuel], 226 King e
Muckleston John S, (J Muckleston & Co), h 81 King e
Mudie John, B A, [Macdonnell & Mudie], h King, cor West
Mudie William, 192 Gordon
Mulholland James, mechanic, 184 Barrie
Mulholland Mrs Thomas, 114 Barrie
Mulally Cornelius, laborer, 114 William
Mulally Denis, cigar maker, 114 William
Mullin Edward, salesman, bds 430 Princess
Mullen James, weighman, 262 Sydenham
Mullen Patrick, carpenter, 392 Barrie
Mullett Miss Catharine, 38 Upper Charles
Mulligan Wm, laborer, Beverly
Mulroney Dennis, laborer, Park, G T R station
Mundell Edward D, M D, 6 Victoria Terrace, Montreal
Mundell John, M D, 11 Montreal, h 59 Arch
Mundell Mrs Mary (wid David) 59 Arch
MUNDELL WILLIAM, B A, Barrister, Solicitor, Conveyancer, etc. Residence 59 Arch, Office 139 Princess, near City Hotel
Munro Charles, engineer, 58 Wellington
Munro Frederick, laborer, n side Cataraqui

Munro John, mechanic, 232 Barrie

Munro Mrs Margaret (wid John) 286 Johnston

Murch W S R, com traveller, 66 Earl

Murphy James, carpenter, 189 Montreal

Murphy James, laborer, Bagot

Murphy John, carpenter, 181 Alfred

Murphy John B, summer residence, Edge Hill, 305 King w; winter residence, Montreal, P O Box 1116

Murphy Jos, laborer, 212 Earl

Murphy L W, grocer, Princess, cor King

Murphy Thomas, mariner, 35 Rideau

Murphy Thomas, painter, Cataraqui

Murphy Thos, laborer, 256 Earl

Murphy William, laborer, head Princess

Murphy Wm, wheelwright, 122 Clarence

Murray Mrs Catharine [wid James], 231 Wellington

Murray Charles, old No 104, Bagot

Murray Edward, salesman, 104 Bagot

Murray Miss Eliza, dressmaker, 105 Brock

Murray Francis, laborer, 12 Rideau

Murray Geo, mariner, 48 O'Kill

Murray Capt James, mariner, 6 Barnstaple Terrace, Clergy

Murray James, engineer, 336 Division

Murray James jr, clerk, 336 Division

Murray John, supervisor, K & P Railway, old No 104, Bagot

Murray John, 17 Upper Charles

Murray Mrs John C, 186 Barrie

Murray Jos, mariner, 20 Rideau

Murray Mrs Mary, 217 Bagot

Murray Randall, teamster, r258 King e

Murray & Taylor [W J Murray, A D Taylor] staple and fancy dry goods, 176 Princess

Murray Wm, clerk, 527 Princess

Murray W J [Murray & Taylor] h 217 Bagot

Murray William J, carpenter, 11 Vine

Myers H J, grocer, cor Colborne and Barrie

Myers Mrs Mary [wid Henry] 227 Sydenham

Nancollas Mrs A [wid Robert] 151 Brock

Nash Major Edward, R A, R M C, res College

Nash Mrs Mary [wid Wm] 268 Johnston

Nash T W, sec-treasurer K & P Ry, 144 Union

Neelon Sylvester [D Hutchison, manager], flour and feed, 113 Brock

Neill John, traveller, 218 King e

Neill Wm, letter carrier, 127 Division

Neilson Surgeon-Major J L H, R S G, res Barracks

Neilson Matthew, civil engineer, 73 Colborne

Neish Wm, clerk customs, 302 Gordon

Neish William E, jeweller, 302 Gordon

Nelson Miss Catharine, dressmaker, 169 Bagot

Nelson Miss Eliza, school teacher, 65 Sydenham w

Nelson John, jr, carter. 150 Rideau

Nelson John, sr, 152 Rideau

Nesbit Duncan, carpenter, 29 Main

Nesbit Robert, policeman, 260 Alfred

Neville M J, accountant K & P Ry, 116 Rideau

Nevens Wm, yard boss K & P Ry, n s Cataraqui

Newberry Hy, salesman, Queen

Newell Napoleon, laborer, 37 Upper Charles

Newell Mrs Sophia [wid Robt] 2 Rideau

Newell William, mariner, 307 Earl

Newlands Francis, contractor, 343 Barrie

Newlands George, architect, 506 Princess

Newlands Isaac, contractor, 184 Ordnance

Newlands John, contractor, 506 Princess

Newlands John, mason, 163 Nelson

Newlands Richard, tobacconist, 70 Princess, h 148 Division

Newlands W, architect, 332 King e, h 291 Gordon

Newman Henry, carpenter, 118 Montreal

Newman R & J H, contractors, Bagot

Newman William, guard K P, King w

Newman Wm, carpenter, 218 Barrie

Newnham T, riding instructor, R S G

Newton John, carpenter, 58 Colborne

Newton Thomas, cab driver, 111 Picard

Newton Thomas jr, carter, 111 Picard

Nichol John, bookkeeper, 295 Alfred

Nicoll Jno, carpenter, 91 Bay

Nickle Wm, 130 Earl

Nicholls Charles, laborer, 225 Wellington

Nichols Mrs Elizabeth, [wid Samuel], 10 Anglin's Cottages, Bay

Nicholson A B, Prof, Queen's University, 128 Union

Nicholson Alex, moulder, 37 Bagot north

Nicholson Capt C Howard, mariner, 210 Gordon

Nicholson D, plasterer, 425 Brock

Nicholson Mrs Margaret [wid Mark], 92 Bay

Nicholson Thomas, laborer, 41 Bagot n

Nicholson Thomas [McConville & Nicholson], 136 Ontario

Nicholson Thomas, carpenter, 346 Gordon

Nicholson William, blacksmith, 13 Redan

Nimmo Rev J H, M D, 141 Barrie

Nisbet F, bookseller and stationer, Brock, cor Wellington

Nobbs Wm, carpenter, 52 Union

Nobes John, carpenter, 236 Wellington

Nolan J, sexton St Mary's Cathedral, 329 Brock

Nolan John, scroll sawyer, 51 Bagot n

Nolan John, laborer, 278 Sydenham

Nolan M, sailor, 348 Brock

Noon John, 59 George

Noonan Capt Daniel, mariner, 59 Rideau

Norris James, prop Ottawa Hotel, Ontario, cor Princess

Norris, Joseph, carpenter, 219 Earl

Norris Marshall, coal heaver,397 King e

Norris W H, com traveller, 315 Brock

Norris Miss W H, 315 Brock

Northmore Geo H, baker, 22 York

Northmore Wm H, carpenter, 22 York

Norton Fred G, bookkeeper, Collingwood

Noxon B D, (Noxon & Rockwell), h 3 Victoria Terrace, Montreal

NOXON & ROCKWELL, (B D Noxon, J Rockwell), wholesale and retail dealers in Fine Boots, Shoes, Rubbers, Trunks and Valises. Fine Goods a Specialty. 145 Princess, cor Bagot.

Nugent, Edward, engineer, 793 Montreal

Nugent Edward, machinist, 241 Gordon

Nugent Mrs Eliza (wid Peter), 241 Gordon

Nugent Mrs Elizabeth (wid T), 19 Johnston

Nugent Mrs Esther (wid Patrick), 292 Montreal

Nugent James (Nugent & Taylor), 391 Brock

Nugent Peter, customs dept, 19 Johnston

Nugent Robert, laborer, 131 Montreal

Nugent & Taylor (Jas Nugent, Henry Taylor), stoves and tinware) 183 Wellington

O'Barny Daniel, laborer, 68 Cherry

O'Brien Alex, merchant tailor, 265 Princess

O'Brien Edward, laborer, 25 Division

O'Brien George, mariner, 111 York

O'Brien Jno, laborer, 21 Young

O'Brien Jno, laborer, Markland

O'Brien Jno, carter, John north

O'Brien John, machinist, 22 Young

O'Brien Lawrence, engineer, 67 Union

O'Brien Patrick, laborer, 304 Princess

O'Brien Thos, printer, 74 Earl

O'Brien Thos, ship carpenter, 1 Union e

O'Brien Thomas, laborer, 34 Cherry

O'Brien Timothy, shoemaker, 275 Montreal

O'Connor Daniel, laborer, 216 Sydenham

O'Connor Mrs Helen, (wid Patrick), Artillery Park, Barrack

O'Connor James O, salesman, Walsh & Stacey

O'Connor Jno, laborer, 291 Earl

O'Connor John, shoemaker, 168 Ontario

O'Connor Maurice, carpenter, Dufferin

O'Connor Patrick, miller, 23 Rideau

HORSESHOE ISLAND. | Lots Certain to Rapidly Enhance in Value. Invest Now!

19

O'Connor Robert, shoemaker, Bagot

O'Connor Capt Thos, mariner, 13 West

O'Donald Mrs Ellen, 25 Young

O'Donnell B, gardener, 254 Earl

O'Donnell Thos, 100 Earl

O'Donnell John, Inland Rev dept, 407 King e

O'Donnell Patrick, storekeeper K P, 10 O'Kill

O'Donnell Wm, laborer, r 24 Johnston

O'Gorman Daniel, carter, 8 John

O'Grady Sergt J, R S G

O'Hagan Alex, r 170 Bagot

O'Harra Henry, King

O'Hearn John, engineer, 35 John

O'Hern Patrick, plumber, 23 Ontario

O'Neil Arthur, laborer, 263 Sydenham

O'Neill Chas, laborer, 53 Bay

O'Neil Jas, laborer, 54 Elm

O'Neill Michael, laborer, r 428 up stairs, King e

O'Neil Patrick, mechanic, 110 Barrie

O'Neil Mrs Patrick, 8 Colborne

O'Neill Patrick, laborer, Bagot

O'Neill Patrick, laborer, 142 Rideau

O'Neill Terrence, laborer, r 81 Wellington

O'Neill William, laborer, 63 Queen

O'Reilly D, musician, 159 Brock

O'Reilly Felix, laborer, 202 Montreal

O'Rielly George, mechanic, 172 Barrie

O'Reilly Miss, 66 Barrie

O'Reilly P, shoemaker, 259 Division

O'Reilly T, engineer, 813 Johnston

O'Shea John, trader, 37 Johnston

O'Shea W J, bookkeeper, Queen

O'Sullivan Jeremiah, laborer, 76 Earl

O'Toole Charles, engineer, 281 Sydenham

Oberndorffer H, cigarmaker, 88 Queen

Oberndorffer S, cigar manufr, 89 Princess, h 88 Queen

Ockley A E [V Ockley & Sons] h 332 Montreal

Ockley J V [V Ockley & Sons] h 115 Princess

Ockley Vincent [V Ockley & Sons] h 115 Princess

Ockley Vincent & Sons [Vincent, J V, T G, and A E] grocers, 115-17 Princess

Ockley T G [V Ockley & Sons] h 332 Montreal

Odd-Fellows' Relief Association, R Meek, Secretary, Montreal, cor Princess

Odette John, teamster, n side Cataraqui

Odwin Rev Bro, Christian Brothers' School, 89 Clergy

Offord G jr, traveller, 464 Brock

Offord George sr, wholesale and retail boots and shoes, 117 Brock & 127 Princess, h 46 Clergy

Offord Jas, clerk, 46 Clergy

Offord Jonathan, accountant, 45 Upper Bagot

Ohlke P, art decorations, 182-184 Wellington. (See side lines.)

Oldfin John, gasfitter, 280 Wellington

J. B. PAGE & Co. Fashionable Hatters & Furriers
138 Princess Street.

ALPHABETICAL DIRECTORY. 147

Oldfin Mrs Mary Ann (wid John) 282 Wellington

Oil & Enamel Cloth Co, G W Amey, manager, North, cor Rideau

Oldham Mrs Jane (wid John K) 35 Wellington

Oliver Chas, marine diver, Barrack, cor King

Oliver A S, M D, F R C P S K, 351-53 King o

Oliver Chas, clerk customs, bds 286 Queen

Oliver Isaac, carpenter, n side Dufferin

Oldrieve George S (Oldrieve & Horn) 7 Wellington

Oldrieve & Horn (G S Oldrieve, Alex Horn) sailmakers, etc, 263 Ontario

Olsen Alex, steward, York

Ontario Bank, T Y Greet, manager, Wellington, cor Clarence

Ontario Building and Savings Society, James McArthur, manager, 67 Clarence

Oram John, bookkeeper, 185 Colborne

Orr Jas A, printer, bds St Lawrence Hotel

Orr John, (Richmond, Orr & Co), h 213 Bagot

Orr John, caretaker, fair grounds Nelson

Orr John L, blacksmith, 357 Princess

Orr —, Ontario

Orrel, Mrs Ann, 19 Gordon

Orser Edward, musician, 135 Colborne

Orser Horace, laborer, 139 Colborne

Orser Wm, laborer, 147 Pine

Orser Sidney, carpenter, 445 Princess

Osborne George, sec'y K & P Mining Co, Bartlett s

Ostler Fred, accountant, agent London Life Ins Co'y, Brock, cor Wellington, h 1 College

Ottawa Hotel, Jas Norris, prop, Ontario, cor Princess

Otto C H, bookbinder, 11 Montreal, h 82 Frontenac

Otto J J, bookbinder, 34 Frontenac

Outram Mrs Susan, 225 Wellington (upstairs)

Overend T, contractor, 241 Brock

Packer Joseph, machinist, 24 Division

Packer Thomas, clerk, 24 Division

Paddon Thomas, laborer, 296 Division

Page J B, (J B Page & Co) h 191 Johnston

Page J B & Co, hatters and furriers, 138 Princess *(See top lines.)*

Page John D, car inspector, K & P R'y, North

Page J P, merchant, 191 Johnston

Paine S H, 165 King w

Paladeau Henry, 106 Ontario

Palmer Edward, cigar maker, 330 Montreal

Palmer Geo F, ship carpenter, 84 Johnston

Palmer Miss Jane, 262 Earl

Palmer Mrs N [wid John] boarding house, 330 Montreal

Palmer Timothy, confectioner, 51 Princess

Pappa Jas, printer, 140 Queen

Pannell William, carpenter, 248 Alfred

Paradis Joseph, ship carpenter, 22 Place d'Armes

Parent N, paymaster K & P R, 217a Montreal

Parker Mrs Ann (wid Bennett), 318 Division

Parker Mrs Fanny [wid E H], 198 King e

Parker William, engineer, 299 Montreal

Parkin Geo H, farmer, 42 Division

Parkin T M, confectioner, 94 Brock

Parks George, piano maker, bds Windsor Hotel

Parks George, laborer, Barrack

Parsons Mrs Harriet H (wid Wm) 12 Earl

Parsons Mrs John, r42 Johnston

Parsons Mrs, 307 Barrie

Patch J S, manager Canadian-American Express Co, h 86 Union

Patterson David J, carpenter, 601 Princess

Patterson Miss Ellen, 91 Queen

Patterson Mrs Eliza (wid Wm) r 161 Bagot

Patterson Mrs Elizabeth (wid Henry) 219 Gordon

Paterson Capt Frank, mariner, 163 Union

Patterson Geo, moulder, head Princess

Paterson H M, manager Federal Warehouse, bds City Hotel

Paterson John, laborer, 15 Upper William

Paterson Mathew, mariner, 1 Hales' Cottages, King w

Patterson Robert, grocer, 303 Division

Patterson Robt H, blacksmith, King e

Patterson R S, commission, 46 Princess

Patterson William, student, 55 Arch

Patton Charles T G, agent, 237 Queen

Patton John, insurance agent, 242 Gordon

Patrick Rev Bro, Christian Brothers' School, 89 Clergy

Paul Rev Bro, Christian Brothers' School, 89 Clergy

Paul James, moulder, 26 Upper William

Paul John, sup't harbor, 276 Johnston

Paul Wm J, jeweller, 26 Upper William

Payne Jos R, laborer, 210 Queen

Peart W H, agent K & P R, 39 Gore

Pedler Herbert, clerk, 16 Deacon

Pellchie S, tailor, Stephen

Pelow Dennis, laborer, 13 Ontario

Pellow Thos H, manager J McParland, bds American Hotel

Penner Miss Eliza, 60 William

Pense Edward J B, prop *British Whig,* h 49 King e

Pense James, clerk P O, 190 Clergy

Percival C M, horseshoer, 38 Princess

Percy John, cab driver, 106 Gore

Percy John, mechanic, 40 Division

Percy Thomas, boilermaker, 211 Sydenham

Percy Wm, tailor, 247 Earl

Perley Geo E, asst engineer dry dock, 80 Wellington

Perry Alfred, machinist, caretaker drill shed, Union

Perry Edward, moulder, 215 Gordon

Perry Mrs Ellen (wid William), bds 106 Gore

Perry Norman H, carter, 225 Montreal

Perry Wesley, laborer, 33 First

Perryman John, plasterer, 50 John

Perryman John, mechanic, 72 Arch

Peters H, mason, 7 Pine

Peters Henry, mariner, 220 Division

Peters H J, carpenter, 408 Barrie

Peters Hugh, carpenter, 12 Cowdy

Peters Mrs J [wid Hugh], grocer, cor Princess and Victoria

Peters John, shoemaker, Chadwick's yard, Bagot

Peters Thos, hairdresser, 343 King e

Peters Wm, engineer, Bagot

Pettigrew Alexander D, 151 Colborne

Petrie J D, teller Bank B N A, 102 Bagot

Phelan Daniel, M D, 246 Bagot

Phelan Thos, currier, Bagot

Phillips Mrs Cinderella, [wid Philip], **r87 Johnston**

Phillips Thomas, shoemaker, end Barrie

Phillips Thomas H, bookkeeper, Bagot

Phillips Wm, laborer, Beverly

Phippen Mrs Betsy (wid Samuel) 204 Bagot

Phippen S S, secretary Public Schools, 115 Stuart

Pickering Thos, r 87 Johnston

Pickering Wm, milk dealer, head Princess

Pidgeon George, messenger customs dep't, Wellington, cor Gore

Pigiou J, piano maker, 361 Brock

Pigeon Mrs Jane (wid Nathaniel) 436 Barrie

Pigion Mrs R, ladies' furnisher, 297 Princess

Pigion Richard, gardener, cor Elm and Alfred

Pierce Mrs Margaret, 2 Gray's Lane

Pike Richard, blacksmith, Bagot

Pillar Wm, 435 Princess

Pillar Wm sr, 629 Princess

Pipe Mrs Margaret, dressmaker, 333 Queen

Pipe Wm, prop Kingston Bottling Works, 261 Princess, h 285 Princess

Piper Albert, checker G T R, 23 Wade's Lane

Pitton J, clerk, 363 Brock

Pitt Samuel, porter British American Hotel, 38 Clarence

Plant Edwin, bookkeeper, 200 Queen

Plees Mrs Kate [wid Rev Henry] 183 Division

Plunkett Isaac, laborer, old No 119 Bagot

Pogue Geo, mason, 28 Main

Pogue Robert, shoemaker, 115 Albert

Pollie Hugh, bookkeeper, bds 190 Ordnance

Pollie John, tinsmith, bds 190 Ordnance

Pollitt Frank, baker, 27 Pine
Pollitt Thos, baker, 29 Pine
Pollitt Wm, baker, r69 Earl
Polson N C [N C Polson & Co], h 317 Gordon
Polson N C & Co, druggists, 232 Princess
Pope Jno, laborer, bds 6 Quebec
Pope Thomas, shoemaker, 23 Ellice
Porter Arthur, salesman, 280 Queen
Porter Charles, storeman, 133 Bagot
Porter Frank, gardener, 42 Young
Porter Rev T G, Church of England, 136 Union
Porter John G, painter, 131 Queen
Porteous C E L, manager Bank of Montreal, res Bank
Porteous Rev Geo, 300 Gordon
Potter A, sailor, 418 Johnston
Potter H, engineer, 16 Pine
Potts John, carter, Ontario
Potts Wm, bartender, 77 Gore
Pound Geo, baker, 400 Barrie
Pound John, baker, 271 Division
Powell Charles, carpenter, 103 Picard
Powell James W, photographer, 165 Princess
Powell Mrs, 105 Picard
Power Mrs John, Montreal, cor Queen
Power J W [Power & Son] h 72 Sydenham
Power & Son, architects, Golden Lion Block, Wellington
Power T R P [Power & Son] Queen
Power William, ship builder, 64 Gore

Powers J, 131 Colborne
Powers John, laborer, end Alfred
Powley Joseph, salesman, 309 Brock
Pratt Mrs Matilda [wid James] 111 Ordnance
Prevost Z, merchant tailor & gents' furnisher, 55 Brock, h 113 Earl
Price Cornelius V, County Judge, 150 King e
Price R B, M D, Vaughn Terrace, 426 Princess
Prime Rev Frederick, rector All Saints Church, 89 York
Primo J, laborer, 261 Johnston
Prince Mrs Eliza [wid James], 258 King e
Pringle John, moulder, 217 Montreal
Prittie Thos, rope maker, 451 Princess
Pugh David John, harnessmaker, 220a Division
Pugh Fred J, salesman, Walsh & Steacy
Pugh Wm, sexton St George's, Wellington, cor Johnston
Purcell, Patrick, hairdresser, 73 Clarence
Purcell Michael, 262 Earl
Purdue John, laborer, 47 Upper William
Purdy Elijah, agent, 34 Division
Purdy Frank D, salesman, 246 Gordon
Purdy James, piano agent, 246 Gordon
Purtell John, laborer, 25 Ontario
Purtell Michael, clerk, 25 Upper Charles
Purtell Wm, blacksmith, 25 Upper Charles

Purtenn James, carter, 58 Upper Charles

Purtenn James jr, piano maker, 58 Upper Charles

Purvis Charles, traveller, 165 Clergy

Putman Harry, baker, bds 70 Princess

Pyke Miss Nellie, stenographer, 205 William

Pyman Thos, packer, 14 Ann

Pymer John, laborer, 3 Young

Pynter John, engineer, 262 Queen

Pynter Wm John, machinist, 260 Queen

Queen's University and College, Stuart, cor Arch

Quelish Stephen, plaster worker, r 87 Johnston

Quigley Jas, prop Depot House, G T R station, Montreal

Quigley Jas, engineer, 31 Upper Charles

Quigley James, laborer, 20 Johnston

Quigley Joseph, Custom House, 141 William

Quigley Thomas, laborer, 278 Sydenham

Quinliven John, laborer, 4 Anglin's Cottages, Bay

Quinn Rev John S, Roman Catholic, 225 Johnston

Quinn Mrs M, grocer, 312 King e

Quinn Mrs Maria, 282 Bagot

Quinn P J (Cousineau, Quinn & Corrigan) h 270 Wellington

Rail Frederick, mariner, Ontario

Ramsay James, Victoria

Randal Jas, sawyer, 176 Montreal

Randall Wm, mason, 24 Upper Charles

Randall G, laborer, 428 Johnston

Randalls Henry Jas, sailor, 29 Division

Randalls Richard, laborer, 97 Picard

Rankin Andrew, carter, 21 Rideau

Rathbun The Co'y, A Hoppins agent, foot Queen, and 300 King w

Rastrick E L, architect, bds 331 King e

RATTENBURY J R, dealer in Hats, Caps, and Gents' Furnishings. Laundry Work done in First-class Style, on short notice. 206 Princess, h 21 Union

Rattray J L, manager A F Brabant, h 43 Brock

Ravenscroft Walter, carter, 164 York

Raymond C Nelson, student, 293 Alfred

Rea Andrew, mariner, 200 Alfred

Rea David, laborer, 47 Division

Redden J, carpenter, Albert

Redden James, grocer, 178 Princess, h 111 Union e

Redmond Joseph, laborer, 16 Young

Redmond Martin, Bagot

Redmond Miss, 14 Bagot n

Redmond Thomas, salesman, Walsh & Steacy

Redmond William, carpenter, 198 Alfred

Rees Allan John, com traveller, 196 Queen

Rees Bros, confectioners, 177 Princess

Rees Miss, 250 Barrie

Rees C F, traveller, 224 Johnston

Rees F S, [Rees Bros], h 177 Princess

Rees Wm J L, clerk, 250 Barrie

Reeve John, hotel, 35 Brock

Reeves Daniel, engineer, 281 Montreal

Reeves Frederick, merchant, King e, h cor Gore

Reeves Robt, carter, head Princess

Reeves W, gents' furnisher, 352 King e, h King, cor Gore

Regan Mrs E (wid John) 52 O'Kill

Regan Mrs, grocer, Beverly

Regan John, guard K P, 98 William

Regan Thos, foreman, 280 Sydenham

Reid Frank C, upholsterer, 254 Princess

Reid James, furniture manufacturer and undertaker, 254-256 Princess. *(See back cover.)*

Reid James, grocer, Bay, cor Rideau

Reid James, hatter, 224 Gordon

Reid J B, architect, Brock, cor Wellington, h 94 Queen

Reid John, machinist, 94 Bay

Reid Joseph W, cabinet maker, 10 Garrett

Reid Mrs M (wid M), 430 Johnston

Reid Paul, shipwright, 35 Union

Reid R J, undertaker, 254-256 Princess, h 12 Garrett

Reid Samuel son, printer, *Whig* Office

Reid Samuel F, upholsterer, 254 Princess

Reid Wm, carter, 165 Alfred

Reid W H, butcher, King, cor Brock

Reid Wm, salesman, 639 Princess

Rendle Mrs, Victoria

Renton John L, mail clerk, 319 Gordon

Renton Mrs L (wid James), 276 Earl

Renton T T, bookkeeper, 272 Earl

Renton W J, clerk, 272 Earl

Rescorla Edwin, laborer, Victoria

Retallack E H, ledger keeper Bank Montreal, Maitland

Revell Edward, laborer, 274 Ontario

Reyner J, pianos, etc, Golden Lion Block, Wellington, h 131 Union

Reynolds Mrs Anne [wid Samuel], 321 Victoria

Reynolds Geo, sailor, 7 York

Reynolds John, moulder, Victoria

Reynolds Sampson, broom maker, 329 Victoria

Reynolds Robert, mason, end Nelson

Reynolds William, moulder, 321 Victoria

Ricard Wm E, printer, 39 Upper Bagot

Rice Miss Harriet, 69 Sydenham w

Rice Thos, laborer, 318 Barrie

Rice —, 133 Union

Richards Samuel, mason, 98 York

Richards Stephen, boilermaker, 40 York

Richardson George [Jas Richardson & Sons] 98 Gordon

J. B. PAGE & Co. Fashionable Hatters & Furriers
138 Princess Street.

ALPHABETICAL DIRECTORY. 153

Richardson Henry [Jas Richardson & Sons] 102 Stuart

Richardson James [Jas Richardson & Sons] 100 Stuart

Richardson James & Sons (Jas, Geo, Henry), grain buyers, phosphate, etc, foot Princess

Richardson Mrs Jane (wid Wm) boarding house, 62 Earl

Richardson Miss Lizzie, dressmaker, 216 Division

Richardson Miss Matilda, hair works, 108 Princess

Richardson W, carpet weaver, 208 Division

Richardson W L, cabinet maker, 263 Princess, h 432 Brock

Richmond Jas [Richmond, Orr & Co] h 17 Union

Richmond, Orr & Co, dry goods, millinery, carpets and house furnishings, 120-122 Princess

Ridout Fred, carpenter, bds 117 Ordnance

Rigg Major R A, R A, R M C, res College

Rigley James, laborer, 310 Earl

Rigney & Hickey, groceries and liquors, 136 Princess and 239 Bagot

Rigney Wm [Rigney & Hickey] h 126 Johnston

Rikley Edward, baker, 19 York

Riley James, spinner, 307 Montreal

Riley John, laborer, Picard

Riley Michael, laborer, Ontario

Risbger Thomas, 363 Division

Rivers Lieut V B, R S G, 98 Wellington

Roach Edward, laborer, Beverly

Roach John, laborer, 68 York

Roach Miss, 140 Barrie

Roach William, fireman, 39 King w

Roadly Jos, steward, 92 Earl

Robb Mrs Mary Ann [wid Alexander], 107 Wellington

Robbs James, butcher, 292 Princess

Robbs Wm, carter, 17 Balaclava

Roberts Ernest T, clerk, City Engineer's Office, 119 Barrack

Roberts Jas, laborer, Barrack

Robertson Bernard, painter, Stephen

Robertson Bros, crockery, china and glassware,187 Princess

Robertson B W, (Geo Robertson & Son), 161 Earl

Robertson D S, broker, 190 Ontario

Robertson Miss Eliza, 146 Wellington

Robertson Mrs Euphemia [wid George], Sydenham w, cor Earl

Robertson George & Son, wholesale grocers, 183 Ontario

Robertson John, tailor, Stephen

Robertson Thos McKean, (Robertson Bros), h 82 Union

Robertson Wm, blacksmith, 377 Earl

Robertson Wm J, boiler maker, 395 Division

Robinson Alex, com traveller, 75 Colborne

Robinson Alex, carpenter, 286 Princess

Robinson Alex, boiler maker, 107 King e

Robinson Bros, [Thomas D & James S], painters and paper hangers, 275-277 Bagot

SCHOOL BOOKS OF ALL KINDS
At McAuley's.

20

Robinson Andrew, watchman, 348 Division

Robinson Benj, (J G King & Co), 3 Park Place, 100 Bagot

Robinson Benj, mechanic, 75 Colborne

Robinson C, merchant tailor, 185 Wellington, h 429 Brock *(See side lines.)*

Robinson George, boat builder, King w

Robinson G W, carriage manfr, 233-35 Princess, h 247 Queen

Robinson J, painter, 88 Division

Robinson Jas, heater, 81 Queen

Robinson James, machinist, 212 Queen

Robinson James S, (Robinson Bros), h 279 Bagot

Robinson Lewis, salesman, 329 Montreal

Robinson L C, salesman, Montreal

Robinson Robert, painter, Victoria

Robinson Robert, carpenter, 25 Gordon

Robinson Robert, ship builder, 27 King w

Robinson Samuel, baker, old No 115 Bagot

Robinson Thos, clerk, 7 Ann

Robinson Thos D [Robinson Bros] h 108 Queen

Robinson Webb, builder, 28 Upper Charles

Robinson Wm, clerk Division Court, 273 Bagot, h 279 do

Robinson Wm jr, clerk customs, 123 Colborne

Robinson Wm, bartender Stanley House

Robinson W W, bookkeeper, 28 Upper Charles

Robson Geo, car inspector C P R, 5 Dunn Terrace, Bay

Rochefort Alfonse, carpenter, 35 Upper William

Rockwell J [Noxon & Rockwell] h 151 Sydenham

Rockwell W A, com traveller, Alice

Roddy Edw, carter, 131 Durham

Rogers Frank, bartender British American Hotel

Rogers Mrs J B, 60 O'Kill

Rogers R V [Kirkpatrick & Rogers] h 148 Barrie

Rogers T X, messenger Ontario Bank, res bank

Rogers W H, contractor, Albert

Rollands Mrs, 35 George

Rollinson Robt, blacksmith, 114 Picard

Rolow Jos, ship carpenter, 69 Cherry

Ronan T, undertaker, 244 Bagot

Roney A F [Roney & VanLuven] h 175 Montreal

Roney Henry, old 107 Bagot

Roney James, ship carpenter, 12 Charles

Roney Miss Norah, dressmaker, 217 Montreal

Roney Miss Susan, dressmaker, 12 Charles

Roney & VanLuven [A F Roney, A P VanLuven] props Grand Union Clothing Store, 122 Princess

Rooney Benhard, stonemason, 284 Sydenham

Rooney Patrick, 284 Sydenham

Rooney Timothy, r 87 Johnston

Root Chas, signal man G T R, 44 Grove

Roothame G T, bds Lake's, Brock

Rose Mrs Catharine (wid Alex) 161 Sydenham

Rose R M, Co'y registrar, 170 Barrie

Roseau Joseph, carpenter, 70 Ontario

Ross Alex, staple and fancy dry goods, millinery, carpets, & oilcloths, 128-130 Princess, h 238 Johnston

Ross Prof Donald, Queen's University, 185 Queen

Ross Mrs J B [wid Walter] 317 Earl

Rothwell C G, clerk, 207 William

Rothwell H C, mariner, 207 William

Rourke C, stovefitter, 17 Young

Rourke Owen, laborer, 24 Earl

Rourke Peter, laborer, 42 Elm

Roushorn Almond, old No 121 Bagot

Rousseau Edward, laborer, 107 Ordnance

Routley John, dealer in sporting goods, 173 Princess

Routley W K, tobacconist, 173 Princess

Rowan R F, civil engineer, 297 Barrie

Rowan R F F, laundry, 190 Wellington, h 247 Brock

Rowatt ——, foreman, 208 Gordon

Rowcroft Samuel, spinner, 246 Montreal

Rowe Charles, carpenter, 214 Bagot

Rowe Ernest, clerk, 36 Elm

Rowe Robert K, school teacher, r164 Bagot

Rowe Wyman, laborer, 361 Alfred

Rowland Fleming, collector inland revenue, Mozart Place, 160 Earl

Roy Richard, tailor, 245 Queen

Rubery Patrick, laborer, Wellington

Rudd T G, merchant, 146 Johnston

Runians N E, grocer, 242 Princess

Rushford Alexander, mariner, 90 Ontario

Rushford Alexander, engineer, 65 Queen

Rushford James, laborer, old No 106 Bagot

Russell Ed, bds Stanley House

Russell John, grocer, 189 Clergy

Russell John, salesman, 189 Clergy

Rutherford C, stove mounter, 379 Brock

Rutherford J, carpenter, 382 Johnston

Rutherford Jas, guard K P, 7 Pembroke

Rutherford Mrs Jane (wid Thos), 192 Colborne

Rutherford John, grinder, r286 Division

Rutherford Robt, blacksmith, 270 Division

Rutherford T, moulder, 391 Johnston

Ruttan Henry M, bookkeeper, 183 Brock

Ryan Andrew, saddler, 219 Princess

Ryan Mrs C [wid J] 257 Johnston

Ryan Mrs Eliza [wid John], 11 York

Ryan John, laborer, 3 Wellington Terrace, Montreal

Ryan John, carpenter, 2 Quebec

Ryan Wm Jos, fitter, 22 Wade's Lane

Ryan Patrick, laborer, Newman's Cottages, King w

Ryan W F, laborer, 25 Wade's Lane

Ryder John, laborer, Patrick

Rynard Mrs, 220 Barrie

St George's Hall, Wellington, cor Johnston

St John Mrs Rosette, 270 Sydenham

St Lawrence Hotel, Elder Bros, props, King e, cor Queen

St Thomas John, laborer, 11 Ontario

Sabas Rev Bro, Christian Brothers' School, 89 Clergy

Salcy Mrs Harriet (wid Martin) 27 Ontario

Salsbury Benj, laborer, Victoria

Salter Joseph, auctioneer, &c, 58 Brock and 288 Princess

Salvation Army, Major Wm Woolley, divisional officer, res Barracks

Sammon Isaac, laborer, 2 Adelaide

Sands Henry, hide buyer, 144 Montreal

Sands John, 13 Colborne

Sands J S [J S Sands & Son] h 13 Colborne

Sands J S & Son [J S and W C] merchant tailors, 171 Wellington

Sands Thomas, shoveller, 438 King e

Sands Thomas, grain shoveller, Ordnance

Sands W C [J S Sands & Son] h 50 Clergy

Sangster C, 358 Brock

Sangster Wm, baker, 275 Queen

Sargent F R, accountant, 28 Frontenac

Sarsfield Geo, boots and shoes, 107 Princess, h 9 Upper Bagot

Saunders B, laborer, 50 Elm

Saunders Edward, prop Dublin House, 144 Ontario

Saunders Hy, carpenter, 98 Pine

Saunders H J, M D, M R C S, Eng, coroner, 214 King e

Saunders Jas, butcher, bds 214 Colborne

Saunders James G, butcher, 348 Gordon

Saunders Mrs Jane (wid Rev J C) 246 King e

Saunders John, butcher, 338 Princess, h 730 do

Saunders John, laborer, head Princess

Saunders John, mariner, 251 Queen

Saunders John, laborer, 46 Earl

Saunders John O, laborer, Beverley

Saunders Robert, laborer, head Princess

Saunders William, tinsmith, 101 Chatham

Saunders Wm, salesman, 101 Chatham

Savage Brothers [Henry B and Thomas] painters and dealers in wall paper, 78 William

Savage Henry B [Savage Bros] h 76 William

Savage John, 79 York

Savage Thos [Savage Bros], h 80 William

Savage W J, painter, 18 Vine

Sawberry Sam'l, laborer, Picard

Sawyer A O, salesman, 334 Brock

Sawyer John, painter. 72 Earl
Sawyer W A, salesman, 72 Earl
Sawyer Wm, artist, 72 Earl
Scales Thos, M D, 20 George
Scanlan Mrs Ellen [wid Patrick], 206 Montreal
Scanlan John, printer, John n
Scanlan Mrs, 101 Albert
Scanlan Wm, printer, old No 88 Bagot
Schermerhorn Charles, mason, 416 Johnston
Schonfieldt Henry, spinner, Collingwood
Scholfield James, baker, 370 Princess
Schroder John, pork butcher,78 Brock
Schultz Solomon, carpenter, Corrigan
Scobell F R, 95 York
Scobell Mrs Mary [wid Sydney], bds 53 Clergy
Scobell S W, accountant K P, 288 Barrie
Scott Charles, plasterer, 448 Division
Scott D, clerk, 315 Johnston
Scott Mrs E (wid R) 255 Johnston
Scott James, laborer, 72 Ontario
Scott Mrs James, 14 Johnston
Scott Nathaniel K, traveller, 51 Clergy
Scott Thos, baker, 27 Division
Scott W, carpenter, 318 Brock
Scott Capt Wm, mariner, 283 Wellington
Scouse J, painter, 267 Johnston
Scouton Levy, carpenter, 152 Pine
Scrivens J, carpenter, Victoria
Scrutton Edmund, laborer, Orchard

Scrutton James, teamster, 8 Quebec
Seale C, laborer, 316 Quebec
Seale John, carpenter, Picard
Seale Wm, 30 Frontenac
Sears Mrs Ester (wid Alonzo) Patrick
Sears George [J Muckleston & Co] h 38 Clergy
Seaton Richard, laborer, 133 Queen
Seeley David, carpenter, 274 Ontario
Selby Charles, blacksmith, Victoria
Self S, laborer, 289 Earl
Sellars Robt, J P, 201 Queen
Shales Robert J, blacksmith, old No 125, Bagot
Shanahan John, laborer, 41 Young
Shanahan John, Ocean Saloon, 298 King e
Shanahan Miss Mary Ann, huckster, 91 Rideau
Shanahan William, Terrapin Hotel, 76 Princess
Shangrow Peter, ship carpenter, 292 Barrie
Shangrow W Peter, laundryman, 292 Barrie
Shannessy Mrs Mary, 50 Rideau
Shannon James, Postmaster, 47 George
Shannon James, carter, Albert
Shannon L W, publisher *Daily News*, 47 George
Shannon R W, M A, barrister, 297 King e, h 47 George
Shannon Samuel, clerk, 281 Queen
Shannon Wm, 281 Queen
Sharman Mrs Jacob, 187 Ordnance

Horseshoe Island. Boats twice a day each way. Liquor prohibited from being sold.

Sharman Thomas N, boat builder, etc, foot Simcoe. (See advt.)

Sharow Adolphus, blacksmith, 22 James

Sharpe A B, machinist, 331 Brock

Sharpe Alex, storekeeper, 51 Union

Sharp Chas, grocer, 44 Colborne

Sharp Daniel, sailor, 1 Division

Sharp Mrs Elizabeth (wid Andrew) grocer, 64 Ontario

Sharp Harry, grocer, 286 Princess, h 44 Colborne

Sharp John, student, 285 Sydenham

Sharp Joseph, rag dealer, 132 Clarence, h 362 Brock

Shaw A, surveyor customs, 190 Gordon

Shaw Mrs A (wid John) 135 William

Shaw Alex, salesman, 301 Alfred

Shaw F & Co, dry goods and carpets, 174 Princess. (See top lines)

Shaw Felix [F Shaw & Co] h 113 Bagot

Shaw James, 301 Alfred

Shaw James jr, clerk, 301 Alfred

Shaw J D G, teller Bank Montreal, bds British American Hotel

Shaw Jos, laborer, Ordnance

Shaw Robert, barrister, 332 King e, h 128 Bagot

Shaw J Morgan [H Skinner & Co] h 303 Barrie

Shaw Samuel, baker, 288 Earl

Shaw Samuel, carter, 291 Earl

Shaver James, laborer, Patrick

Shaver Wm, fireman K & P Ry, Bagot

Shea Mrs Margaret (wid Michael) Bagot

Shea Michael, mariner, bds 238 Ontario

Shea Wm, keeper Asylum, 29 Arch

Shean Dan'l, laborer, 27 Ontario

Shedden The Co (Geo Young, agent) cartage agents, foot of William

Sheldon & Davis, photographers, 334 King e

Shepherd John, Court House keeper, res Court House

Sherbino Robt, carpenter, 236 Alfred

Sheridan Bernard, grocer, 235 Wellington

Sherlock J M, merchant tailor, 225 Princess, h 254 Queen

Sherlock J M, jr, pianos and organs, 281 Princess, h 254 Queen

Sherman James F, clerk, 33 Colborne

Sherman W E, clerk, Wellington

Sherratt Mrs Anna (wid S O) 338 Montreal

Sherwood James, cabman, 35 King w

Sherwood Sherman, laborer, bds 6 Quebec

Shibley Henry T, B A, barrister, 44 Clarence, h 94 Bagot

Shibley Schuyler, 94 Bagot

Shook Edward, 18 Up Charles

Shook Henry, grocer, 212 Montreal

Shore Loynes & Co, grocers, Princess, cor Montreal (See top lines.)

Shorey E C, chemist, bds 266 Princess

F. SHAW & CO.'S DRESS GOODS
PLEASE THE MOST FASTIDIOUS.

Shortt Adam, prof, Queen's University, 63 West

Shortt Mrs E Smith, M D, 63 West

Short Rev W, First Methodist Church, 308 Johnston

Shufflebotham Walter, quarry owner, 466 Montreal

Siddall Joseph, mariner, 154 Rideau

Silver Benjamin, clothier, 93 Princess

Siler John, machinist, 196 Colborne

Simmonds A D, book collector, stationer, etc, 208 Princess, h 142 Ordnance

Simmonds Capt Wm, mariner, 145 Montreal

Simmonds W J, salesman, 142 Ordnance

Simons Mrs A, [wid J], 300 Brock

Simmons Alfred, Kingston Candle Works, Livingston ave

Simmons Jacob, carpenter, Bagot

Simmons John, salesman, 145 Montreal

Simmons Mars, carpenter, 25 Rideau

Simpson Archibald, hotel keeper, 286 Ontario

Simpson Bernard, carpenter, 4 Rideau

Simpson Isaac, J P, private banker, 93 Clarence, h 132 King e

Simpson Mrs Jane (wid James) Markland

Sinclair John, laborer, Collingwood

Sinclair Robert, teamster, 86 Frontenac

Sine Arnold, fancy goods and branch office G N W Tel Co, 202 Princess, h 187 Clergy

Sine M W, Veterinary Surgeon, 155 Brock

Singer Manufacturing Co, J Laishley, manager, 213 Princess

Singleton Thos, laborer, 26 York

Sinnott Miles, cabman, 41 King w

Sinnot Mrs Mary (wid John) 32 Johnston

Sinnott Thomas, cab driver, 34 Johnston

Sissons Wm, laborer, 30 Charles

Skeggs Jos, laborer, cor Gordon

Skelton Anthony, laborer, 480 Montreal

Skinner Henry & Co, wholesale druggists and importers, 171 Princess

Skinner James A, finisher, 23 Union

SKINNER J S, B A, Barrister, Solicitor, Notary, etc. 81 Brock, cor Wellington, h 13 Maitland.

Skinner Will B, druggist, 171 Princess

Skinner Wm [Henry Skinner & Co] h 9 Wellington

Slater Thos, laborer, 5 Cherry

Slavin Jas [Slavin & Mackin] h Gore

Slavin & Mackin [Jas Slavin, Arthur Mackin] tailors, 175 Wellington

Sleeman Wm H, plasterer, 158 Frontenac

FOR BOOKS AND STATIONERY
TRY McAULEY'S BOOKSTORE.

Sleeth James, mason, 304 Johnston

Sleeth Samuel, bds 70 Princess

Slimmons John, fireman K & P R'y, Montreal

Sloan Alexander, laborer, 293 Montreal

Sloan Bros (Thos & John) props City Hotel, 129 Princess

Sloan, David, billiardist, City Hotel

Sloan J, painter, 323 Johnston

Sloan Robt, engineer, King e

Sly Alex, blacksmith, 32 James

Sly Franklin, carpenter, 32 James

Small Philip, policeman, 193 Alfred

Smalbridge Geo, carpenter, 159 Alfred

Smalbridge William, mason, 320 Earl

Smart John, laborer, 276 Wellington

Smeaton Charles, currier, 40 Picard

Smeaton J R, grocer, 59 King w

Smeaton Thomas, tanner, 21 Charles

Smilie John, watchman, 118 Picard

Smyth A J, salesman, 128 Johnston

Smyth Alex, harbor master, 128 Johnston

Smith A T, local manager Bell Telephone Co, 49 Colborne

Smith Bros (Charles & John), watchmakers, 345 King e, h 125 Bagot

Smith Rev Buxton B, curate St George's Church, Bagot, cor Gore

Smith C F, (Smythe, Smith & Lyon), 56 William

Smith Miss Anne, 86 Division

Smith Arch, laborer, 188 Barrie

Smith Charles, painter, Anne, cor Stephen

Smith Daniel, ragman, 38 Upper Charles

Smith Edward, machinist, 99 Chatham

Smith Edward jr, machinist, 99 Chatham

Smythe E H, Q C, LL D, [Smythe, Smith & Lyon], h 3 Westbourne Terrace, 59 West

Smith Mrs Eliza [wid John], 149 Colborne

Smith Miss Etta, school teacher, 125 Bagot

Smith Frederick, clerk water works dep't, 84 Ontario

Smith George, 428 Princess

Smith Geo, com traveller, bds 125 Bagot

Smith H, laborer, 65 York

Smith Henry, laborer, 50 Division

Smith Lieut-Col H R, 14th Batt, "Ringwood," King w

Smith H Stalleraffe, bookbinder, 43 Brock, h 65 Gore

Smith Isaac, carpenter, Victoria

Smith J, laborer, 439 Barrie

Smith Capt James, mariner, 55 William

Smith Jas, mason, 6 Quebec

Smith Jas, carpenter, 49 Bay

Smith Jas, 85 Division

Smith John, book and job printer, 153 Wellington, h 337 Johnston

Smith John G, teamster, Gore

Smith Joseph, laborer, 146 Bay

Smith Joseph A B, merchant tailor, etc, 259 King e

Smith Miss M, dressmaker, 184 Wellington

Smith M, deputy sheriff, 830 Brock

Smith Mrs Margaret (wid Jno), 62 Colborne

Smith Mrs Mary, 134 Clarence

Smith Mrs Mary (wid Patrick) 84 Ontario

Smith Mrs Mary (wid Robt) 97 Wellington

Smith Patrick, engineer G T R, Park, G T R station

Smith Robt, teamster, 56 Albert

Smith Samuel, teamster, old No 128 Bagot

Smith Samuel, spinner, Stephen

Smythe, Smith & Lyon, (E H Smythe, Q C, LL D, C F Smith, H V Lyon, B A), barristers, 192 Ontario

Smith Thomas, carpenter, bds Windsor Hotel

Smith Rev D Thomas, 518 Princess

Smith W C, clerk, 122 Clarence

Smith Wm, laborer, 50 Bagot u

Smyth Wm S, clerk P O, 136 Johnston

Snider Damon, laborer, 71 Cherry

Snyder J, whitewasher, 370 Brock

Snider Jehiah, carpenter, 243 Montreal

Snodden Alex, policeman, 178 Alfred

Snook T L, barrister, Ontario, cor Clarence

Snowden William, mason, 234 Gordon

Soles Venandus, currier, Grove

Somerville Frank, engineer, 195 Colborne

Somerville Frank, carpenter, McAuley's Cottages, Dufferin

Sommerville Fred, salesman, 195 Colborne

Somerville George, mariner, 55 Earl

Somerville Mrs Jane (wid Alex), 55 Earl

Sowards James, wood and coal merchant, n s Place de Armes, cor Ontario

Sowards James, Maple Leaf Hotel, 240 Montreal

Spafford Arch, Albion Hotel, Montreal, cor Queen

Spangenberg F W, jeweller and watchmaker, 347 King e, h 36 Wellington

Spankie Wm, 716 Princess

Sparks R E, dentist, 230 Princess, h 132 Gordon

Spence & Crumley [D M Spence and E Crumley] dry goods, millinery and mantles, 132-134 Princess. (See advt front cover)

Spence D M [Spence & Crumley] h 132 Princess

Spence John, laborer, 12 Upper William

Spence John, currier, River, n side

Spence R A, carpenter, 170 Queen

Spence Wm, grocer, cor Gordon and Johnston

Spencer Rev A, clerical secretary Synod Diocese of Ontario, St George's Hall, h 186 Queen

Spencer Mrs Jane (wid Abraham) 290 Montreal

Spencer L B, prop paint works, 104 Bagot

Spencer Lewis, boilermaker, 6 Rideau

Spencer Mrs Maria (wid Robt) 8 Redan

Spencer R, merchant tailor, 79 Brock, h Balaclava, cor Redan

Spencer Robert, cutter, Balaclava, cor Redan

Spenceley A J, blacksmith, 325 Johnston

Spriggs H J, librarian Mechanics Institute, 64 Arch

Spooner Edward, carpenter, 206 Alfred

Spooner Frank, carpenter, 10 Ann

Spooner John, ship carpenter, 289 Wellington

Spotten Mrs Mary (wid George) r 127 Montreal

Spottswood G A, St Nicholas Club, 186 Wellington

Sproule John, laborer, Ontario

Squire Mrs Hattie (wid Geo H) 79 Division

Stacey James, manager *Daily News*, 335 Division

Stacey John, gardener, 207 Alfred

Stackhouse A, L D S, dentist, Bagot, cor Princess

Stackhouse J H, dental student, Bagot, cor Princess

Stafford Jas, carriagemaker, 379 Division

Stafford R, messenger Bank B N A, res bank

Stagg John, laborer, 18 Elm

Staley Chas D, caretaker dry dock office, 30 Union

Staley Henry, musician, 78 York

Stanford Mrs Mary (wid Thos) 79 Bay

Staley Horatio, painter, 82 Queen

Staley Martin, hotel, Barrack, cor Wellington

Staley Morton B, carpenter, 101 King

Stallard Mrs Sarah (wid James) Corrigan

Stanley Thomas, laborer, n side Cataraqui

Stansbury John, driver, 441 Barrie

Steacy Edward T [Walsh & Steacy] h 197 Johnston

Steacey James, traveller, 316 Barrie

Steacy J J, salesman, 197 Johnston

Stearne Philip, fur dealer, 223 King e

Steel John, carpenter, 31 Main

Stethem W J, buyer, King, cor George

Stephens Willard, mariner, 85 Pine

Stevenson A W, Steward, 359 Brock

Stevenson & Co, piano manfrs, Princess, corner Ontario

Stevenson H S, [Stevenson & Co], h 58 William

Stevenson Mrs Margaret [wid John], r 91 Earl

Stevenson Robert, tinsmith, Orchard

Stevenson Thos, bookkeeper, 47 Rideau

Stewart Alex, hotel, lower station G T R, Montreal

Stewart Colin, telegraph operator, G T R, 283 Montreal

Stewart John, watchman, 123 Picard

Stewart James, agent K & M Forwarding Co, bds British American Hotel

Stewart John, M D, 309 Barrie

Stewart Joseph, carpenter, 630 Princess

Stewart Wm, station master K & P Ry, Barrack

Stigney Thos, laborer, Barrack

Stigney William, laborer, 434 King e

Stinson Mrs Daniel, 250 Montreal

Stirling Miss Lizzie, 141 King e

Stitt Gilbert, blacksmith, 34 Union e

Stoba Mrs E, 108 Earl

Stokes Benj, teamster, 22 Place d'Armes

Storey Edgar, carpenter, 304 Barrie

Stoughton Miss, 4 Hales' Cottages, King w

Stover Hiram, laborer, Victoria

Stowell H F, artist, 43 Brock

Strachan David, blacksmith, 81 Queen

Strachan Arch, hardware, Princess, cor Montreal, h 98 Bagot

Strachan Gordon, mason, Upper Victoria

Strachan Jas, carpenter, Upper Victoria

Strachan John, broom maker, Upper Victoria

Strachan Martin, sawmill owner, 95 Queen

Strachan Mrs Nellie (wid Martin D) 178 Clergy

Strachan Mrs Sarah (wid John) 248 Division

Strachan Thos, blacksmith, 81 Queen

Strachan John, Upper Victoria

Strange Frank, clerk, 34 Barrie

Strange J M [Dalton & Strange] h 172 King e

Strange John, barrister, 95 Clarence, h 34 Barrie

Strange Capt M W, 95 Clarence, h 34 Barrie

Strange Orland S, M D, 156 King e

Strange & Strange, insurance agents, 95 Clarence

Strainge William, grocer, 149 Montreal

Stratford Mrs H, grocer, 284 Princess

Stratford Henry, taxidermist, 354 Princess

Stratford Henry, carpenter, 144 Pine

Strathy James B, Emily

Stratton Ira, teacher, Kingston Business College Co, Wellington

Stretch Wm, sewing machine agent, Barrack

Strong Anthony, machinist, Bagot

Strong W O, engineer in charge public works, bds at British American Hotel

Stroud Bros, T B Hawley manager, teas and coffees, 109 Princess

Stroud W, Sergt-Major R S G

Stunden Fred, clerk Windsor Hotel

Sturgess Manuel, carter, 334 Montreal

Suddard Edward, laborer, 22 Elm

Suddard James, carter, 122 Montreal

Suddard John, laborer, 36 Main

Suddard John, 22 Elm

Sughrue John, laborer, 33 Johnston

Sullivan Miss Annie, 11 Arch

Sullivan Mrs Catharine (wid Hugh) 225 Wellington

Sullivan Mrs Catharine (wid Michael) 169 Montreal

Sullivan Dennis, old 126 Bagot

Sullivan Mrs Eliza [wid M] grocer, Ontario

Sullivan Mrs Jane [wid Roger] grocer, 94 Gore

Sullivan Jeremiah, laborer, old 50 Bagot

Sullivan John, laborer, 407 Barrie

Sullivan Hon M, M D, Princess, cor King

Sullivan Michael, carpenter, 167 Montreal

Sullivan Miss, dressmaker, 295 Princess

Sullivan W H, barrister, 36 Clarence, h 89 William

Sullivan William, engineer, 72 William

Sutherland Alex, boots & shoes, 103 Princess, h 4 Victoria Terrace, Montreal

Sutherland Miss Annie M, 193 Gordon

Sutherland Jas T, bookkeeper, 4 Victoria Terrace, Montreal

Sutherland J, clerk, 295 Barrie

Sutherland John H, salesman, 4 Victoria Terrace, Montreal

Sutherland Malcolm S [Fenwick, Hendry & Co], h 55 West

Sutherland R, shoemaker, 105 Princess

Sutherland Samuel, com traveller, 11 Colborne

Swain John C, carpet weaver, 140 York

Swane Mrs M, [wid J], 314 Johnston

Swales Mrs Jane [wid Wm] 265 Gordon

Swan Geo T, grocer, 27 Ellice

Swan Samuel D, machinist, 47 Elm

Swauston A, baker, 356 and 258 Princess

Swanston Mrs Harriett, 294 Johnston

Sweetman, John, laborer, end Montreal

Sweetman Thomas, laborer, G T R station, Montreal

Swift James, (James Swift & Co), h 140 King

Swift James & Co, wharfingers, commission and coal merchants, foot Johnston

Swift John, machinist, 242 Barrie

Swift Joseph F, general agent King, cor Clarence, h 44 William

Swift Mrs, 224 King e

Swindlehurst William, weaver, Rideau

Switzer Fletcher, boarding, 288 Queen

Switzer Nelson, 170 Bagot

Switzer Peter, laborer, lower 63 Queen

Sykes Alexander V, tanner, 200 Rideau

Sykes Victory, tanner, 200 Rideau

Tait Joseph, mason, 37 Upper Charles

Tait Joseph, plasterer, 21 Ellice

Tallon John, section boss G T R, 675 Montreal

Talbot Miss E, 251 Victoria

Tandy Mrs M J [wid Wm] 201 Brock

Tarrant James A, carpenter, 8 Ann

Tarrant John, carpenter, 209 Alfred

Tassell Mrs Elizabeth [wid R] 220 Johnston

Taylor A D [Murray & Taylor] 133 William

Taylor Edward J, machinist, 95 Picard

Taylor Mrs Eliza [wid John] Bagot

Taylor F D, ledger-keeper Ontario Bank, 230 Wellington

Taylor Geo, barber, 34 Upper William

Taylor Henry [Nugent & Taylor] h 361 Johnston

Taylor J H, secondhand dealer, 238 Barrie

Taylor J H, asst supt K & P R, 54 Johnston

Taylor John, laborer, 425 Division

Taylor Jno, jr, engineer, 18 Ellice

Taylor Jno A, carter, 8 Ellice

Taylor Jos, steamboat inspector, 63 George

Taylor Mrs Mary [wid John] 82 Division

Taylor Mrs P [wid J R] 430 Brock

Taylor Samuel, machinist, 26 Stuart

Taylor Thos F, marine inspector, 77 Arch

Taylor W R, jr, salesman, 75 Arch

Taylor Capt William R, jr, 241 Queen

Telgmann Miss Agnes, music teacher, 1 Victoria Terrace, Montreal

Tenney John W, laborer, Victoria

Tetlock John, salesman, Picard

Tetlock John, carpenter, Picard

Tetro Michael, laborer, 37 Wellington

Tetro Michael D, engineer, 37 Wellington

Thacker N G, clerk Bank Montreal, Maitland

Theobald J M, hairdresser, 167 Wellington

Theobald Geo E, painter, Victoria

Thibodeau Augustus, 22 Ontario

Tholst Wm, laborer, 1 Albert

Thomas John, mason, 16 Cowdy

Thomas Samuel, plasterer, 272 Queen

Thompson Alexander, ship carpenter, Ontario

Thompson Alex, salesman, bds Albermarle House

Thompson Andrew, carpenter, 279 Sydenham

Thomson David, grocer, 83 Earl

Thompson Francis, mariner, 190 Sydenham

Thompson Geo, ship carpenter, r 35 Wellington

Thompson Geo, collector, 284 Johnston

Thompson James, salesman, bds Union Hotel

Thompson J Duncan, Mayor City of Kingston, 22 Colborne

Thompson Robert, knitter, 400 Division

Thompson Robert, porter City Hotel

Thompson Robert, wholesale liquors, 45 Clarence

Thomson Robert, cashier, 308 Gordon

Thomson Mrs Susan (wid Adam) 173 Sydenham

Thompson Thomas, guard K P, 85 Frontenac

Thompson, Thomas J, student, 85 Frontenac

Thompson Timothy, salesman, Walsh & Steacy

Thompson Wm, freight agent G T R, foot William, h 308 Gordon

Thompson Wm, ship carpenter, Ontario

Thompson ——, 254 King e

Thornton E, prop Union Hotel, Ontario, cor Brock

Thornton Mrs Mary [wid A], 2 First

Thornton John, grocer, cor Chatham and Princess

Thurston Henry, engineer, 92 Barrack

Tierney Bros [Owen and John] grocers, 25 Brock

Tierney James, grocer, 261 Ontario, h 380 Barrie

Tierney John [Tierney Bros] h 86 Queen

Tierney Owen [Tierney Bros] h Johnston, cor Clergy

Tilson Robert, fireman, 358 Montreal

Timberlake Rev Wm, pastor 3d Methodist Church, 1 Barnstaple Terrace, Clergy

Timmerman Nicholas, policeman, Victoria

Titus Geo, mariner, Union e

Toban Michael, dyer, 38 Union

Toby —, laborer, r35 Wellington

Toland Mrs Mary (wid John) 353 Princess

Tooher Thos, grocer, 312 Montreal

Torkington Wm, turnkey jail, 78 Ontario

Towers William, laborer, 279 King e

Townsend Wm, carpenter, 836 Princess

Townsend Wm H, bricklayer, Victoria

Toye R H, baker and confectioner, 302 King e, h 82 Gore

Tracy Francis, trade instructor K P, 21 Division

Tracy Frank, jr, tinsmith, 21 Division

Tracy Wm, basket maker, 21 Division

Treneer John, carter, 220 Earl

Trenheill Mrs Eliza (wid Benj) Barrack

Trowell Capt John, mariner, 122 Wellington

Truesdell Walter, carpenter, 46 James

Tucker J, mason, 347 Brock

Tucker Thos, laborer, North

Turbett Jno, grocer, 228 Barrie

Turcott Alpheus, ship carpenter, 83 Division

Turcott Augustus, 83 Division

Turcott Geo, car builder, Quebec

Turcott J, Plum

Turcott Jno, laborer, 35 Young

Turnbull Thomas, laborer, 21 Arch

Turnbull Thos, engineer, King w

Turner Jas, laborer, 13 Upper William

Turner Mrs, 103 Wellington

Turpin Henry G, carter, 29 Bagot

Turpin Mrs Jane [wid Henry], 335 Queen

Tuttle Isaac, lumberman, Beverly

Tuttle John, policeman, 107 Stuart

Tweddell John, merchant tailor, 131 Princess, h 102 Queen

Tweed Thos, grocer, 47 Arch

Tweed Wm, painter, 76 York

Twigg Jno, laborer, 29 Gordon

Twigg John E, clerk, 27 Lower Gordon

Twinkler Miss, 212 Sydenham

Twiss Francis, carter, 117 Barrack

Twitchell M H, Consul United States, h 26 Wellington

Twohey Mrs, 207 Gordon

Tyner Mrs Anne (wid Wm) 252 Gordon

Tyo Stephen, mariner, 14 Redan

Tyo Stephen, jr, mariner, 336 Montreal

Tyson Hy, laborer, 140 Colborne

Union Hotel, E Thornton, prop, Ontario, cor Brock

United States Consulate, M H Twitchell, Consul, 196 Ontario

Upham Wm, conductor G T R, G T R station, Montreal

Upper Joseph, King e

Urquhart Archibald, com traveller, 1 Wellington Terrace, Montreal

Vail John, laborer, r 170 Bagot

Valdock J G, guard K P, Livingston ave

Vanalstine Alex, Queen's hotel, 127 Brock

Vanarnam C A, confectioner, 350 King e

Vanasky A, laborer, 305 Brock

Varauld Mrs Margaret (wid John) 23 Ontario

Vance James, laborer, 68 North

Vanderwater R W, pianos and organs, 188 Wellington, h 43 George

Vanhooser John, moulder, 50 James

Vanluven Charles, miller, Dufferin

VanLuven Thos F, co treasurer, head Princess

Varney Richard, foundryman, 25 King w

Van Straubenzie Capt A H, R M C, res College

VanTassel Wm A, manager Haines & Lockett, bds Hotel Frontenac

Vanwinkle Jacob, carpenter, 199 Colborne

Vanwinkle Nial, carpenter, 117 Ordnance

Veal Elijah, baker, 628 Princess

Veal John, baker, 198 Barrie

Verbeck Edward, dyer, 266 Earl

Verbeck Leon, electrician, 182 Rideau

Vick David, carpenter, Stephen

Villard Ernest, laborer, Collingwood

Vince William, engineer water works, 19 Ontario

Victoria Foundry, Chown & Cunningham, props, King, cor Queen

Virtue Wm [Bibby & Virtue], h 337 Division

Virtue Mrs Ann [wid Matthew] 337 Division

Voight H C, accountant, 226 Johnston

Volume Jasme, shoemaker, 59 Elm

Waddell D A, harness maker, 83 Princess, h 287 Wellington

Waddell John, contractor, 221 Division

Waddell John, M A, Ph D, R M C, 132 Wellington

Waddell J F, saddler, 249 Division

Waddell Robt, Wellington Place, 82 Wellington

Wade Fred, salesman, 9 Wellington

Wade F C, drug clerk, 89 Gore

Wade Henry, druggist, King, cor Brock, h 89 Gore

Wade Mrs Mary [wid Henry] 89 Gore

Wade Thos V, cabinet maker, Wellington, h 89 Gore

WADDINGTON BROS, (Wm George and Henry) wholesale and retail dealers in Beef, Mutton, Pork, Smoked Tongues, Bologna and other Sausages, Hams, Lard, etc. Venison in season a specialty, 322 King e

Wafer Peter, 112 Ordnance

Waggoner John, Albermarle Hotel, 22-24 Market Sq

Wah Long, laundry, 88 Clarence

Waldie A, gen agent Confederation Life, 111 Wellington

Waldren George, broom maker, 222 Division

Waldron Richard, dry goods, Wellington, cor Brock, h 80 Barrie

Waldron R S, salesman, 80 Barrie

Waldren W M, salesman, 222 Division

Wales Robert, 119 William

Walkem J B [Walkem & Walkem] h 40-foot road, Tp Kingston

Walkem R T, Q C, [Walkem & Walkem], h 72 Barrie

Walkem & Walkem, [R T Walkem, Q C, J B Walkem], barristers, 93 Clarence

Walker Charles, bar tender, 35 York

Walker D J, county clerk, 205 Colborne

Walker Duncan, blacksmith, 21 Pine

Walker Mrs Ellen, 286a Division

Walker Herbert, machinist, 88 Wellington

Walker Mrs Jane [wid John], 62 Arch

Walker John, salesman, 205 Upper Colborne

Walker J S, clerk, 220 Queen

Walker Marcus, laborer, 398 Montreal

Walker Mrs Robert, 232 Sydenham

Walker ——, 35 Main

Wallace Ernest, painter, Ann, cor Stephen

Wallace Mrs Marie [wid Andrew], 92 Division

Wallace William, fireman, 206 William

Waller Geo, laborer, 22 Cowdy

Walsh Arthur, salesman, 118 Colborne

Walsh Edwin, [Lambert & Walsh], 118 Colborne

Walsh George W, loom fixer, 2 Montreal

Walsh J, tobacconist, 179 Wellington

Walsh James, porter British American Hotel, 57 Arch

Walsh John, 3 Barnstaple Terrace, Clergy

Walsh John J, 76 Gore

Splendid Value in Black & Colored Henriettas at Shaw's

ALPHABETICAL DIRECTORY. 169

Walsh Lawrence, guard K P, 23 Division
Walsh Michael, butcher, 314 King e
Walsh Miss, 55 King w
Walsh Patrick, coal and wood dealer, Barrack, cor Ontario
Walsh Patrick J [Walsh & Steacy] h 3 Barnstaple Terrace, Clergy
Walsh & Steacy [Patrick J Walsh and Edward T Steacy] dry goods and carpets, 106-108 Princess
Walter William, laborer, 375 Division
Waltham Wm, umbrella repairer, 181 Clergy
Wandell Mrs, Victoria
Ward George, lumberman, 182 Victoria
Ward Hy, painter, 134 Victoria
Ward John (John Ward & Co) h 162 Johnston
Ward John, salesman, bds 27 Brock
Ward John, laborer, Bagot
Ward John & Co, grocers, 341-43 Princess
Ward Owen, laborer, Bagot
Ward Presley, blacksmith, 14 Wade's Lane
Ward Thos, sailor, Bagot
Ward Wm, engineer, 41 James
Wartman R, mason, 322 Brock
Wartman Mrs S J [wid Horace] 371 Princess
Warwick Chas J, carpenter, 86 Arch
Waterbury W B, accountant, Merchants Bank
Waters John, baker, 33 Rideau
Waters John, knitting mill, 89 King w

Waters John, baker, Bagot
Watkins George, Victoria
Watson Alexander, laborer, 74 Ontario
Watson Benj, 250 Gordon
Watson George C, tailor, 226 Gordon
Watson Henry B, machinist, 19 West
Watson John, M A, LL D, professor Queen's College, res College
Watts James, shoemaker, 234 Wellington
Watts John, laborer, 230 Wellington
Watts William, gardener, Victoria
Way Daniel, agent, 473 Princess
Weaver S, fancy goods and picture framing, 125 Princess, h 136 Queen
Weaver Saul D, clerk, 136 Queen
Weber G M, piano maker, 360 Johnston
Weber Piano Factory, E J B Pense, prop, cor Gordon and Princess
Webster W A, emigrant agent, 106 Stuart
Webster & Co, miners, 43 Brock
Weir John, laborer, Rideau
Weir Mrs M (wid W) 470 Brock
Wemp John, laborer, old 120 Bagot
Wemp Mrs Mary, dressmaker, 120 Bagot
Welsh A, clerk Union Hotel
Welsh Charles, 185 Division
Welch E R (E R Welch & Son) h 179 Division
Welch E R & Son (E R and Fred), marble cutters, 300 Princess

Horseshoe Island. Boats twice a day each way. Liquor prohibited from being sold.

C. Robinson, Fashionable Tailor, 185 WELLINGTON, Near Princess.

22

Welch Frederick (E R Welch & Son) h 421 Princess
Welch John, cashier, 63 Earl
Welch Michael, butcher, 624 Princess
Welch Thos, teamster,77 Queen
Weller Miss, fancy goods, 227 Princess
Wells C A, carriage painter, bds 53 Princess
Wells H, harness maker, 53 Princess
Wells H P, livery, 36 Princess, h 437 do
Wells William J, clerk P O, 288 Wellington
West Wm S, auctioneer, Ontario, cor Princess
Westcott Wm, laborer, 28 Elm
Whale Luke, mariner, Patrick
Whalen Jas, mariner, 52 North
Whalen Mrs Margaret [wid Daniel], 58 Earl
Whalen Patrick, tanner, 17 John
Wheeler Joseph, piano maker, old No 90 Bagot
Whims Peter, laborer, 12 Earl
Whinton John, plumber, McAuley's Cottages, Dufferin
Whitcomb Mrs M, (wid J), 330 Brock
White Benjamin, prop Montreal House, 242 Ontario
White Miss Eliza, r184 Bagot
White J T, fire and life insurance agent, 92 Brock, h Earl cor Gordon
White R, dyer, 79-81 Princess
White Mrs Sophia (wid John), 100 Barrack
White Thos, laborer, Stephen
White W J B, city agent Canada Life Assurance Co'y, 92 Brock

Whitebread John, bookkeeper, Bagot
Whitebread John, laborer,Markland
Whitebread Mrs Sarah E (wid James), 79 Colborne
Whiting J L, B A (Britton & Whiting) h Clergy
Whitfield Albert W, baker, old No 117 Bagot
Wilder Geo A, grocer, Bagot, cor Earl
Wylie George C, carpenter, 403 King e
Wilkes Rev Arthur B, Congregational, 140 Union
Wilkins H, painter,410 Johnston
Wilkinson C P, clerk,165 Queen
Wilkinson G E [G M Wilkinson & Son] h 165 Queen
Wilkinson Geo M, 165 Queen
Wilkinson G M & Son (H J and G E) grocers and wine merchants, 180 Wellington
Wilkinson H J (G M Wilkinson & Son) h 130 Bagot
Wiley Mrs C [wid John] 412 Princess
Wiley Jas, engineer, 212 Barrie
Williy J W, laborer, John north
Williams Edward, lumber dealer, 23 Earl
Williams Edward, coal & wood, end King e
Williams Fred, steamfitter, bds American Hotel
Williams George, sec Y M C A, h 13 Mack
Williams J, laborer, 395 Johnston
Williams Manley,prop Pittsburg House, 282 Ontario
Williams Mrs Martitia (wid Geo H), 48 Earl

Williams Cornelius, Victoria

Williamson Adam, contractor, 115 Gore

Williamson Fred, 118 Ordnance

Williamson George, laborer, 27 Union

Williamson J W, prof, Queen's College, 134 Earl

Williamson Mrs M (wid J), Collingwood

Williss John, 99 King w

Wilson Mrs Andrew, manager Orphans' Home, Union

Wilson Bramwell, agent, 196 Sydenham

Wilson B S, sewing machine agent

Wilson Major E B, 126 Union

Wilson Miss Elizabeth, 1 Gray's Lane

Wilson Francis, laborer, r91 Earl

Wilson Geo, A Battery, Bagot

Wilson George, machinist, 24 Chatham

Wilson George, boiler maker, King w

Wilson Geo, laborer, 12 Deacon

Wilson, G F, stone cutter, 29 Colborne

Wilson G F, stone cutter, 15 u Charles

Wilson Henry, Victoria

Wilson H W, chemist, 75 Union

Wilson James, laborer, 43 Earl

Wilson James, Centre

Wilson Miss Jane, Bagot

Wilson J B E, clerk Merchants Bank, 126 Union

Wilson John, gardener, 9 James

Wilson John F, manager The Rathbun Co, 302 King e

Wilson R J, manager Can Pac Tel Co, h 334 Brock

Wilson Richard, laborer, Rideau

Wilson Robt, laborer, 25 Chatham

Wilson Mrs Sarah [wid Thos] 146 King e

WILSON T C, the largest and longest established Livery in the city. Vehicles ready night and day at a moment's notice. Telephone 291. 120 Clarence, h 202 Queen

Wilson Thos, laborer, Barrack

Wilson W J, druggist, 185 Princess

Wilson Wm, 198 Queen

Wilson Wm, jr, Cataraqui

Wilson William, sr, manager cotton mill, 'Briarfield House,' Rideau

Wilmot Edward, boarding house, old 82 Bagot

Wilmot Henry, contractor, Bagot

Wilmot Henry F, clerk P O, 63 Sydenham w

Wilmot N, blacksmith, 39 Montreal, h 181 Colborne

Wiltse Thomas, carpenter, 29 Union

Wiltshire Walter, baker, n s Princess

Wilton H A, tinsmith, 243 Bagot

Wilton Henry, saddler, 243 Bagot

Windsor Hotel, P McLaughlin prop, Princess, cor Montreal *(See advt.)*

Wintrup John, machinist, 46 Division

Wiseman Francis, mason, 168 Gordon

Wood Mrs Abby Ann [wid Dennis], 29 Charles

Wood Bros, watchmakers, 236 Princess

Wood Chester, carpenter, 44 Grove

Wood H A [Wood Bros], h 236 Princess

Wood Isaac, 236 Princess

Wood Mrs Mary (wid William), 134 Chatham

Wood Robert, tobacconist, 238 Princess

Wood Samuel, laborer, Park, G T R station

Wood Wm, laborer, 51 Chatham

Woodhead Thos, laborer, military stores dept, 54 Place de Armes

Woodrow Wm H, engineer, 89 Wellington

Woodrowe Sergt T, R S G

Woods Charles, printer, 310 Queen

Woods John, laborer, Beverly

Woods John, laborer, Miller's Lane

Woods L M, Wood's Fair, 101 Princess

Woods Miss M, fancy goods, 107 Brock, h 120 Johnston

Woods W H V, driver, end Frontenac

Woods William, laborer, 224 Wellington

Wolliver Mrs, 4 Brewery Lane

Wolf Z, mariner, 218 Wellington

Woolard Wm J, salesman, end Frontenac

Woolley Major William, divisional officer, res barracks

Wootten James, agent, Artillery Park Barracks

Wormworth Wm, piano maker, 117 Earl

Worth Mrs Ellen [wid Thos], Bagot

Worth Thomas, caretaker riding school, Place d' Armes

Wotten ——, carter, 216 Alfred

Wrenshall Charles, artist, 81 Albert

Wright Mrs Caroline [wid Jno] 278 Johnston

Wright Clark & Son, hatters and furriers, 178 Wellington

Wright Clark W, [Clark Wright & Son], h 25 Colborne

Wright George, carter, 110 Barrack

Wright G F, dental student, 33 Colborne

Wright James, clerk, bds Wellington

Wright John, city foreman, 303 King w

Wright Robt, mason, 305 Bagot

Wright Wm, butcher, 270 Johnston

Wright Zedoc, currier, 188 Rideau

Wurtele Capt A G G, R M C, 140 Johnston

Yateman Henry, engineer, 100 Pine

Yatos Mrs Bessie (wid Dr Octave), 64 William

Yates Mrs, Centre

Yeddo Henry, engineer, 28 Ontario

Yeomans Mrs Anne [wid Joseph], 210 Bagot

Yolden Henry, machinist, 60 Wellington

Young Men's Christian Association, Geo E Williams, sec'y, 129 Princess

Young Miss F E, 201 Earl
Young George, agent The Shedden Co'y, 216 Gordon
Young George, shoemaker, 198 Colborne
Young Henry, mason, 93 York
Young Henry, laborer, 15 Gordon
Young Jas, laborer, 405 King e
Young Mrs Jane (wid William), dressmaker, 395 King e
Young Leon, laborer, 23 Elm

Young Miss Martha, dressmaker, 72 Wellington
Young Miss M L, 201 Earl
Young Remie, laborer, 25 Elm
Young Richard, guard K P, 269 Gordon
Young Stephen, tanner, Rideau
Young Women's Christian Association, Miss Machar, sec'y, 128 Clarence
Yule James, com traveller, 71 Colborne

SUBSCRIBERS'

CLASSIFIED BUSINESS DIRECTORY.

ARCHITECTS.

Gillen & Gillen, Bagot, cor Brock
Power & Son, Golden Lion Block, Wellington
Reid James B, 81 Brock

AUCTIONEERS.

Martin E R, 20 Market Sq
Salter J, 58 Brock and 288 Princess

BAKERS.

Carnovsky T R, Princess, cor Victoria
Toye R H, 302 King e

BANKS.

Bank British North America, City Hall
Merchants, King, cor William
Montreal, King, cor William
Ontario, Wellington, cor Clarence

BANKERS.

Carruthers J B, King e, over King's drug store
Cheque Bank of London, Donald Fraser, agent, 344 King e
Fraser Donald, 344 King e
Mills & Kent, 91 Clarence

BARRISTERS AND SOLICITORS.

Agnew James, City Hall
Britton & Whiting, 69 Clarence
Givens D A, 43 Brock
Kirkpatrick & Rogers, 194 Ontario
Macdonnell & Mudie, 38 Clarence
Machar J M, 38 Clarence

McIntyre Donald, 304 King e
McIntyre John, 304 King e
Mundell Wm, 139 Princess
Shannon R W, 297 King e
Shaw Robert, 332 King e
Skinner J S, 81 Brock
Smythe, Smith & Lyon, 192 Ontario
Snook T L, 200 Ontario
Shibley H T, 44 Clarence
Sullivan W H, 36 Clarence
Walkem & Walkem, 93 Clarence

BLACKSMITH.

Cockburn Wm, 277 Ontario

BOAT BUILDERS.

Knapp A C, Cataraqui Bridge
Sharman T N, foot Simcoe

BOOK BINDERS.

McAuley Thomas, 356 King e
Smith H Stalleraffe, 43 Brock

BOOKSELLERS AND STATIONERS.

British & Foreign Bible Society Depository, G S Hobart, 155 Princess
Henderson John & Co, 86 Princess
McAuley Thomas, 356 King e
Nisbet Francis, Brock, corner Wellington

BOOTS AND SHOES.

Abernethy J & Co, 260 Princess
Armstrong D F, 141 Princess
Cunningham Thos, 267 Princess
Dick W J & Son, 168 Princess
Haines & Lockett, 116 Princess
Noxon & Rockwell, Princess, cor Bagot
Offord Geo, sr, 127 Princess & 48 Brock

BOTTLING WORKS.

Hinds Bros, 10 Market Square
Pipe William, 261 Princess

BREWER.

Bajus Philip, 308 Wellington

BUILDING AND LOAN COMPANIES.

Frontenac Loan & Investment, 49 Clarence
Ontario Building and Savings, Clarence

BUTCHERS.

Green John, Bagot, cor Earl
Waddington Bros, 318 King e

CARPENTER AND JOINER.

Brookes Thomas S, 94 Albert

CARTAGE AGENTS.

Shedden The Co, foot William

CHEMISTS AND DRUGGISTS.

Chown & Mitchell, 124 Princess
Hobart G S, 135 Princess
King J G & Co, Market Square
Polson N C & Co, 232-34 Princess
Skinner Henry & Co, wholesale, 171 Princess
Wade Henry, cor King & Brock
Wilson W J, 185 Princess

CHINA, GLASSWARE, ETC.

Oakley Vincent & Sons, 115-17 Princess
Robertson Bros, 187 Princess

CIGAR MANUFACTURER.

McGowan George A, 43 Brock

COAL AND WOOD.

Anglin W B & S, Wellington, cor Bay

Breck & Booth, Ontario, corner Clarence
Crawford R & Co, foot Queen
Joyce John L, Bay, cor Rideau
Mallen M, Ontario, cor Barrack
Rathbun The Co, foot Queen & 300 King w
Sowards James, Place d'Armes, cor Ontario
Walsh P, Barrack, cor Ontario

CONFECTIONERS.

Crothers H & W J, 207 Wellington
Toye R H, 302 King e

COTTON MILLS.

Kingston Cotton Manufacturing Co, foot Cataraqui

DENTISTS.

Clark J H, M D, 190 Wellington
Clements Leonard, 142 Wellington
Stackhouse A, Bagot, cor Princess

DRY DOCK.

Davis R & Son, end Wellington

DRY GOODS.

Bowes & Bisonette, 204 Princess
Cousineau, Quinn & Corrigan, 80 Princess
Doran B & Co, 126 Princess
Federal Warehouse, 114 Princess
Hardy John C & Co, 88 Princess
Laidlaw J & Son, 191 Princess
McMahon A J, 112 Princess
Macnee & Minnes, wholesale, 251 Bagot
Minnes & Burns, Princess, cor Bagot
Murray & Taylor, 176 Princess

Richmond, Orr & Co, 120-122, Princess
Ross Alex, 128-130 Princess
Shaw Felix & Co, 174 Princess
Spence & Crumley, 132-134 Princess
Waldron Richard, 174 Wellington
Walsh & Steacy, 106 Princess

ELECTRIC LIGHTING.

Kingston Electric Lighting Co, foot Brock

ENGINE WORKS.

Canadian Locomotive & Engine Co, Ontario

EXPRESS COMPANIES.

American, King, cor Brock
Canadian, King, cor Brock
Dominion, King, cor Clarence

FANCY GOODS.

Sine A, 202 Princess
Weaver S, 125 Princess

FIRE AND BURGLAR PROOF SAFES.

McDowall R J, 220 Princess

FLOUR AND FEED.

Baker W F, 12 Market Sq
Campbell J G & Son, foot Brock
Franklin J, 213 Princess
McNeill W J, 61 Brock
Neelon S, 113 Brock

FORWARDING COMPANIES.

Kingston & Montreal Forwarding Co, Portsmouth
Montreal Transportation Co'y, foot Queen

FOUNDERS AND MACHINISTS.

Chown & Cunningham, Victoria Foundry, cor King and Queen

Pure Teas. Shore Loynes & Co.

Davidson, Doran & Co, 37 Ontario

FURNITURE MANUFACTURERS AND DEALERS.

Brame Henry, 251 Princess
Drennan W M, 75 Princess
Reid James, 254 Princess

GENTS' FURNISHERS.

Ashley W G, 121½ Princess
Dunbar John, 100 Princess
Grand Union Clothing Co, 122 Princess
McMahon A J, 112 Princess
McNaughton & Co, King, cor Princess
Rattenbury J R, 206 Princess

GROCERS.

Crawford James, 182 Princess
Gibson David, 345-7 Princess
Gunn A & Co, wholesale, 125-7 Ontario
Henderson J S, 61 Brock
Johns Thos H, 270 Princess
McRae Bros, cor Wellington and Brock
McRae W R & Co, wholesale, Wellington, cor Brock
Redden James, 178 Princess
Robertson Geo & Son, wholesale, 183 Ontario
Shore Loynes & Co, 200 Princess
Stroud Bros, 109 Princess
Ward J & Co, 341-3 Princess
Wilkinson Geo M & Son, 180 Wellington

HAIR DRESSER.

Johnson Jas B, 155 Wellington

HARDWARE.

Bibby & Virtue, 335 King e
Chown A & Co, 252 Bagot

Horsey R M & Co, 189 Princess
McMahon Bros, 85-7 Princess
Martin W C, saddlery, 216 Princees
Muckleston J & Co, 71-3 Princess
Strachan Arch, 193 Princess

HATS AND CAPS.

Galloway James, 84 Princess
Mills Geo & Co, 170 Wellington
Page J B & Co, 138 Princess
Wright Clark & Son, 178 Wellington

HOTELS.

Albion, A Spafford, Montreal, cor Queen
Anglo-American, Joseph Little, Ontario, cor Johnston
American, W H Hunter, 27 Brock
British-American, J E Dunham, King, cor Clarence
Collender, T Doolan, 324 King e
Hotel Frontenac, E H Dunham, Ontario
Stanley House, Johnston Brown Ontario, cor Market
Terrapin, Wm Shanahan, 76 Princess
Union, E Thornton, Ontario, cor Brock
Windsor, P McLaughlin, 205-209 Princess

INSURANCE COMPANIES AND AGENTS.

Accident Ins Co of North America, J P Gildersleeve, 42 Clarence
Ætna Fire Ins Co, Hartford, J F Swift, King, cor Clarence
British Empire Mutual Life Co, C H Martin, 86 Brock

Caledonian Fire, J P Gildersleeve, 42 Clarence

Canada Life Association, W J B
White, city agent, J T White,
special agent, 92 Brock

Citizens' Life & Accident Ins Co,
R J McDowall, 220 Princess

City of London, Fire, Strange
& Strange, 95 Clarence

Commercial Union, Fire,Strange
& Strange, 95 Clarence

Confederation Life, A Waldie,
111 Wellington

Dominion Plate Glass, Strange
& Strange, 95 Clarence

Fire Ins Association, Mills &
Kent, 91 Clarence

Glasgow & London Fire, C H
Martin, 86 Brock

Glasgow & London Fire, J T
White, 92 Brock

Glasgow & London Fire, R J
McDowall, 220 Princess

Guarantee Co of North America,
J P Gildersleeve, 42 Clarence

Hartford Fire Co, J F Swift,
King, cor Clarence

Imperial Fire, London, Eng, C
H Martin, 86 Brock

Lancashire Fire Ins Co, J P Gildersleeve, 42 Clarence

Liverpool & London & Globe
Ins Co, Thos Briggs, 87 Clarence

Lloyd's London & Liverpool Marine, Thos Briggs, 87 Clarence

Lloyd's Plate Glass Ins Co,
Mills & Kent, 91 Clarence

London Accident & Guarantee,
J T White, 92 Brock

London & Lancashire, Fire, E
C Hill, 43 Brock

London Assurance Corporation,
Mills & Kent, 91 Clarence

London & Lancashire Life Co,
Mills & Kent, 91 Clarence

Mutual Life Ins Co, N Y, R J
McDowall, 220 Princess

New York Life Ins Co, Donald
Fraser, 334 King e

North American Life, J F Swift,
King, cor Clarence

Northern Assurance Co, Fire,
London, Eng, J B McIver, 38
Clarence

North British Mercantile Ins Co,
M Flanagan, City Hall

Norwich & London Accident Assurance Co, C H Martin, 86
Brock

Ontario Mutual Life, J M Sherlock, 281 Princess

Phenix Fire, Brooklyn, J F
Swift, King, cor Clarence

Phœnix Fire Ins Co, Strange
& Strange, 95 Clarence

Queen Ins Co'y, Mills & Kent,
91 Clarence

Royal Insurance Co, Strange &
Strange, 95 Clarence

Royal Insurance Co, Donald
Fraser, 344 King e

Royal Canadian, fire and marine, C F Gildersleeve, 42 Clarence

Scottish Union & National, Fire,
C H Martin, 86 Brock

Standard Life Assurance, J P
Gildersleeve, 42 Clarence

Sun Life Assurance, Canada, E
C Hill, 43 Brock

Travelers Life & Accident, J F
Swift, King, cor Clarence

LAUNDRY.

Kingston, 206 Princess

LIVERY.

Wilson T C, 120 Clarence

LOCOMOTIVE WORKS.

Canadian Locomotive and Engine Co, F J Leigh, supt, J H Birkett, sec-treas, Ontario

LUMBER DEALERS.

Anglin W B & S, foot Wellington
Caldwell A & Son, Ontario, cor Place d'Armes
McRossie Wm, Princess, cor Ontario
Rathbun The Co'y, foot Queen
Strachan M & Son, Barriefield

MERCHANT TAILORS.

Dunbar John, 100 Princess
Flett A G, 214 Princess
Grand Union Clothing Co, 122 Princess
Lambert & Walsh, 110 Princess
Livingston C & Bro, 75-77 Brock
McNaughton & Co, King, cor Princess
Moore Thomas, 354 King e
O'Brien Alex, 265 Princess
Prevost Z, 55 Brock
Robinson C, 185 Wellington
Sands J S & Son, 171 Wellington
Smith Jos A B, 259 King e
Spencer R, 79 Brock

MUSIC DEALERS.

Carey & Son, 156 Wellington
Henderson John & Co, 86 Princess
McAuley Thomas, 356 King e
McDowall R J, 220 Princess
Sherlock J M, jr, 281 Princess
Vanderwater R W, 188 Wellington

NEWSPAPERS.

British Whig, 336 King e
Canadian Freeman, 119 Brock

Chronicle & News, 67 Princess
Daily News, 67 Princess
Weekly British Whig, 336 King e

OIL CLOTH WORKS.

Oil & Enamel Co, Rideau, cor North

PAINTERS AND PAPER HANGERS.

McMahon T & Co, Brock, cor Bagot
Milo Thos W, 41 Montreal
Robinson Bros, 275 Bagot
Savage Bros, 78 William

PHOTOGRAPHERS.

Henderson Henry, 90 Princess
Powell James W, 165 Princess

PHYSICIANS AND SURGEONS.

Anglin W G, 52 Earl
Connell J C, 279 King e
Dupuis Thos R, 7 Montreal
Fee Samuel H, 405 Princess
Fenwick K N, 141 King e
Fenwick T M, Barrack cor King
Garrett Richard W, 52 Johnston
Henderson W H, 95 Wellington
Hemsted Edwin, 424 Princess
Herald John, 199 King e
Irwin Chamberlen, cor King & William
Livingstone Marion, 233 Bagot
McGillivray Alice, 230 Princess
McGillivray T S, 230 Princess
McVety A, 203 Wellington
Oliver A S, 351 King e
Phelan Daniel, 248 Bagot
Saunders H J, 244 King e
Strange O S, cor King & Union
Sullivan M, 360 King e

PIANOS AND ORGANS.

Carey & Son, 156 Wellington
George Joseph, 112-14 Gore

F. SHAW & CO.'S DRESS GOODS
PLEASE THE MOST FASTIDIOUS.

ALPHABETICAL DIRECTORY. 179

McDOWALL R J, Dealer in Bell, Evans Bros, Mors, Wagner, Guild and Fischer Pianos ; Bell, Thomas, Uxbridge, Excelsior, Doherty, Bridgeport & New England Organs, No. 220 Princess
Sherlock J M, jr, 281 Princess
Vanderwater R W, 188 Wellington
Weber Factory, cor Gordon and Princess

PICTURES AND FRAMES.

Ohlke P, 184 Wellington

PLANING MILLS, SASH AND DOORS.

Anglin W B & S, foot Wellington
Strachan M & Son, Barriefield

PLUMBERS AND STEAM FITTERS.

Dunn Wm, 229 Princess
Elliott Bros, 77 Princess
McKelvey & Birch, 71 Brock
McNeil Neil, 66 Brock

PORTRAIT PAINTER.

Stowell H F, Brock, cor King

PRINTING, BOOK AND JOB.

Bailie Bros, 190 Wellington
British Whig, 336-340 King e
Canadian Freeman, 119 Brock
Daily News, 67 Princess
Smith John, 153 Wellington

RAILROAD TICKET AGENT.

Canadian Pacific, J P Gildersleeve, 42 Clarence
Kingston & Pembroke, J P Gildersleeve, 42 Clarence

REAL ESTATE AGENTS.

Cliff George, 95 Clarence
Hill E C, 43 Brock

Moore Wm, 90 Brock
Swift J F, King, cor Clarence

ROOM PAPER AND PAPER HANGERS.

McMahon T & Co, cor Brock & Bagot
Milo Thomas S, 41 Montreal
Robinson Bros, 277 Bagot
Savage Bros, 78 William

SEWING MACHINES.

Cunningham John, 348 King e
George Joseph, 112-14 Gore
New Home, R J McDowall, 220 Princess
New Raymond, R J McDowall, 220 Princess
Singer, J Laishley, 213 Princess
White, John Cunningham, 348 King e
Wanzer, R J McDowall, 220 Princess

SPORTING GOODS.

Routley John, 173 Princess

STEAMSHIP LINES (OCEAN.)

GILDERSLEEVE J P, agent for the Allan, Beaver, Black Diamond, Cunard, and Inman Steamship Lines, 42 Clarence
Dominion, C F Gildersleeve, 42 Clarence

STOVES, TINWARE, ETC.

Bibby & Virtue, 337 King e
Chown & Cunningham, 248 Bagot
Chown Edwin & Son, 250 Bagot
Dunn Wm, 229 Princess
Elliott Bros, 77 Princess
Horsey R M & Co, 189 Princess
McKelvey & Birch, 71 Brock

New Home, New Raymond & Wanzer Sewing Machines.
AT McDOWALL'S MUSIC ROOMS.

Horseshoe Island. Boats twice a day each way. Liquor prohibited from being sold.

TELEGRAPH AND TELEPHONE COMPANIES.

Bell Telephone Co, 186 Ontario
Canadian Pacific Telegraph Co, Clarence, cor Ontario, branch office, H A Liffiton, 167 Princess
Great North Western Telegraph Co, 34 Clarence, branch office, A Sine, 202 Princess

UNITED STATES CONSUL.

Twitchell M H, Ontario, cor Clarence

UNDERTAKERS.

Brame Henry, cor Princess and Sydenham

Drennan W M, 75 Princess
Reid James, 254 Princess.

WATCHMAKERS AND JEWELLERS.

Johnston Albert E, 192 Wellington
LeHeup J A, 57 Brock
Liffiton H A, 167 Princess
Spangenberg F W, 347 King e

WHARFINGERS.

Breck & Booth, foot West
Calvin Co, foot Brock
Gunn A & Co, Ontario
Richardson & Sons, foot Princess
Swift Jas & Co, foot Johnston

VILLAGE OF BARRIEFIELD.

A Village in the Township of Pittsburg, on the east side of the Cataraqui River, 1½ miles from Kingston, with which it is connected by a bridge. Here are situated Fort Henry and Point Frederick, on which is the Royal Military College. Population of the Village about 300.

Anderson C, waiter R M C
Anderson Wm, carpenter
Batten Geo, mariner
Belwa Charles, township clerk
Belwa Mrs Charles
Birtle Sergt-Major II, R M C
Bowman Chas, boat builder
Bowman John, boat builder
Brogan Sergt Peter, R M C
Brough Sergt A, R M C
Butcher M, butler R M C
Butlin C, express driver
Butland Charles, laborer
Byrnes John, laborer
Byrnes John, printer
Byrnes Miles, grocer
Byrnes Wm, salesman
Caverly Nathaniel, blacksmith
Cherry Wm, machinist
Dick Geo, sailor
Dowler Richard
Esford James, machinist
Esford Robert, laborer
Forbes Mrs Robt, grocer
George Fred G, deputy registrar
Graham John, laborer
Grange W, waiter
Halen Miss Rose
Hines Mrs S A
Hutton John, cabinet maker
Hutton Wm, carpenter
Jacobs Sergt, R S G

Jones Rev K L, M D, Episcopal
Knapp H J, boat builder
Knapp Jas, boat builder
Leader Edward, sawyer
LeHeup Harry, oil, bones, etc
Lister J, waiter R M C
McCormick J, waiter
McCrosbie Wm, blacksmith
McGregor C, waiter R M C
Martin John, retired
Medley Miss Elizabeth, grocer
Medley George, butcher
Medley Wm, drover
Medley W H, druggist
Minogue W, head-class servant, R M C
Mitchell Wm, carpenter
Morgans Sergt-Major J, R M C
Muller George, sailor
Nash Major Edward, R M C
Norman William, laborer
Parkhill M J, salesman
Pound West, engineer
Rea Henry, machinist

Rickey Alex, carriagemaker
Rickey George, carriagemaker
Ridy J, waiter R M C
Ryan John, postmaster
Ryan John, quarryman
Salsbury J, waiter R M C
Sedford Jas, laborer
Smith Joseph, bricklayer
Stanton Mrs
Strachan Martin, quarry owner
Strachan Martin & Son, planing, sash, and door mills
Thompson Sergt T, R M C
Thompson Thomas
Tisdale Alexander, carpenter
Tisdale John, laborer
Vallincourt Octave, teamster
Watts Mrs Eliza
Williams L J, messman R M C
Wilson Richard, quarryman
Wilson Wm, laborer
Young A, waiter R M C

VILLAGE OF GARDEN ISLAND.

An Island in the St. Lawrence, directly opposite Kingston, being 1¾ miles distant. A station of the Great North-Western Telegraph Co. Here are located the extensive shipyards of The Calvin Co. (limited), who own all the Island. Connected in summer by ferry boat four times a day, and in winter by a stage twice a day. Population about 450. H. A. Calvin, Reeve; A. H. Dugdale, Clerk.

Abrieu Thomas, carpenter
Achee Joseph, sailor
Adsit Samuel, carpenter
Allen Fred, carpenter
Andre Henry, raftsman
Blanchette Hyacituth, raftsman

Calvin The Co'y, (Limited), merchants and ship owners
Calvin Hiram A, The Calvin Co'y
Calvin Sanford C, The Calvin Co'y

Clement Joseph, mariner
Compo E, raftsman
Compo Felix jr, mariner
Compo Felix sen, mariner
Compo Joseph, raftsman
Compo Melien, raftsman
Compo Seraphin, raftsman
Crosby James, mariner
Crosby Robert, mariner
Cushen John, teamster
Dalzell James, carpenter
Dalzell Thomas, carpenter
Desforges J B, raftsman
Dix John, sailor
Dutemple Edward, raftsman
Fahey John, mariner
Ferguson John, mariner
Ferguson Thomas jr, clerk
Ferguson Thos sen, carpenter
Garand John, carpenter
Garipey Fred, raftsman
Glenn Andrew, blacksmith
Gobeil Edward, carpenter
Gray Thos, engineer
Harris John, machinist
Harris Thos, machinist
Jones Peter, machinist
Kennedy David sen, carpenter
Kennedy James, watchman
Kennedy John, engineer
Kennedy Samuel, carpenter
Kenosh Joseph, raftsman
Lacasse Moses, carpenter
Lalond Napoleon, raftsman
Lambert George, raftsman
Lappin Thos, carpenter
Lariviere, Joseph, raftsman

Larush Anthony, mariner
Lawrence Francis, mariner
Lefave David jr, mariner
Lefave David sen, mariner
LeRiche Hugh, raftsman
Lewers David, farmer
McGarity George, blacksmith
McGarity James, machinist
McMasters Andrew, teamster
McQuarrie Hugh, teacher
McReady Wm, engineer
Malone A H, mariner
Malone Anthony, postmaster
Marshall Wm, J P
Martin Ephraim, mariner
Marton George, sawyer
Marton Wm, culler
Menard George, raftsman
Mullin John, machinist
O'Reilly Luke, mariner
Owens Wm, mariner
Phelix C E, engineer
Rogey Wm, butcher
Sauve George, engineer
Sauve J R, mariner
Sauve Joseph, blacksmith
Simons John, engineer
Simons Robert
Simons William
Smith Thomas C, engineer
Snell Mrs John
Sweet H N, mariner
Theriault Francis, engineer
Trickey Antoine, raftsman
Veech Robert, machinist
Veech Stannis, engineer

VILLAGE OF PORTSMOUTH.

An incorporated village adjoining the city on its western boundary, connected with it by the street railway. Here is located the Kingston Penitentiary, a very handsome building, situated at the eastern end of the village, on the river's banks. At the western end is the Kingston Asylum for the Insane ; the building is a very fine and handsome structure of cut stone ; the grounds are most beautiful, and are tastily laid out. Among the other principal buildings are the Warden's residence, a most beautiful structure, surrounded by ornamental grounds well laid out, and the Episcopal and Methodist Churches, Orange Hall, Town Hall, and a number of private residences. The Kingston & Montreal Forwarding Co.'s shipyards, docks and warehouses are located in the village. Population, exclusive of the Asylum and Penitentiary, about 900. Assessed value, $120,000.

COUNCIL :—John Fisher, Reeve ; Joseph Porter, John Marks, George McAuley, Robert Dodds, Councillors ; Thos. Kelly, Clerk ; Thos. McCammon, Treasurer ; Edward Beaupre, Collector ; Adam Tait, Constable.

Adams James, trade instructor K P
Alexander John, sausage maker
Alexander Philip, grain buyer
Allen Joseph A
Anglin Wm, bursar Asylum for Insane
Appleton Robert, guard K P
Arundell Wm, carpenter
Arthurs Robt, laborer
Arthurs Wm, mechanic
Asylum for the Insane, C K Clarke, superintendent
Atkins Alex, guard K P
Atkins Richard, guard K P
Ault Franklin, guard K P
Baiden Eli, gardener
Baiden Henry, gardener
Baiden Richard, gardener
Baker John, accountant
Bannister Mrs Ann
Bannister Henry, surveyor
Bannister John, guard K P
Bateson Thos, keeper Asylum

Baugh Francis, carpenter
Beaupre Alfred, sailor
Beaupre Mrs Ann
Beaupre Charles, sailor
Beaupre Edward, hotel keeper
Beaupre Peter M, guard K P
Belanger Maxime, carpenter
Betts John H, M D
Betts Mrs Mary
Buck Mathew, carpenter
Burke Edward F, butcher
Burke Henry, laborer
Cameron Alex, contractor
Campbell James, P M, grocer
Carlton Wm, mechanic
Carr Wm, gardener
Clarke C K, superintendent Asylum for Insane
Clark James, laborer
Collins Alfred, laborer
Connolly Henry, mechanic
Convery Thos, carpenter
Cooper Thos, laborer
Cottle Mrs L P

Craig Mrs Margaret
Craig Miss Mary E
Craig Capt Thos J, mariner
Crawford Miss Fanny
Crawford Wm, gardener
Crimmons Frank, clerk
Crimmons Patrick, keeper Asylum
Culcheth Ernest, baker
Culcheth Mrs John
Dearing Miss Bridget
Dearing Wm, laborer
Dennison James, carpenter
Dennison John, carpenter
Dillon Miss Margaret
Dillon Mrs Mary
Dobbs Rev F W
Dodds James H, blacksmith
Dodds Robert, boiler maker
Donnelly John, guard K P
Dooley Wm, laborer
Doyle James, guard K P
Duncan Miss Mary
Duncan Wm, bookkeeper
Elliott Mrs Elizabeth
Elliott Thos C, guard Asylum
Evans Thos, guard Asylum
Evans Thos, printer
Ewart Thos, laborer
Fahey Miss, matron Penitentiary
Ferguson George, laborer
Fisher Mrs Eliza
Fisher Miss Eliza
Fisher John, Portsmouth Brewery
Fisher Wm, brewer
Fitzgerald Patrick, carpenter
Fitzgibbon Daniel, guard
Flynn John, laborer
Friendship John, gardener
Gibson Miss Ann
Gillespie James, keeper Asylum
Goulding Timothy, laborer

Graham Jethro, salesman
Graham R M, accountant
Graham Thos F, carpenter
Graham Wm, carpenter
Graham Wm, jr, carpenter
Halliday Jas, hospital steward K P
Harrigan Hugh, laborer
Hatrick John, keeper Asylum
Henstridge Josephus, teacher
Hewton Fred C, clerk
Hewton Robert, chief instructor K P
Hogan Wm, blacksmith
Holland George, jr, laborer
Holland George, sr, guard K P
Holland James, laborer
Holland Wm, carter
Hooper Jos W, carpenter
Houghton Isaac, gardener
Howard Thos, carpenter
Hughes David, keeper Asylum
Hurst Wm, guard K P
Johnson Edward, guard Asylum
Kelly Mrs Susan
Kelly Thos, village clerk
Kennedy Mrs Ann
Kennedy John, guard Asylum
Kennedy Michael, messenger
Kennedy Patrick, laborer
Kennedy Thomas, laborer
Kennedy W J, clerk
Kerr Hugh
Kingston & Montreal Forwarding Co (Limited), A Gunn, president, Jas Stewart, agent
Kingston Penitentiary, M Lavell, warden
Kirkpatrick Miss E, matron Asylum
Knight Henry, laborer
Koen Mrs Hannah
Koen Michael, guard Asylum

Lavell M, Warden Kingston Penitentiary
Leahy Edward, jeweller
Leahy Michael, keeper K P
Lewis Calvin, carter
Liddell Joseph, carpenter
Liddle Mrs Mary
Lindsay Robert, builder
Lonergan Thos, keeper Asylum
Lowe Samuel, general merchant, telegraph and express agent
McAuley Geo, jr, carpenter
McAuley Robert, guard K P
McCammon Robert, baker
McCammon Thomas, jr, keeper K P
McCammon Thomas, sr, baker
McCauley Geo, sr, guard K P
McConnell Wm, grocer
McConville Charles, guard K P
McGeehan D J, clerk
McGeehan Richard, carpenter
McGeein Bernard, keeper K P
McGeein Daniel, carpenter
McLean Allan, steward Asylum
McLeod John, contractor
McManus Mrs M A
McManus Mrs Maria
McManus Miss Mary J
McNulty Wm J, laborer
McWater Alex, laborer
McWater John, mechanic
McWater Thos, laborer
Marks John R, carpenter
Marks Richard, carpenter
Marks Wm, carpenter
Mathewson J B, teacher K P
Mathewson John P, carpenter
Matier Samuel, baker
Metcalf Mrs Mary
Mills John, guard K P
Mooney Edward, guard K P
Mooney John

Mooney Wm S, guard K P
Moore Jas W, laborer
Moore John, shoemaker
Moore Thos, guard K P
Moreland A, hotel
Newman John, laborer
Nicholson Amos, carpenter
Newman George, laborer
Nicholson John, carpenter
Nicholson Thos, carpenter
Norris Robert, carpenter
O'Brien Mrs Bridget
O'Neil John, boilermaker
O'Neill Richard, keeper K P
Payne Geo A, clerk
Payne John, mason
Payne Thos, guard K P
Porter Andrew, laborer
Porter William, laborer
Potter Joseph, gardener
Power Mrs Bridget
Pugh Mrs Mary
Pugh Thomas, guard K P
Rattray Rev Jas, Presbyterian
Redmond John jr, clerk
Redmond Patrick, keeper, Asylum
Robb Henry, carpenter
Robinson J, assistant medical sup't, Asylum for Insane
Sampson Thos, keeper, Asylum
Scally John, guard K P
Scott John, painter
Sexton Geo, fisherman
Seymour Isaiah, boilermaker
Shine Henry, carpenter
Short James, hotelkeeper
Simpson J, M D, ass't physician, Asylum
Smith John, sawyer
Smith Thos, keeper K P
Smith Wm, laborer
Stewart John, carpenter
Stoness Robert, laborer

24

Sullivan Wm, deputy warden, K P
Swift Michael, moulder
Swift Mrs Ruth
Thompson Andrew, carpenter
VanStraubenzie Col B, D A G
Walsh Lawrence, guard K P
Watts John, gardener
Watts Samuel jr

Williamson John, laborer
Wishart Edward, carpenter
Wishart Mrs
Wishart Wm, pianomaker
Wolfred Mrs Julia
Wood Nial, farmer
Woodhouse Henry, guard K P
Woods Wm, laborer

MISCELLANEOUS DIRECTORY.

CITY COUNCIL.

Mayor, James Duncan Thompson ; W. Adams, Wm. Carson, George Creeggan, W. M. Drennan, G. S. Fenwick, John Gaskin, C. F. Gildersleeve, Wm. Harty, Joseph Hiscock, James Minnes, John S. Muckleston, John McCammon, Donald McIntyre, John McLeod, N. C. Polson, F. S. Rees, Chris. Robinson, Wm. Robinson, R. W. Shannon, J. F. Swift, Wm. Wilson, aldermen.

CITY OFFICIALS.—Michael Flanagan, clerk ; F. C. Ireland, treasurer ; James Agnew, solicitor ; Thomas O. Bolger, engineer ; Wm. S. Gordon, assessor and commissioner ; George Thompson, collector ; Alex Smyth, clerk of market and harbor master ; Andrew Lanigan, messenger ; John Duff, police magistrate ; James P. Gildersleeve, registrar ; F. J. George, deputy registrar.

POLICE FORCE.— Edwin Horsey, chief ; Robt. Carson, sergeant ; Robt. Nesbitt, sergeant; Samuel McCullagh, Alexander Snodden, Philip H. Small, James Megarry, John Tuttle, Orlando Burnett, Robert E. Aiken, John Ballentine, Jas. A. Craig, Nicholas Timmerman, policemen.

FIRE DEPARTMENT. — 20 men.— Henry Youklen, chief ; P. Devlin, assistant ; John Lemmon, foreman ; Thomas Kirkpatrick, assistant foreman ; Wm. Burk, secretary; J. Lemmon, treasurer.

FIRE ALARM.—No. 1, for a section from the west side of Princess street to Clarence, and from Bagot street to the water's edge ; 2, for a section from east side of Princess to Bay, and from Bagot to the water's edge ; 3, corner Queen and Montreal ; 4, corner Rideau and Bay ; 5, on Division, (All Saints Church); 6, on Princess, near Gordon ; 7, cor Alma and Redan ; 8, corner Earl and Barrie ; 9, Knitting Mill ; 12, Montreal, near Charles ; 13, corner River and Rideau ; 14, Military College ; 15, Hospital ; 17, corner Earl and Gordon ; 18, corner King and Union ; 21, corner John and Montreal ; 23, corner Princess and Barrie ; 24, Williamsville ; 25, corner Arch and Deacon ; 26, Bagot, near William ; 27, Grove Inn ; 28, Adelaide, above Patrick ; 29, corner Brock and Albert ; 32, corner Colborne and Upper Bagot ; 35, corner West and Sydenham ; 42, corner Victoria and Alfred.

KINGSTON BOARD OF TRADE.

J. S. Muckleston, president; Thos. Mills, secretary.

TRUSTEES.

COLLEGIATE INSTITUTE.— Edward J. B. Pense, Chairman; E.H.Smythe, LL.D., sec.; Hon. G. A. Kirkpatrick, Dr. C. A. Irwin, Robert Gardiner, Dr. Phelan, Prof. N. F Dupuis.

PUBLIC SCHOOLS.— W. Dunlop, chairman; W. Allen, S. Anglin, W. J. Arniel, Dr. S. H. Fee, Dr. Herald, A. Horne, H. Hunter, J. A. Macdonald, A. R. Martin, H. B. Savage, J. A. B. Smith, A. Williamson, T. C. Wilson; W. G, Kidd, inspector; S. S. Phippen, secretary; F. C. Ireland, treasurer.

SEPARATE SCHOOLS.—Rev. Father Twomey, chairman; M. Brennan, D. Driscoll, S. Lambert, J. Tierney, R. Beaupre, B. Leahy, J. Campbell, E. Dwyer, J. Behan, O. Tierney, E. Garvin; W. H. Sullivan, secretary.

CITY CORONERS.—John Stewart, M.D.; C. A. Irwin, M.D.; H. J. Saunders, M.D.

POST OFFICE.

James Shannon, postmaster; Robert T Burns, ass't postmaster; John Kelly, senior clerk; Wm S. Smyth, British and Foreign mail clerk; A. T. Deacon, money and savings bank; Robert J. D'Arcy, registered letter clerk; James McBride, general delivery; F. Macdonald, J. P. Pense, Thomas Moore, W. J. O'Reilly, A. J. Chamberlain, Wm. Wells, G. G. Meagher, distributing and forwarding clerks; A. H. Miller, sup't of letter carriers; John Collins, Robert Lewers, P. J. Howland, Robert Gilmour, Robert Keans, Wm. Neill, R. Elliott, R. E. Genge, letter carriers; John Morrisey, messenger.

POST OFFICE INSPECTOR'S OFFICE—KINGSTON DIVISION.

Gilbert Griffin, Post Office Inspector; Allan Jones, ass't P. O. Inspector; J. E. Hopkirk, P. H. Macarow, J. C. Strange, H. F. Wilmot.

RAILWAY MAIL CLERKS.

H. F. Ketcheson, John L. Renton, John Hoyland, D. J. Walker, jr, W. J. Doller, J. R. Sayers, M. McKinnon, Angus Gillies.

CUSTOM HOUSE.

(King, cor. Clarence St. Examining Warehouse—188 Ontario St.)

C. Hamilton, collector; A. Shaw, surveyor; R. D. Anglin, chief clerk; Thomas Gaskin, second clerk; W. Neish, third clerk; M. J. Haddigan, fourth clerk; T. Driver, appraiser; T. Meagher, J. Kidd, S. Angrove, J. Quigley, W. Robinson, landing waiters; G. H. Pidgeon, messenger and packer; P. Nugent, packer in examining warehouse.

INLAND REVENUE.

(South Market Square.)

F. Rowland, collector; T. Grimason, deputy-collector; C. T. Dickson, accountant; A. Hanley, bookkeeper; G. W. Browne, John O'Donnell, C. M. Hamilton, officers; E. Fahey, canals and excise.

CANAL OFFICE.

(Clarence Street.)

Wm. Burrows, collector.

STEAMBOAT INSPECTOR'S OFFICE.

(Clarence Street.)

Thomas Donnelly, inspector; Edward Adams, boiler inspector

GAS INSPECTION OFFICE.

(Clarence Street.)

Wm. Burrows, inspector.

WEIGHTS & MEASURES OFFICE

(Clarence Street.)

J. A. McDonald, inspector.

HIDE INSPECTOR'S OFFICE.

(Clarence Street.)

P. S. McKim, inspector.

CHURCHES.

Church of England.

DIOCESE OF ONTARIO.

St. George's Hall—Clerical Secretary's Office. Rev. A. Spencer, sec'y. Depository—Rev. Fred Prime, manager.

Cathedral of St. George.—(King cor. Johnston street.)—Rev. Buxton B. Smith, rector; Rev. Mr. Harding and Rev. A. Spencer, curates.

St. James' Church.—(Union, cor. Arch.—Rev. J. K. McMorine, M.A., rector.

St. Paul's Church.—(Queen, cor. Montreal.)—Rev. Rural Dean W. B. Carey, M. A., rector.

All Saints'—(320 Division.)—Rev. Frederic Prime, rector.

Hours of service—11 a. m. and 7 p. m.

Methodist.

First Methodist. — (Sydenham St.)—Rev. W. W. Carson, pastor.

Second Methodist.—(Queen St.)—Rev. J. Kines, pastor.

Third Methodist.—(Brock, cor. Montreal.) Rev. W. Timberlake, pastor.

Fourth Methodist.—(Brock, between Clergy and Barrie.)—Rev. D. C. Sanderson, pastor.

Fifth Methodist—(Williamsville)—Rev. L. M. England, pastor.

Hours of service—11 a. m. and 7 p. m.

Congregational.

First Congregational—(Wellington, cor. Johnston)—Rev S. N. Jackson, pastor. Services, 11 a. m. and 7 p. m.

Bethel Church.—(Johnston, cor. Barrie.) Rev. A. L. McPhayden, pastor. Services, 11 a. m. and 6.30 p. m.

Charles Street Congregational Church.

Presbyterian.

Cooke's 201 Brock St.) Rev. S. Houston, pastor. Services, 11 a.m. and 6.30 p.m.

Chalmers—(129 Earl St.)—Rev. Malcolm McGillivray, B.A., pastor. Services, 11 a.m. and 7 p.m.

St. Andrew's—(corner Princess and Clergy)—Rev. John Mackie, pastor. Services, 11 a.m. and 7 p.m.

Baptist.

(95 Johnston)—Services, 11 a.m. and 6.30 p.m.

Roman Catholic.

St. Mary's Cathedral—(corner Clergy and Johnston)—Hours of service: Mass every day at 7.30 a.m. Sundays—Summer, Low Mass, 7.30 a.m.; children's mass, 9.15 a.m.; High Mass, 10.30 a.m.; vespers, 7.30 p.m. Winter—Low Mass, 8 a.m., children's Mass, 9.30 a.m.; High Mass, 11 a.m.; vespers, 7.30 p.m. Right Rev. James Vincent Cleary, Bishop of Kingston; Rev. Thomas Kelly, secretary; Revds. John S. Quinn, Thomas Carey, Alex. Carson.

Catholic Apostolic—(285 Queen St.)—Rev. J. E. Gilmour, pastor. Services, 10 a.m. and 5 p.m.

SALVATION ARMY.

(Barracks, Queen, cor Bagot.)

Major Wm. Woolley, Divisional officer; Mary A. Ilett, captain; Martha Caldwell, lieutenant. Services every evening at 8 p.m. Sundays, 7, 11 a.m.; 3, 7.30 p.m.

EDUCATIONAL.

QUEEN'S UNIVERSITY AND COLLEGE.

Sandford Fleming, C.E., C.M.G., LL.D.,Chancellor; Very Rev. George Monro Grant, M.A., D.D., Principal and Vice-Chancellor; Rev. James Williamson, M. A., LL.D., Vice-Principal; Rev. George Bell, B.A., LL.D., Registrar; J. B. McIver, Sec.-treasurer.

Registrar of University Council, R. W. Shannon, M.A. Observatory Board, the Principal, Prof. Williamson, M. Flanagan, Esq. Director of Observatory,Professor of Astronomy. Curators of the Library, Professors Marshall and Ross. Librarian, Adam

Shortt, M.A. Curator of Museum, Lecturer on Natural Science. Examiner for Matriculation in Medicine, Rev. James Fowler, M.A. Examiners in Gaelic, Evan MacColl, Esq., R. M. Rose, Esq., Rev. M. MacGillivray, M.A. Janitor, John Cormack.

OFFICERS OF INSTRUCTION.

In Divinity.

The Principal, Primarius Professor of Divinity ; Rev. Jno. B. Mowat, M.A., D.D., Professor of Hebrew, Chaldee and Old Testament Exegesis ; Rev. Donald Ross, M.A., B.D., Professor of Apologetics and New Testament Criticism ; Rev. James Carmichael (King), Lecturer on Church History.

In Arts.

Rev. J. Williamson, M.A., LL.D., Professor of Astronomy ; Rev. J. B. Mowat, M.A., D.D., Professor of Hebrew ; Nathan F. Dupuis, M.A., F.B.S., Edin., Professor of Mathematics ; Rev. Geo. D. Ferguson, B.A., Professor of History ; John Watson, M.A., LL.D., Professor of Logic, Mental and Moral Philosophy ; John Fletcher, M.A., Oxon, Professor of Classical Literature ; D. H. Marshall, M.A., Edin., F.R.S.E., Professor of Physics ; Wm. L. Goodwin, B.Sc., Loud., D.Sc., Edin., Professor of Chemistry and Mineralogy ; James Cappon, M.A., Professor of English Language and Literature ; John McGillivray, Ph.D., Professor of Modern Languages ; Rev. Alex. B. Nicholson, B.A., Assistant to Professor of Classics ; Rev. Jas. Fowler, M.A., John Kay Lecturer on Natural Science ; Adam Shortt, M.A., John Leys Lecturer on Political Science ; W. J. Patterson, B.A., William Nickle Tutor in Mathematics ; Omar L. Kilborn, B.A., R. G. Reid Tutor in Chemistry ; Thos. G. Allen, B.A., Hiram Calvin Tutor in Chemistry ; Adam Shortt, M.A., A. M. Cosby Tutor in Philosophy ; William Gunn, T. A. Dawes Tutor in Modern Languages.

In Law.

J. Maule Machar, M.A., Lecturer on Roman Law ; Byron M. Britton, M.A., Q.C., Lecturer on Criminal Law ; R. Vashon Rogers, B.A., Lecturer on Common Law ; G. M. Macdonnell, B.A., Q.C., Lecturer on the Law of Real Property ; Richard T. Walkem, Q.C., Lecturer on Equity ; John McIntyre, M.A., Q.C., Lecturer on Medical Jurisprudence.

ROYAL COLLEGE OF PHYSICIANS AND SURGEONS.

(In affiliation with Queen's University and University of Trinity College, Toronto.

Fife Fowler, M.D., L.R.C.S., Edin., Professor of the Theory and Practice of Medicine, and President of the Faculty. Michael Lavell, M. D., Emeritus Professor. Hon. Michael Sullivan, M.D. (Surgeon to the Hotel Dieu), Professor of Principles and Practice of Surgery. Alfred S. Oliver, M.D. (Surgeon to the Kingston Hospital), Professor of Materia Medica, Therapeutics and Pharmacy. Thos. R. Dupuis, M.D., F.R.C.P.S., and M.R.C.S., Eng., (Surgeon to the Kingston Hospital), Professor of Clinical Surgery and Histology. The Professors of Chemistry and Botany in Queen's University, Professors of Chemistry, Practical Chemistry and Botany. Kenneth N. Fenwick, M.A., M.D., M.R.C.S., Eng., (Surgeon to the Kingston Hospital), Professor of Obstetrics and Gynæcology. Chamberlen A. Irwin, M.D., (Surgeon to the Kingston Hospital), Professor of Clinical Medicine and Sanitary Science. W. H. Henderson, M.D., M.R.C.S., Eng., Professor of Physiology. R. W. Garrett, A.M., M.D., Professor of Anatomy. H. J. Saunders, M.D., M.R.C.S., Eng., Professor of Medical Jurisprudence. D. E. Mundell, M.D., Demonstrator-in-Chief of Anatomy. Omar L. Kilborn and A. Gandier, Associate Demonstrators of Anatomy.

WOMEN'S MEDICAL COLLEGE.

Affiliated to the University.

City Buildings.

M. Lavell, M.D., President of the Faculty. Hon. M. Sullivan, M.D., F.R.C.P.S.K., (Surgeon to the Hotel Dieu), Professor of Principles and Practice of Surgery. A. S. Oliver, M.D., F.R.C.P.S.K., (Surgeon to the Kingston Hospital), Professor of Materia Medica, Therapeutics and Pharmacy. Thomas M. Fenwick, M.D., Professor of Theory and Practice of Medicine. D. Phelan, M.A., M.D., (Surgeon to the Hotel Dieu and House of Providence), Professor of Physiology and Histology. (Mrs.) Alice McGillivray, M.D., Professor of Obstetrics and Diseases of Women and Children. W. G. Anglin, M.D., M.R.C.S.E., Eng., Professor of Anatomy, Descriptive and Surgical. (Mrs.) Elizabeth Smith-Shortt, M.D., Professor of Medical Jurisprudence and Sanitary Science. Chemistry, the Professor of Chemistry, Queen's College. Botany, the Professor of Botany, Queen's College. Clinical Surgery, the Lecturer on Clinical Surgery in the General Hospital. Clinical Medicine, the Lecturer on Clinical Medicine in the General Hospital. Demonstrators of Anatomy to be appointed in October.

KINGSTON COLLEGIATE INSTITUTE.

Established 1791.

TEACHING STAFF. — Rector and Science Master, A. P. Knight, M.A.; Classical Master, E. O. Sliter, B.A.; Mathematical Master, W. H. Irvine, B.A.; Modern Language Master, A. J. Dales, M.A.; English Master, Brough; Drawing Master, Charles Wrenshall; Drill Master, P. McGhie.

KINGSTON BUSINESS COLLEGE COMPANY.

82 Princess St.

Graduating courses in Commercial Science, including Practical Penmanship, Commercial Law, Composition, Commercial Arithmetic, Practical Grammar, Business Correspondence, Bookkeeping and Spelling. Plain and Ornamental Penmanship, including the art of teaching it. Phonography, Type-Writing and Telegraphy. J. B. McKay, president; Amos McDonald, secretary.

CONVENT OF THE CONGREGATION DE NOTRE DAME.

Cor. Bagot and Johnston.

Mother St. Wilfred, Superioress.

ST. MARY OF THE LAKE.

King Street West.

Mother St. Cecilia, Superioress.

CHRISTIAN BROTHERS' SCHOOL.

89 Clergy Street.

Rev. Bro. Halward, director; Rev. Brothers Patrick, Odwin, Paul, Mark, Frederick and Anthony, teachers; Brother Sabas, domestic. Registered number of pupils, about 410.

MECHANICS' INSTITUTE.

Princess, cor. Montreal.

James Redden, president; Neil McNeill, R S. Dobbs, vice-presidents; C. E. L. Porteous, cor. sec.; W. Neish, treasurer; H. Crothers, rec. sec.; H. J. Spriggs, librarian.

CATHOLIC LITERARY SOCIETY

Rooms — McRae's Block, Wellington St.

Meets 2nd Monday in each month. J. J. Behan, president; T. J. Hennessey, vice-president; W. J. O'Rielly, secretary; M. J. Neville, treasurer.

Reading room and library are open every day and evening.

MILITARY.

Royal School of Gunnery, "A" Battery, C. A., Tete du Pont Barracks. Commandant and Assistant Inspector of Artillery, Lieut.-Col. W. H. Cotton; Lieut. and Brevet-Major John Fraser, Quartermaster; Adjutant, Major Drury; Lieutenants, V. B.

Rivers, J. A. G. Hudon, W. P. Burroughs ; Surgeon-Major, J. L. H. Neilson ; Veterinary Surgeon, James Massie.

Establishment of "A" R. S. G.—1 Lt.-Col., 1 major, 4 lieutenants, 1 surgeon, 1 vet. surgeon, 1 quartermaster, 1 master gunner, 1 sergeant-major, 1 laboratory foreman, 1 ordnance armourer, 2 assistant gunnery instructors, 1 trumpet major, 1 riding instructor, 1 quarter-master sergeant, 6 sergeants, 4 corporals, 4 bombadiers, 8 acting bombadiers, 5 trumpeters, 115 gunners, and 16 horses, making a total of 160 men.

In addition to the above, 10 officers and 20 non-commissioned officers and men are allowed to join a short course of instruction.

There are three short courses during the year.

ROYAL MILITARY COLLEGE OF CANADA, KINGSTON.

Commandant, Major-Gen. D. R. Cameron, C. M. G. ; Staff-Adjutant, Lt.-Col. S. C. McGill ; Professor of Surveying, Military Topography and Reconnaisance, Major C. B. Mayne, R. E. ; Professor of Mathematics and Mechanism, Major R. A. Rigg, R.A.; Professor of Fortifications, Military Engineering, Geometrical Drawing, and Descriptive Geometry, Major S. Davidson, R. E. ; Professor of Military History, Administration and Law, Major Edward Nash, R. A. ; Instructor in Mathematics and Professor of Artillery, vacant ; Instructor in Fortification, Military Engineering, Geometrical Drawing and Descriptive Geometry ; Capt. A. H. Van Straubenzie ; Instructor in Mathematics, Geometrical Drawing and Descriptive Geometry, Capt. A. G. Wurtele ; Assistant Intructor in Surveying, Military Topography, Physics and Chemistry, Capt. John B. Cochrane ; Professor of English Literature, Rev. K. L. Jones, M. A., B. D. ; Professor of Drawing and Painting, Forshaw Day, Esq., R. C. A. ; Professor of French, Arthur D. Duval, Esq., M. D. ; Professor of Civil Engineering, R. C. Harris, Esq., C. E. ; Professor of Physics, Chemistry and Geology, John Waddell, M. A., Ph. D. ; Medical Officer, J. L. H. Neilson, M. D., Surgeon-Major "A" Battery, R. S. G. ; Paymaster, Capt. M. W. Strange.

4TH REGIMENT OF CAVALRY.

John Duff, Col. ; H. Smith, Adjt. ; H. R. Duff, Surgeon ; M. W. Strange, Paymaster ; Edward Ming, Vet. Surgeon ; Alex. W. Strange, Riding Master ; Thos. Todd, Quartermaster. No. 1 Troop.—Capt. A. Knight, 1st Lieut. Geo. Purcell, 2nd Lieut. Joseph Scriven.

KINGSTON FIELD BATTERY.

W. M. Drennan, Major, Commanding ; J. A. Wilmot, Captain ; R. E. Kent, 1st Lieutenant ; Geo. Moore, 2nd Lieutenant ; H. J. Saunders, Surgeon ; M. W. Sine, Vet. Surgeon.

14TH BATTALION, PRINCESS OF WALES' OWN RIFLES.

H. R. Smith, Lt.-Col. ; J. W. Power, Major ; Dr. W. H. Henderson, Surgeon ; Dr. J. H. Betts, Assistant Surgeon ; Major H. J. Spriggs, Quartermaster ; Major J. Galloway, jr., Adjutant.

Captains.—Jas. Murray, jr., L.W. Shannon, J. S. Skinner, W. G. Hinds, A. G. Farrell.

1st Lieuts.—W. Nicol, W. Hera, F. Strange, D. A. Givens.

2nd Lieuts.—H. H. Gildersleeve, R. J. McKelvey, D. F. Armstrong, John Newlands, W. J. White, John Marshall.

Military District Staff No. 3.—Lt.-Col. VanStraubenzie, D. A. G. ; Major W. King, District Paymaster and Superintendent of Stores.

SOCIETIES.

MASONIC.

Rose of Sharon Sovereign Chapter of Rose Croix de H. R. D. M.—Meets first Wednesday in each month.—Bro. F. Day, 18°, M. W. S. ; Bro. Kinghorn, 18°, P. M. W. S.; Bro. Birtles, 18°, Prelate ; Bro. F Welch, 18°, 1st

General; Bro. H. J. Wilkinson, 18°, 2nd General ; Bro. C. B. Mayne, 18°, Raphael ; Bro. F. Gillen, 18°. M. C.

Kingston Lodge of Perfection, No. 7. —Meets 3rd Thursday of each month. —Ill. Bro. Bajus, 32°, P. T. P. G. M.; Bro. H. Birtle, 18°, T.P.G.M.; Bro. F. Welch, 18°, J. G. W.; Bro. John Kinghorn, 18°, Sec'y ; Bro. George Thompson, 18°, Treas.; Bro. F. Day, 18°, O.; Bro. F. B. Gillen, 18°, Al.; Bro. C. B. Mayne, 18°, M. C.; Bro. W. J. Wilson, 18°, Expert ; Bro. A. M. McMahon, 14° Ass't E.; Bro. G. Somerville, 14°, Captain Guard ; Bro. E. H. Ball, 18°, Tyler.

Knights Templar— Hugh de Payens Premier Preceptory, No. 1.—Assembles in the Masonic Hall, King St., at 8 p. m., on the second Monday in January, April, July, October, and December, and on the 18th of March. Em. Fr. Allan McLean, Presiding Preceptor ; R. Em. Fr. J. A. Henderson, D.G.M., Past E. P.; Fr. W. M. Drennan, Constable ; Fr. James Walters, Marshal ; Em. Fr. Edmund W. Case, Captain of Guard ; R. Em. Fr. John Kerr, Treasurer ; R. Em. Fr. F. Rowland, Registrar ; Em. Fr. S. W. Scobell, Almoner ; Fr. D. W. Allison, R. A. Irwin, Standard-bearers ; Fr. E. H. Ball, Guard.

Ancient Frontenac and Cataraqui Chapter, No. 1.—Meets 3rd Wednesday in each month.—R. T. Walkem, Z.; G. Somerville, H.; J. Adams, J.; J. B. Reid, S. E.; W. Wilson, S. N.; W. H. Carnovsky, P. S.; D. Milne, S. S.; W. Pugh, J. S.; E. Law, M. 1st V.; G. Thompson, M. 2nd V.; A. Hanz, M. 3rd V.; E. Ball, Janitor.

Ancient St. John's Lodge, No. 3, G.R.C.—Meets 1st Thursday of each month. —John Waddell, W. M.; John Kinghorn, I.P.M.; Walter H. Macnee, S.W.; Richard W. Garrett, J.W.; E. R. Welch, Treasurer ; Jno. Sutherland, Sec'y ; W. J. Wilson, S. D.; A. Brough, J. D.; R. E. Burns, I.G.; W. Massie, D. C.; W. J. Renton, W. J. Livingston, Stewards ; E. H. Ball, Tyler.

Cataraqui Lodge, No. 92, G. R. C. —Meets second Wednesday in each month.—Richard Bunt, W.M.; Geo. Somerville, I.P.M.; S. Angrove, S. W.; W. H. Carnovsky, J. W.; Rev. J. Gallaher, Chaplain ; James Shannon, Treas.; D. Callaghan, Secretary ; W. Lowe, S.D.; H. D. Bibby, J D.; W. Wilson, D. of C. ; W. Pugh, R. McMillan, Stewards , D. Milne, I.G.; E. H. Ball, Tyler.

Minden Lodge, No. 253, G. R. C. —Meets 1st Monday of each month. H. Mowat, W. M.; J. Hewton, I. P. M.; James Adams, S.W.; J. P. Oram, J.W.; Rev. M. Macgillivray, Chaplain ; J. F. McEwen, Treas.; J. B. Reid, Sec'y ; A. McMahon, S. D.; J. Bunt, J. D.; John Newlands, I. G.; John Newton, T. Minnes, Stewards ; R. F. Hyland, D. of C. ; W H. L. Atkins, Organist ; E. H. Ball, Tyler.

ODD-FELLOWS.

Canton Kingston, No. 6, Patriarchs Militant.—Meets first Thursday, in hall over Curtis' Drug Store, cor. of Princess and Montreal Sts. Wm. Saunders, Captain ; R. F. Elliott, Lieutenant ; Wm. J. Moore, Ensign ; George Parks, Standard Bearer ; J. F. Dillon, Clerk ; William Healey, Accountant.

KINGSTON ENCAMPMENT, No. 15.— 2nd and 4th Monday. Hall, Princess, cor. Montreal. L. Milks, C.P.; J. S. R. McCann, S.W.; Capt. J. Saunders, H.P.; K. McIver, J. W.; George Wright, Sec.; W. Healey, F. S.; R. F. Elliott, Treasurer.

KINGSTON LODGE, No. 59.—Meets every Friday. Hall, over Curtis' drug store, Princess, cor. Montreal. William Healey, N.G.; Thomas Donnelly, V.G.; N. P. Joyner, R.S.; W. Saunders, P.S.; John Pollie, Treasurer.

CATARAQUI LODGE, No. 10. —Meets every Tuesday. Hall, Wilkinson's block, Princess, cor. Montreal. W. J. Moore, N.G.; K. McIver, V.G.; F. R. Sargent, R.S.; J. S. R. McCann, Treasurer ; H. Brouse, W.; H. Walker, C.; F. X. Rogers, O.G.; F. Forsythe, I.G.

ODD-FELLOWS' RELIEF ASSOCIATION OF CANADA, Montreal, cor. Princess. —Fife Fowler, M.D., President ; W. Dunn, Vice-President ; Robt. Meek, Secretary ; Daniel Callaghan, Treas.

DAUGHTERS OF REBECCA, LOUISE LODGE, No. 10.—Meets 1st and 3rd Monday.

FORESTERS.

COURT FRONTENAC, No. 59. —Independent Order meets every 2nd and 4th Thursday. Hall, Princess, cor. Montreal. T. W. Moore, C.D., H. C.R.; R. Meek, C.R. ; Wm. McNaughton, V.C.R.; J. S. R. McCann, R.S.: J. R. Rattenbury, Treasurer ; S. Lowe, F.S.

I. O. O. F., M.U.—Loyal Forward Lodge, No. 6,873 W. Lowe, N.G. ; A. E. Fields, V.G. ; E. Roberts, F.S. ; G. H. Booth, R.S. ; Dr. McVety, T.

CANADIAN ORDER OF ODDFELLOWS, MANCHESTER UNITY, ST. LAWRENCE LODGE, No. 113.—Meets 1st and 3rd Tuesday, S.O.T. Hall, cor. Princess and Montreal. C. D. Chown, N.G. ; Lake, Secretary ; Robt. W. Allen, Treasurer.

A. O. U. W.
(Hall, Princess, cor Montreal.)

KINGSTON LEGION SELECT KNIGHTS, No. 10.—Meets 4th Monday. W. Stewart, Select Commander ; Thos. King, V.C. ; W. H. Godwin, Secretary ; A. G. Flett, Treasurer ; John Hopkirk, Recording Treasurer.

LIMESTONE, No. 91.—Meets 2nd and 4th Thursday. Thos. King, M. W. ; Charles Smeaton, O. : Wm. Stewart, Foreman ; W. H. Godwin, Recorder ; J. B. Forsyth, Financier.

ROYAL ARCANUM.

ST. LAWRENCE COURT, No. 905.— Meets 1st and 3rd Mondays. Wm. Dunlop, Regent ; J. M. Shaw, V.C.; R. D. Anglin, Secretary ; G. S. Fenwick, Treasurer; A. Shaw, Collector.

LOYAL ORANGE ASSOCIATION.
(Hall, 82 Princess.)

No. 6 meets 2nd Wednesday in each month. Joseph S. Gould, W. M.; J. Spooner, Secretary.

No. 291 meets 2nd Friday in each month. J. Featherston, W.M.; W. Cook, Secretary.

No. 316 meets 1st Tuesday in each month. Geo. Pigion, W. M ; Joseph Anderson, Secretary.

No. 325 meets 1st Thursday. Robt. Moxley, W.M.; W. McCammon, Secretary.

No. 352 meets 1st Friday. John Gaskin, W.M ; W. Dunlop, Secretary.

No. 577 meets 2nd Monday. Wm. Corbett, W. M.; J. Shanessy Secretary.

No. 1, DERRY LODGE 'PRENTICE BOYS.—F. W. Eward, W.M. Meets 1st and 3rd Monday.

No. 16, BOYNE LODGE, TRUE BLUES —Wm. McKee, W.M ; J. Graham, Secretary. Meets last Monday in each month.

ORANGE YOUNG BRITONS, GASKIN LODGE, No 261.—Meets 2nd Thursday. J. Shanessy, W.M.; J. McCammon, Secretary.

ROYAL SCARLET DISTRICT CHAPTER. —James Marshall, W. C.; Samuel Swann, Com S. Meets on the 14th of each month.

ROYAL BLACK PRECEPTORY, No. 139.—Sir Kt. Wm. McCammon, C.; Sir Kt. James Marshall, reg. Meets every 3rd Thursday.

CANADIAN ORDER FORESTERS.

COURT STANLEY, No. 199.—Meets 2nd and last Tuesday. J. E. Hopkirk, C.R ; H. T. Shibley, V.C.R ; F. A. Birch, F.S ; J. S. Skinner, R. S.; J. A. Minnes, T.; P Hunter, S. W.; E. B. Loucks, J.W.; J. S. Hume, M.

ORDER CANADIAN HOME CIRCLE.

KINGSTON CIRCLE, No. 105.—Meets 1st and 3rd Monday. Hall, Wilkinson's Building, Montreal, cor. Princess. W. M. Drennan, P.L., Donald Fraser, L.; F. A. Forsyth, V.L.; C. T. Dickson, Secretary; A. F. McVety M.D.; Treasurer ; W. H. Godwin, F.S.; J W. Madden, M ; Jos. Theobald, W.; J. Crawford, G.; David Rae, S.

25

TEMPERANCE SOCIETIES.

ROYAL TEMPLARS OF TEMPERANCE.

HAND IN HAND COUNCIL, No. 273. —Meets every Monday, corner of Wellington and Clarence. William Kelly, S.C. ; H. M. Hawley, Rec. Sec.

INDEPENDENT ORDER OF GOOD TEMPLARS.

HOPE OF KINGSTON LODGE, No. 152.—Meets every Monday, corner of Montreal and Princess. Robert Allen, L.D.

WOMEN'S CHRISTIAN TEMPERANCE UNION.

Mrs. Dr. McCammon, President.

SONS OF TEMPERANCE.

ST. LAWRENCE, No. 2.— Meets every Thursday, Montreal, corner of Princess. Geo. Gordon, W.P.; Jos. George, Fin. Scribe.

NATIONAL SOCIETIES.

ST. GEORGE'S SOCIETY.

E. H. Smythe, LL.D., President ; Joseph Salter, 1st Vice-President ; John Green, 2nd Vice-President ; J. A. B. Smith, Secretary ; Wm. Pipe, Treasurer ; Revs. F. Prime and C. E. Cartwright, Chaplains; Dr. Saunders, Physician.

SONS OF ENGLAND.

LEICESTER LODGE, No. 33.—Meets 2nd and last Tuesday. Jos. Salter, President ; John Green, Vice-President ; William Allison, Secretary ; Thos. Lambert, Treasurer.

TYNE LODGE, No. 79.—Meets 2nd and 4th Tuesday. E. Smith, President ; John Porter, Vice-President ; J. Siler, F.S.; T. H. Phillips, Secretary ; J. Beauchamp, T.

SONS OF SCOTLAND.

SIR WM. WALLACE CAMP, No. 13. —Meets 4th Friday over Toye's bakery, King e. W. Dunnett, Chief ; A. Waldie, Chieftain ; J. B. Reid, Rec. Secretary; W. Gibb, F.S.; Capt. Paul, Tr.; Geo. Gordon, Marshall ; Robert Weir, Piper ; John McMillan, Standard Bearer ; Wm. Stewart and A. G. Flett, Guards.

ST. ANDREW'S SOCIETY.

Captain Murray, Secretary.

CATHOLIC SOCIETIES.

CONFRATERNITY OF THE HOLY FAMILY

Men's branch meets 1st Sunday in each month at 3.30 p.m. Women's, 1st Friday at 7.30 p.m.

ST. VINCENT DE PAUL SOCIETY.

(Purely charitable)—Meets every Sunday afternoon in St. Mary's vestry at 2.30 p.m. F. Crimmons, President ; Lawrence O'Brien, Vice-President ; M. E. Brennan, Secretary ; Edward Fahey, Treasurer ; Rev. D. A. Twomey, Chaplain.

CHILDREN OF ST. MARY.

Miss Fahey, President.

CATHOLIC MUTUAL BENEFIT ASSOCIATION, BRANCH NO. 9.

Meets 1st and 3rd Wednesday in each month. J. J. Behan, President ; Edward Steacy, 1st Vice-President ; Rev. T. Kelly, 2nd Vice-President ; M. Brennan, Secretary ; George Gruber, Fin. Secretary ; W. Shanahan, Treasurer ; John Crowley, Marshal.

I. C. B. U., BRANCH 483.

President, W. P. Kilcauley ; 1st Vice-President, R. J. James ; 2nd Vice-President, T. Feeney; Chaplain, Rev. Father Quinn ; Marshal, John Fitzgerald ; Secretary, M. P. Murphy ; Fin. Secretary, Jas. Gallivan, Treasurer, E. J. Clayton ; Tyler, W. Taylor.

EMERALD CLUB.

Regular meeting 2nd Monday in each month. Rooms over Horseshoe, Market Square. Manager, D. McGeein ; ass't Manager, E. Amond ; Treasurer, T. Redmond ; Secretary, P. J. Lawless ; entertainment committee's officers : J. P. Walsh, Chairman ; M. Foley, Treasurer ; W. P. Kilcauley, Secretary.

BANKS.

BANK OF BRITISH NORTH AMERICA, City Hall.—F. Brownfield, Manager ; W. Bayly, Accountant ; J. D. Petrie,

Teller ; R. R. F. Harvey, Ledger ; H. Cartwright, Clerk ; R. Stafford, Messenger.

MERCHANTS BANK OF CANADA, King, Cor. William.—G. E. Hague, Manager ; W. B. Waterbury, Accountant ; T. R. Merrett, Teller ; A. M. Gildersleeve, Ledger ; J. B. E. Wilson, Clerk ; W. C. Kent, Clerk ; G. W. McQuarrie, Clerk.

BANK OF MONTREAL, King, Cor. William.—C. E. L. Porteous, Manager ; H. S. Dupuy, Accountant ; J. D. G. Shaw, Teller ; E. H. Retallack, Ledger-keeper; N. G. Thacker, Clerk ; P. G. W. H. Harvey, Clerk.

ONTARIO BANK.—T. Y. Greet, Manager ; W. J. C. Harvey, Accountant ; J. H. Mitchell, Teller ; F. D. Taylor, Ledger-keeper ; J. A. McArthur, Clerk ; T. X. Rogers, Messenger.

MISCELLANEOUS.

KINGSTON HOSPITAL.—Governors *ex Officio :* The County Judge, the Mayor of Kingston, the Warden of Frontenac, the Sheriff of Frontenac. The Eleven Life Governors : Sir John A. Macdonald, Sir R. J. Cartwright, Hon. M. Sullivan, M. D., B. M. Britton, Jno Duff, Edwin Chown, Wm. Ford, J. B. Carruthers, Dr. O. S. Strange, E. J. B. Pense, B. W. Robertson. The Subscription Governors : Hon. A. Campbell, Hon. G. A. Kirkpatrick, Ira A. Breck, Alex. Gunn, H. A. Calvin, K. N. Fenwick, M. D., Dr. C. A. Irwin, Principal Grant, E. H. Smythe. Officers : Chairman of the Board of Governors, Dr. O. S. Strange ; attending Medical Officers, Dr. T. R. Dupuis, Dr. A. S. Oliver, Dr. K. N. Fenwick, Dr. J. C. Connell ; Sec'y-Treas., J. E. Clark ; Medical Superintendent, Dr. E. Hooper.

HOTEL DIEU, Brock street.—Sister Margaret Doran, Superioress. The Hotel Dieu Female Orphan Asylum is in connection.

HOUSE OF PROVIDENCE, Montreal street. Sister Mary Edward, Superioress.

PROTESTANT ORPHANS' HOME, Union street, opposite Drill shed.—Mrs. Andrew Wilson, Manager.

HOUSE OF INDUSTRY, 326 Montreal street.—John Harkess. Superintendent.

KINGSTON PENITENTIARY.—M. Lavell, Warden; Wm. Sullivan, Deputy Warden ; O. S. Strange, M. D., Surgeon ; S. W. Scobell, Accountant ; Rev. C. E. Cartwright, Protestant Chaplain ; Rev. John S. Quinn, R.C. Chaplain ; Miss Fahey, Matron ; R. Hewton, Chief Instructor ; Robert R. Creighton, Clerk ; P. O'Donnell, Storekeeper ; Jas. Weir, Steward.

ASYLUM FOR THE INSANE (Post Office, Kingston).—C. K. Clarke, Medical Superintendent ; J. Robinson, M.D., Assistant Medical Superintendent ; J. Simpson, M. D., Assistant Physician ; Wm. Anglin, Bursar; Allan McLean, Steward ; Miss E. Kirkpatrick, Matron.

REGIOPOLIS BRANCH ASYLUM FOR THE INSANE.—John Davidson, Supervisor.

YOUNG MEN'S CHRISTIAN ASSOCIATION, 123 Princess.—W. G. Anglin, M.D., President ; G. M. Macdonnell, Q.C., Vice-President ; G. E. Hague, Treasurer ; G. E. Williams, General Secretary. Meetings—Sunday, 4.15 p.m., young men's gospel meeting ; Monday, 7.30 p.m., training classes ; Thursday, social evening ; Friday, 7.30 p.m., junior department ; Saturday, 8 p.m., Bible study. Free reading room, open every day.

YOUNG WOMEN'S CHRISTIAN ASSOCIATION, 128 Clarence—Miss Machar, Secretary.

HUMANE SOCIETY.—R. S. Dobbs, Sec.-Treasurer.

LIMESTONE CITY TYPOGRAPHICAL UNION, No. 204.—Chas. Woods, President ; Wm. E. Ricard, Secretary.

RAILWAYS.

KINGSTON & PEMBROKE.—(Offices, Ontario street, opposite City Hall), C. F. Gildersleeve, President ; John D. Flower, Vice-President ; T. W. Nash, Sec.-Treasurer and Chief Engineer ; B. W. Folger. Superintendent ; J. H. Taylor, Assistant Superintendent ; Kirkpatrick & Rogers, Solicitors ; F. Conway, Assistant Freight and Passenger Agent ; Wm. Erwin, Road Master ; N. Parent, Paymaster ; M. J. Neville, Auditor.

STAGE ROUTES.

BATTERSEA STAGE.—Wm. Arthur, proprietor, leaves Windsor Hotel, corner Princess and Montreal, Tuesday, Thursday and Saturday, at 3 p.m. Battersea stage, Tunis Ferguson, proprietor, Monday, Wednesday and Friday, from Windsor Hotel, at 3 p.m. Fare, 25 cents.

KINGSTON & GANANOQUE STAGE.— J. B. Brennan, proprietor. Leaves Windsor Hotel daily at 3 p.m.

NEWBORO STAGE. Webb Copeland proprietor. Leaves Windsor Hotel daily at 7 a.m. ; arrives at 3 p.m. Fare, $1.50.

INVERARY STAGE. J. Stoness, proprietor. Leaves Windsor Hotel daily at 4 p.m.

NAPANEE STAGE.— H. Finkle, proprietor. Leaves Windsor Hotel daily at 3 p.m.

SYDENHAM STAGE.—Leaves Albion Hotel, Montreal street, daily.

BATH STAGE (winter only).—A. Ailsworth, proprietor. Leaves American Hotel daily at 3 p.m. Fare, 50 cents.

DIVISION COURT CLERKS.

No. 1, Wm. Robinson, Kingston ; No. 2, P. McKim, Cataraqui ; No. 3, Charles Ruttan, Sydenham ; No. 4, Alex. Grant, Verona ; No. 5, John McGrath, Inverary ; No. 6, Jesse Shibley, Sharbot Lake.

COUNTY OFFICIALS.

Hugh Rankin, Warden ; C. V. Price, Judge ; Wm. Ferguson, Sheriff ; B. M. Britton, Clerk of the Peace and County Attorney ; Arch McGill, County Court Clerk and Deputy Clerk of Crown and Peace and Registrar Surrogate Court ; R M. Rose, Registrar ; Thomas F. Vanluven, Treasurer ; D J. Walker, County Clerk ; Wm. Spankie, B.A , M.D., Inspector Public Schools ; C. H. Corbett, Governor of Jail ; A. S. Oliver, M.D , Surgeon County Jail ; John Shepherd, Court House Keeper.

www.ingramcontent.com/pod-product-compliance
Lightning Source LLC
Chambersburg PA
CBHW030837270326
41928CB00007B/1098